# The Book of Good Love

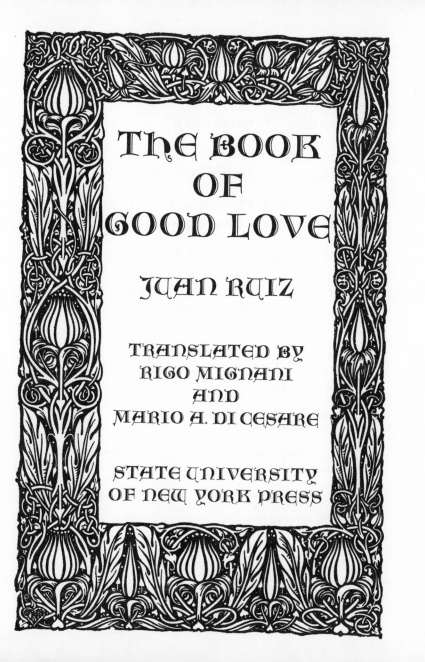

# THE BOOK OF GOOD LOVE

## JUAN RUIZ

TRANSLATED BY
RIGO MIGNANI
AND
MARIO A. DI CESARE

STATE UNIVERSITY
OF NEW YORK PRESS

First Edition

First Paperbound Printing 1972

Published by State University of New York Press,
99 Washington Avenue, Albany, New York 12210

The Library of Congress catalogued the original
printing of this book as follows:


RUIZ, JUAN, *Arcipreste de Hita, fl.* 1343
    The book of good love. Translated by Rigo Mignani and
Mario A. Di Cesare.

    Translation of Libro de buen amor.
    Bibliography: p. ₁361₁–365.

    I. Mignani, Rigo, 1921–        tr. II. Di Cesare, Mario A., tr.
III.  Title.

PQ6430.A5E5    1970        868′.1            69–14644
ISBN 0–87395–048–8                            MARC
ISBN 0–87395–148–4 (microfiche)
ISBN 0–87395–223–5 (pbk)

# CONTENTS

## ACKNOWLEDGMENTS

*We wish to express particular thanks to The Research Foundation of State University of New York, which provided a Summer Fellowship in the early stages of this work, and to the Harpur College Foundation, which provided funds for typing. Among many individuals who gave generously of their time and help, we wish to thank especially Professor Bernard F. Huppé, who read an early version of our work and offered many useful suggestions; Miss Janet Brown, of the State University of New York at Binghamton Library; and Mrs. Hazel Bell, who patiently typed the manuscript.*

*For this reprint, we have made ten minor changes, none of them substantively affecting the translation. We wish to acknowledge with thanks, the suggestions of Edward M. Wilson (Medium Aevum, XL, 80 f.), some of which we have adopted.*

# INTRODUCTION

he *Libro de Buen Amor* [1] shares with *La Celestina* and *Don Quijote* the distinction of being one of the great masterpieces of Spanish literature. Unlike these, however, the *Libro* has not been generally familiar to English readers. [2] A long narrative poem of 1,728 stanzas, mainly in *cuaderna vía* (quatrains with verses of fourteen or sixteen syllables and single rhyme), with songs in various lyrical meters, the *Libro* was written some time in the fourteenth century by Juan Ruiz, the Archpriest of Hita, a town some miles northeast of Madrid. Ruiz is both narrator and protagonist of the work.

## The Story

The poem opens with a prayer for deliverance from prison. This prayer, following the general form of the prayer for the agonizing in the *Ordo commendationis animae*, is the Archpriest's personal preface, a conventional opening to the work. The long prose discourse that follows is a *sermon joyeux* on the text of Psalm 31:8—"I will instruct thee and teach thee in the way thou shalt go: I will guide thee with mine eyes." [3] The Archpriest distinguishes between *buen amor*, which he here defines as love of God and His commandments, and *amor loco d'este mundo*, the foolish love of this world. Discoursing on the three faculties of the soul (reason, memory, and will), he shows how these can promote salvation—as well as the interests of the man seeking *loco amor!* But after all, he points out, forewarned is forearmed, and his intention is to show human folly so that men may choose the good. Thus he both defends his book and indicates how it should be read.

In his Prayer (11),[4] the Archpriest develops the metaphor of the husk and the kernel, urging upon the reader an allegorical interpretation of the work. Two hymns on the seven joys of the Virgin Mary are followed by the hilarious disputation between the Greeks and the Romans, an *exemplum* with ambivalent meanings (44). The story illustrates the general point made in the sermon-parody —that a sign can be interpreted variously, depending on the reader's enlightenment, but with a guarantee of beneficial results no matter how it is interpreted: as the tale shows, even the crudest signs operate ultimately for the good.

With this last admonition to the reader, the Archpriest assumes his role of the elusive manipulator of ambiguities and ironies. He solemnly invokes the Aristotelian principle that all creatures have two fundamental desires: nourishment and sexual intercourse (71). This is particularly true of human creatures, not the least himself. With this, he begins to narrate his fourteen love-affairs.

The first affair, with a *dueña cuerda,* a prudent woman (77), sets a general pattern. The Archpriest sends a messenger, or go-between, to present his suit; the *dueña* responds with fables (the ailing lion, the earth that moaned). She leads him on, but in the end his suit is unsuccessful. The Archpriest composes songs (which are not preserved in the text). Dejected, the Archpriest reflects on the vanity of worldly things, and then turns his thoughts to another lady.

In his second attempt (112), he sends one Ferrand García as his go-between to a baker-woman named Cruz (Cross); this time, the lady is won— but by García! The Archpriest then reflects on astrology and the destiny of man, and on his own condition, for he was born under the sign of Venus, and he narrates the story of King Alcaraz' son, whose destiny as fixed by the stars could not be averted. (Like many other episodes, this one is replete with doctrine.)

In his third adventure (166), the Archpriest makes advances to a noblewoman; she rejects them, narrating the fable of the burglar and the hounds. Downcast by his failures, the Archpriest turns angrily on his patron, Sir Love (Don Amor, 181), reproaching him for being so mean with his favors, and corroborating his rebukes with *exempla* of the youth who desired three women and of the frogs and

King Jupiter. Gradually, the Archpriest's attack becomes a harsh indictment of Love as the fountainhead of all evil. He describes in detail the sins Sir Love causes, beginning with cupidity, the root of all evil, and then proceeding through pride, avarice, lust, envy, gluttony, vainglory, and accidie. Each description is illustrated by a beast fable; and in the last case, the Archpriest links accidie to hypocrisy and illustrates both with the long beast fable satirizing the contemporary practice of law (321). The hypocrisy that attends love and accidie is further exemplified by the rich, hilarious, blasphemous parody of the *Horae* (372), in which a lascivious cleric pursues his amorous enterprises in concert with tag lines from the hours of the priest's daily office. The Archpriest concludes his attack on Sir Love by comparing his followers to the mouse and the frog, both of whom were destroyed by the hawk.

In his reply (423), Sir Love sweetly and reasonably addresses himself not to the substance of the attack but to the reasons for the Archpriest's failure in his affairs. He delineates the physical qualities that make a woman desirable and describes what the good lover must do if he would win her favors. He urges the Archpriest to employ a go-between who knows the trade, and portrays the type in exhilarating detail. He castigates the vice of laziness—often a cause of the lover's failure—and the mistake of leav-

ing one's lady alone too long; both are illustrated by
*exempla,* the latter by the ribald fabliau of Pitas
Payas. Then Sir Love discourses on the power of
money (490)—its power to corrupt the clergy, its
effectiveness in love affairs. To show what evil results
excessive drink can have, however, he relates the tale
of the hermit.

After further counsel, Sir Love departs
(575). The Archpriest is dejected, for he has never
yet found the kind of lady Sir Love described; yet
he knows he must continue to sing his love songs.
He falls in love again (580) and turns to Lady Venus (Doña Venus) for help, describing to her in detail the present object of his affections—a recently
widowed lady named Lady Sloeberry (Doña Endrina). Lady Venus' advice (608–48) repeats in
part her husband's counsels. (During this episode,
the protagonist assumes the guise of one Sir Badger
of the Orchard—Don Melón de la Huerta; the tran-
sition is made silently in the course of the narrative.)
The Archpriest employs Trotaconventos ("convent-
hopper"), a go-between of remarkable talents, who
is an important figure in the rest of the work and
becomes a prototype for many such figures in later
Spanish literature. Her given name, we learn later,
is Urraca; Trotaconventos is a generic name.

There are some lacunae in the text, but the
major events are clear enough, and the lacunae them-

selves can be reconstructed from the twelfth-century Latin play *Pamphilus*,[5] the general storyline of which is followed in this episode. Lady Sloeberry is attracted to her suitor, but is torn by the conflict between love and honor. And besides, she is afraid of a scandal and of losing her inheritance if she marries too soon. Through the supremely skillful management of Trotaconventos, she finally agrees to meet with Sir Badger. At this point, Trotaconventos leaves Sloeberry and Sir Badger alone, on the pretext of having to answer a neighbor's call. (The *Pamphilus* describes the seduction frankly; in the *Libro*, there is a lacuna, perhaps because the missing pages were torn out.) When Trotaconventos returns, Sir Badger is gone and Lady Sloeberry is in tears. The old crone attends to Sloeberry's misery over her dishonor with a mixture of cynicism and pragmatism—and anyway, the lovers eventually get married. But the marriage is very sudden (891); it would appear that the stanza was added to forestall criticism. Furthermore, this "joyful" marriage is followed by eighteen stanzas (including the fable of the lion and the ass) in which the Archpriest illustrates the failings of Lady Sloeberry and severely enjoins his female readers not to imitate her conduct.

Having moralized sufficiently, the Archpriest forthwith proceeds with his love affairs (910). He is attracted to a very young lady and dispatches

Trotaconventos to win her over. Despite a quarrel between the Archpriest and Trotaconventos—which serves as the occasion for the Rabelaisian catalogue of the forty-one nicknames which one should *not* apply to a go-between—the young lady falls for the Archpriest. But, alas, she dies.

Now begins a series of mountain episodes (950), a hearty burlesque of the *pastourelle*. Wandering in the mountains of the Sierra de Guadarrama, the Archpriest encounters four mountain girls, notable primarily for their belligerence and brawn, their lust and greed, and their ugly features, each one worse than the other. Each episode is told twice, first in *cuaderna vía,* then in a lyrical meter. After these wanderings, the Archpriest arrives at the shrine of St. Mary of Vado (1043) and dedicates two hymns on Christ's Passion to the Virgin.

Since the season of Lent is approaching, the Archpriest returns to his own region (1067). The episode which follows is an allegory of the events in the liturgical calendar between the days before Lent and the Sunday after Easter. The first section is the conflict between Sir Carnival (Don Carnal) and Lady Lent (Doña Cuaresma), presented as a mock-battle between the sea foods of the Lenten fast and the rich fare of worldly tables. Sir Carnival's grand armies—roosters, partridges, and capons, corned beef, peacocks, and pheasants—are roundly defeated by Lady Lent's eels and crabs, oysters and squid, lobsters and dogfish, and Sir Carnival is thrown into prison (1126). As Sir Carnival makes his confession, there is a dissertation on confession and absolution (1131–60). Carnival's penance takes the form of a rigorous diet, each day's fare linked to one of the seven sins.

The next section (1173), after describing the deeds of Lady Lent, narrates the escape of Sir Carnival on Monday of Passion Week, the morning after Palm Sunday. Aided by a rabbi, Sir Carnival takes refuge in various parts of Spain (to the dismay of the cattle) and challenges Lady Lent to a duel. Lady Lent does not accept; in pilgrim's garb, she flees from Castile. On Holy Saturday (1210), Sir Carnival and Sir Love make a triumphal entry into the world and are joyously welcomed by all creatures, especially the clergy and religious. There is a good deal of rivalry among the religious (who are united only in their antipathy toward nuns) as they attempt to please Sir Love, but he finally accepts the humble hospitality offered by the Archpriest. Sir Love has a grand pavilion built in a field near the Archpriest's house; here lovers will be welcome. The pavilion is described in some detail (1266); it is an allegory of the seasons and the months of the year. Then Sir Love describes for the Archpriest his wanderings of the past months.

On the Sunday after Easter (1315), after Sir Love has gone, the Archpriest sends Trotaconventos to find a lady for him. She approaches a rich widow, but without success. On the feast of St. Mark (April 25), the Archpriest falls in love with a widow whom he sees praying and sends Trotaconventos to her. But the widow decides to remarry and the Archpriest's suit is again frustrated.

Trotaconventos now urges the Archpriest to turn his attentions to a nun (1331). She once worked in a convent, she knows the nuns well, she considers them superior to other women for charm, good manners, and discretion, and there is one particular nun—Doña Garoça—with whom the Archpriest should hit it off well. The suit of Doña Garoça is carried on mainly through a lengthy and spirited debate in fables between the nun and Trotaconventos, each trying to cap the other. As Doña Garoça becomes interested in the Archpriest, Trotaconventos describes him in detail (1485) and thus persuades her to see him. The Archpriest's hopes rise. A platonic relationship begins between them. Within two months, however, Doña Garoça dies.

In an effort to forget his grief, the Archpriest sends Trotaconventos to a Mooress, again without success (1508). This is Trotaconventos' last assignment, as she herself dies soon afterward (1518). Her death provokes the Archpriest to a long apostrophe to Death, in which the conventional lament (*planctus*) is combined with a sermon; satiric shafts aimed at the living are interwoven. This outburst is followed by a panegyric and epitaph for Urraca; the two together form a kind of apotheosis. She is a true martyr, for she suffered martyrdom for God's sake and was always faithful to those whom she served: now she is a kind of patroness of men who seek *buen amor*.

Moved by the consideration of death (1579), the Archpriest discourses at length on the armor of Christians against the World, the Flesh, and the Devil. His schema prescribes, as specifics against the seven deadly sins, a whole panoply: the seven Works of Mercy, the seven Gifts of the Holy Spirit, the seven Virtues, and the seven Sacraments. But this sermon also ends in jest: cutting it short, the Archpriest points out that he has always been fond of short things, particularly short women, and he goes on to praise them (1606). The fourteenth affair follows, managed (badly) by a new go-between, Sir Ferret (Don Furón). The narrative proper closes here, with a renewed admonition on the title, contents, and meaning of the book. The Archpriest claims to have presented only the bare text; it is up to the reader to develop the gloss.

The remainder of the work (1635 to the end) seems to be an anthology of ten songs, conclud-

ing with a fragmentary narrative about an episcopal
letter to the clergy of Talavera, ordering them to put
away their concubines, and the reception accorded
this letter by the clergymen.

*The Poem*

The meaning of the work has been the subject of much critical debate. At more than one point
the author warns the reader that his book must be
taken allegorically, invoking the usual images of
the husk and the kernel. In some involved stanzas at
the beginning of the work (65–70), Juan Ruiz
seems to provide the reader with the appropriate
method for interpretation.

Allegorical interpretation of the *Libro* stems
largely from the work of Leo Spitzer.[6] Spitzer argued that the *Libro* belongs completely to the char-
acteristically medieval tradition of didactic works.
The main purpose of the *Libro,* according to Spitzer,
is to teach charity. This purpose is achieved by mani-
festing, in the person of the protagonist, all the sin-
fulness of which man is capable. Thus, Ruiz is like
Dante: both anatomize human weakness in order to
preach charity, which alone can overcome that weakness. The humor that abounds in the *Libro* is also
part of the order established by God and part of the
Archpriest's religious vision of the world.

But critics attempting to interpret the *Libro*

as a moral treatise have produced only partial explanations, which are open to serious criticism. First of all, such interpretations are hardly conclusive. Secondly, the critics often are forced to use Christian symbolism indiscriminately, without adequate attention to modifications or variations in the tradition. Thomas R. Hart's *La alegoría en el "Libro de buen amor"* (Madrid, 1959) is the best example of these attempts. He demonstrates, for instance, that the Doña Garoça episode is a reenactment of the temptation in the Garden of Eden. In the sequences of the mountain girls, Hart finds that the snow-capped mountains represent the lack of charity in nature, while the girls who preside over this harsh world symbolize the Devil. Such interpretations of individual episodes are convincing. However, Hart's work does not show a comprehensive allegorical design in the *Libro.*

The failure to show such a comprehensive allegorical meaning has induced many scholars to believe that the *Libro* is a series of humorous adventures in the Goliardic style. In this view, the religious elements and Ruiz' injunctions to allegorical interpretation would be simply camouflage to mislead the ecclesiastical authorities. Most Spanish critics, from Menéndez Pelayo to Dámaso Alonso, sensing how rare a strictly allegorical work is in Spanish literature, have opted for this opinion, while the opposing one is held mainly by non-Spaniards.

Still, the overall design of the work remains unclear. The *Libro,* loosely unified by the fourteen amorous adventures of the Archpriest, seems to be only a sequence of acceptable pretexts for giving examples of various literary genres. At the same time, a contemporary work like the *Decameron,* although organized more coherently by the frame, seems also to be an encyclopedia of human behavior. At a non-literal level, the *Decameron* can be seen as a series of episodes in which the world is alternately presented as upside down or rightside up; the virtuosity of a Ciappelletto may fool the incautious reader. This sort of trap worked quite well in the *Libro,* catching not only Sánchez (its first editor in 1790), but also most of the critics and commentators of the nineteenth and twentieth centuries. The *Libro* was in fact considered immoral, was expurgated by Sánchez, and was merely tolerated by other nineteenth-century critics, some of whom viewed their own tolerance as exemplifying broadmindedness. But the *Libro* properly belongs to that tradition of great medieval works—the *Divine Comedy,* the *Canterbury Tales,* the *Decameron*—which provoke readers to grasp vital and individual moral truth through the artistic experience of error.

Apart from the person of the protagonist and of his aide Trotaconventos, the only character who has any continuity in the *Libro* is Sir Love. He first appears to the Archpriest in a dream and delivers to him all the advice usually contained in an *Ars amandi*. Much later, after the description of the battle between Lady Lent and Sir Carnival, Sir Love appears again, this time preceded by a white banner on which a woman's figure is embroidered in gold, and followed by practically all mankind, especially by the clergy and religious. It is Easter Sunday, but the Risen Christ is nowhere to be seen. Sir Love has taken his place. At least in this sequence, the *Libro* is a parody, and at the same time an indictment, of courtly love. An erring Archpriest has made a pilgrimage which leads to the worship of a new golden calf.

The *Libro* mixes the comic and the serious, the satiric and the tender, the devout and the blasphemous, without embarrassment. It seems largely autobiographical and born from direct experience, yet every part has been linked to some source or model or convention: the most realistic episode, the story of Lady Sloeberry, derives largely from *Pamphilus*. One can use the internal evidence to argue that the Archpriest was—or was not—in prison when he wrote the opening prayer; or that this prayer is clearly for deliverance from an earthly prison, from the prison of the flesh, or from the prison of love. The ironic narrator is very much in evidence throughout.

The poet's style is by turns tight and padded, punning and homely, grand and racy. At times, his tone is tender, at times sententious and proverbial, at times exuberant and lusty. But he is rarely solemn or self-righteous. Even the laments of the unrequited lover can never fully escape the genial sense of amusement lurking just below the surface. Ruiz is clearly fascinated by the concrete as well as the allegorical. His episodes often have dates and locations; abstractions come alive; popular speech bristles through his verses. An extreme example is the tale of Pitas Payas, in which the characters speak a gay mixture of Catalan, Spanish, and Provençal.

That great encounter between rabbits and sardines—the battle of Sir Carnival and Lady Lent —is an uproarious burlesque of the epic encounter between two great knightly forces. Yet it does not debunk chivalry or directly attack church teaching. As Félix Lecoy says,[7] the episode expresses an admirable and powerful *joie de vivre*. The confession, repentance, and mortification of Sir Carnival may appear to argue a victory for righteousness. But April is at hand, nature is at work, and the penitent escapes —Ruiz' way of turning tears into laughter (cf. James 4:9). Occasionally, Ruiz becomes a bit tiresome with his doctrine and his *sententiae,* but generally his instincts are right. In developing the allegory of the months, he resists the medieval tendency to grand elaboration and concentrates on a single motif, and "he discards the customary static description of allegorical figures, in favor of a dynamic evocation of the chores pertaining to each month." [8]

Despite the episodic and loose structure of the whole work, Ruiz' sense of narrative and character is often superb. He is not of course writing a modern novel; in general, he follows the medieval practice whereby lesser characters are individualized, and major characters are portrayed in universalized terms. "Ruiz individualizes with conspicuous vigor the quite secondary figures . . . : the dancing girl and the weaver, who cannot keep their feet still, the one while operating the loom, the other at the sound of the tambourine (470 ff.); or the month of June, personified as a person who 'had eaten unripe grapes, and now his voice was hoarse,' while 'his hands were stained full red, as there was such plenty of cherries.' " [9]

With only a few details, he lets us see the rascally Ferrand García and the baker-woman Cruz disporting themselves, or the picaresque Sir Ferret, the bungling messenger who makes a shambles of the Archpriest's last attempt at an affair, or the Mooress keeping herself aloof. Doña Garoça is convincingly

THE POEM / 19

drawn as both nun and lady, so that the affair with
her remains platonic without any sense of disap-
pointment, and at the same time she can function as
a foil to the common crowd of ordinary nuns.

The main characters—the protagonist and
Trotaconventos—while universalized, do possess
distinct lives of their own. The character of Trotaconventos, though deriving from the old bawd in the
*Pamphilus,* is fully developed out of a few hints in
the Latin play. (It is worth noting that the *Pamphilus* is 780 lines long, while the Sloeberry episode
occupies stanzas 580 to 891, plus seventy stanzas
missing from the text, plus eighteen more in the
Archpriest's postscript to the ladies: a total of 1,596
lines.) Both Trotaconventos and Sloeberry are viv-
idly realized in this episode; Ruiz does not depend
(as the *Pamphilus* did) on happenstance or coinci-
dence. The great interest in this narrative resides in
the three characters and their shifting and developing
relations to each other. Trotaconventos has to work
not only on Lady Sloeberry but also on the suitor.
While the episode itself is superbly dramatic, at times
mere suggestions call up incidents not directly nar-
rated; the suggestions are enough to induce the sus-
pension of disbelief.

As for the Archpriest (to ignore his *Doppel-
gänger,* Sir Badger), externally he has all the marks
of *l'homme moyen sensuel:* a large head, bushy hair

and eyebrows, small beady eyes, a well-shaped
mouth with full red lips, a stout neck, broad shoulders, and strong wrists; his complexion is dark, his
gait is firm, and his general demeanor is jolly. This
portrait, as painted by Trotaconventos for Doña
Garoça (1485), is conventional enough in medieval
fashion. Too, he undergoes no major development
from beginning to end: this is not a psychological
novel. But the multiple role of the Archpriest—poet,
narrator, moralizer, seducer, protagonist—this is
what fascinates the reader.

The poet explores the contrasts between life
and love as they are and life and love as they ought
to be. One should say, he *exploits* these contrasts;
among other things, they provide insight into the
human comedy and into the figure not least comic in
it, himself. He preaches seriously—and portrays real-
ity faithfully. He is a true Christian, full of doctrine
—and truly a man, the same as any sinner: "E yo,
como so ome como otro pecador" (76). The piety
he purports to practice is not the piety "of abstract
theology and morality; he hates and fears as personal enemies the Devil and above all Death—with
a profound horror which is the reverse of his love of
life. With the absolute confidence of the vassal in his
feudal lord, he confides in the Virgin, his personal
and immediate protector, his intercessor before
Christ." [10] He states his moral aims over and over,

but the longest statement of these aims, the prose prologue, is ambivalent in its total effect. His juxtaposition of moralizing and action provides dramatic counterpoint, as, for example, in the postscript to the Lady Sloeberry story. Here, eighteen stanzas of counsel, in themselves a counterpoint to the suspiciously happy ending of that story, are followed immediately by the renewed passion and roving eye of the lonely lover (910).

The general narrative movement is often marked by "playful surprise" and a "zigzagging" or "associative" structure.[11] These manifestations of the irony of the narrator function to undermine effectively what some critics call the didactic intent of the work. As narrator, the Archpriest implicitly insists on his independent role. He satirizes freely and broadly—clergymen and religious, princes of the Church and princes of the state, lawyers and peasants and mountain girls. Even nuns are not exempt. True, he enters into a platonic relationship with one nun, partly because of Trotaconventos' song of praise to nuns. But the attractive person of Doña Garoça, as both nun and lady, sharply contrasts with the weaknesses and foibles of nuns in general, and the type is satirized in the cutting remarks of the male religious during the triumphal entry of Sir Carnival and Sir Love (1247).

Ruiz' satire never becomes righteous indignation—a fact that has pleased some and distressed other moralist critics. In any case, it is difficult to view Ruiz as a conscious, austere moralist exposing the laxity of his times, or as the scapegoat assuming the guilt of his world. Indeed, Ruiz' satire is effective precisely because he does not assume the role of Jeremiah flaying his contemporaries. Its effectiveness resides within the structure of the whole work, as a function of its art. His protagonist is also the object of the satire.

Ruiz is not solemn, he does not take himself too seriously, but he does take the art of love seriously. The point is important. Love itself is worthwhile, according to common doctrine, even when it fails of its object. Love has many virtues. It refines the coarse, educates the unlearned, makes the lover candid, cheerful, eloquent. It energizes the indolent, refreshes the youth of young men and removes the signs of aging. Most of all, it endows with value that which in itself appears worthless. No matter that one is homely or poor, foolish or disfigured; love sees everything as beautiful and noble.

Such a description contains many of the features of courtly love and suggests further meaning for *buen amor*, meanings borne out in the course of the poem. Though on its highest level, *buen amor* is defined as the love of God, it clearly also means human love that is something more than promiscuity or bought favors. One may go further. The *art* of love is important, as is the whole ritual connected with it—such as the sophisticated advice given by Sir Love and Lady Venus, and the song that love inspires and that inspires love.

Ultimately, courtly love as such is indicated in this poem. But the personality of the protagonist-singer as the artist of love remains, and it is that personality that unifies and gives life to the whole work. Whether he is insisting on the intricacies of good versifying, or on the value of both husk and kernel, or tongue-in-cheek on the necessity of each reader's providing his own many-tomed exegesis of the text, he is essentially an artist.[12] As artist, he considers poetry a high endeavor which must not be ancillary to some other purpose. He can even poke fun at himself as artist: "ella fizo buen seso, yo fiz' mucho cantar" (1508)—"She acted wisely and I wrote many songs." His major tenet is that every man should try everything: "Provar todas las cosas, el Apostol lo manda" (950; see also 76). The "Apostle" cited as his authority here is St. Paul, in I Thess. 5:21: "Omnia autem probate, quod bonum est tenete" ("Prove all things; hold fast that which is good"). Ruiz obviously interprets *probare* in two senses—to experience or try, and to examine or verify.

Only the thought of death makes him lose some of his remarkable poise. But soon enough he recovers, and in the epitaph for Urraca he asserts confidently that she deserves the status of martyr and has become a kind of patroness for *buen amor*. He remains the artist of love; when his preaching goes on a mite too long, he cuts it off with the comment that he prefers short or little things, and he turns to his favorite little thing, the small woman.

## The Text

All these observations are made in full awareness that the *Libro de Buen Amor* presents considerable problems. Let us now turn briefly to those problems—the manuscripts, the author, the order of parts, and the unity of the work. Since the *Libro* was first edited by Sánchez in 1790, most textual and scholarly commentary on the work (the bulk of some two hundred editions, books, articles) has been concerned with discussion of these problems.

Ruiz' work has come down to us in three manuscripts: the Gayoso (G), named for its owner Don Benito Martínez Gayoso, the Salamanca (S) and the Toledo (T), named for the libraries which owned them. All three manuscripts are incomplete. The longest, S, lacks 10 folios. G lacks 49 folios. T is hardly more than a fragment, containing 37 folios out of the original 129.[13]

Many of the gaps in S can be filled from G; the resultant collated work totals 1,728 stanzas. At

three places, however, the lacunae of all three manuscripts coincide; all three of these are in the Sloeberry
episode—between stanzas 765 and 766, 781 and
782, and 877 and 878. Seventy stanzas appear to be
irretrievably lost. Add to this number the twenty or
so lyric songs referred to in the narrative but also lost
(assuming they were actually written) and it would
appear that the *Libro* complete had about 2,100 to
2,150 stanzas.

On the other hand, *S* contains thirteen passages that are not found in the other two MSS.[14]
Since these passages do not fit either at the end or at
the beginning of the lacunae in the other two MSS,
it would appear that they never were included in *G*
or *T*. At the end of *T* the date of composition is
given as 1330; *S*, however, is dated 1343. The copyist of *S*, Alfonso de Paradinas, writing around 1417,
states that the *Libro* was written by the Archpriest
when he was in prison by order of Archbishop Gil
de Albornoz. These data have fostered the conjecture
that Ruiz, after writing a first version of the *Libro*
in 1330, was thrown into prison for having written
so irreverent a book; while there, he added the thirteen passages unique to the *S* manuscript, in 1343,
thus making a second version of his work. The hypothesis seems partly corroborated by the first ten
stanzas, in which the Archpriest implores God to re-
lease him from prison. These stanzas are found only

in S. (However, it is impossible to say whether or not G and T originally contained them also, since both lack some folios at the beginning.)

But comparison of the variants, first by Lecoy and then more extensively by Giorgio Chiarini for his recent critical edition, shows that, apart from the thirteen passages in question, there is no evidence that the text was revised by the author.[15] Rather, it seems clear that all three MSS have only one archetype. Some of the thirteen passages are necessary to the text, and thus seem to be lacunae of G and T; others may be interpolations by readers or minstrels, or they may be passages which the author deleted. The problem of the two versions remains, therefore, unsolved.

The person of Juan Ruiz is also surrounded by mystery. Outside the work, there is no evidence that he ever lived. The *Libro* tells us his place of birth (1510), his name and his occupation (19; 575); he says that, though innocent, he was in prison (1–10); the go-between describes his physical appearance (1485–89). Two documents that seem to have existed in the seventeenth century but are now lost state that in 1350–51, one Pedro Fernández was Archpriest of Hita.[16]

Who then was Juan Ruiz, Archpriest of Hita, the small village about twenty miles northeast of Guadalajara? He was clearly not a prudent man,

broadcasting his name and address in a book bound
to cause him trouble and then, while in prison, perhaps adding scabrous passages to it. Why was he in
prison—because of the book or for some other reason? On the other hand, have we any reason *not* to
suspect that "Juan Ruiz, Archpriest of Hita" is simply a fictitious name for the narrator of the *Libro?*

The present order of parts in the *Libro* is
also a puzzle, quite aside from the question of the
two versions. At the end of the narrative, there is a
small anthology of songs and a satirical fragment on
the clergy of Talavera, a small town northeast of
Toledo. Many of the songs and this fragment do
not seem to be part of the *Libro.* Then there is the
matter of the missing songs: more than a dozen
times, the narrator states that certain songs will follow, but there is no trace of these. Then there are
some inconsistencies—references to earlier episodes or
to earlier dates, as for instance in stanzas 913 and
1618.

The unity of structure of the *Libro* has been
another vexing question. For Menéndez Pelayo, the
*Libro* is a picaresque autobiographical novel, which
extends more or less distinctly throughout the work.
When the action lags, the following are interpolated:
(1) exemplary tales and fables; (2) a paraphrase of
Ovid's *Ars amandi;* (3) a version of the *Pamphilus;*
(4) an allegorical narrative, the battle of Sir Carni-

val and Lady Lent, and its sequel, the triumph of Sir Love; (5) various satires, such as that on money; (6) a collection of lyric poems, sacred and profane, showing versatility in metric forms; (7) ascetic and moral digressions, such as the passages on death and on the armor of the Christian. Menéndez Pelayo's catalogue became standard as a descriptive outline of the contents of the *Libro*.

On the other hand, the many attempts to explain the *Libro* as a structured whole and to find in it a progression in action that leads to a necessary end are quite unconvincing. The hypothesis that we do not have Ruiz' work in its original order does not sufficiently justify this failure to determine the unity of the work; the manuscript tradition as we know it today will not allow extensive or crucial changes in the sequence of parts. There is little reason to believe that the original order of the work differed radically from the text as we now have it.

The lack of a simply defined unity in the work has led some scholars (e.g., Mrs. Malkiel and Américo Castro) to locate the *Libro* in a non-Western tradition, Arabic, Hebraic, or both, in which the juxtaposition of loosely related parts to form a unity is more common than in the Latin West. Mrs. Malkiel argues, for instance, that there are many similarities between the *Libro* and works in the Semitic *maqāmāt* genre, especially the *Tahkemoni* by Yehuda ben Selomo al-Harisi and *The Book of Delights* by Yosef ben Meir íbn Zabarra.[17] But non-Western influences are minor, and one cannot conclude from them that the work belongs to a non-Western tradition. Furthermore, the earlier work done by Otto Tacke, Arthur Whittem, and Félix Lecoy on the sources of the *Libro* reveals little that is directly in the non-Western tradition.[18]

## A Note on the Translation

The translation aims at clarity, simplicity, and fidelity to the original. This is one reason why we have not attempted a verse translation. To reproduce the *cuaderna vía*, with its fourteen-syllable lines and its single rhyme for each quatrain, would be virtually impossible in modern English. Furthermore, many merits of Ruiz' poem would surely be lost in modern idiom; for these, there is no alternative to the original text. It is our hope that this unadorned prose rendering might tempt the reader with some knowledge of Spanish to turn to the original poem. Medieval Spanish is less removed from modern Spanish than Chaucer's English is from our own.

We have translated the proverbs directly rather than attempt to find "equivalents" for them; there are no equivalents with the flavor or relevance that the originals have. Where fidelity quarreled with modern idiom, we have opted for fidelity, even at the

cost of some obscurity. Anyone familiar with the
only other translation in English—that by Elisha
Kane—knows how frolicsome and gay it can be. It
is our view, however, that Ruiz is served better by
a modest translation than by a freewheeling adaptation.

The basic texts used here are the critical editions by Chiarini (1964) and Corominas (1967).
We have adopted Chiarini's order for the last parts
of the poem: after stanza 1660, Chiarini has stanzas
1710–28 and then 1661–1709. We have used sub-
titles as they appear in the Salamanca MS and in
most of the editions.

The notes appended to our version are generally of two kinds: brief philological notes on matters such as disputed readings, sources, and bibliography, which may be useful to the specialist; and
explanatory notes for the general reader. We have
tried to keep both to a reasonable minimum.

Except in the prose sermon section (pp. 35–
41), the stanza number at the top of the inside
margin of each page indicates which stanza begins
the page.

# The Book of Good Love

ord God,
who de-
livered the
Jews, that
wicked people from their capitivity       under the
hand of Pharaoh, and who led Daniel out of Babylon's deep pit, deliver my miserable person from this
wretched prison.

Lord God, who granted special grace to Esther, so that she enjoyed your help before the face of King Assuerus, grant me now your prompt grace and your benevolence; free me from my torment in this prison.

Lord God, who saved the Prophet from the lion's pit, who rescued St. James from Gentile hands and freed St. Marina from the dragon's belly, free me, my God, from this prison where I lie.

Lord God, who delivered the holy Susanna —from the false witnesses you delivered her—my God, deliver me also from this great pain; grant me your mercy, save me from your wrath.

Three days at sea the prophet Jonah dwelt inside the whale. But you led him out safe and sound as if from his own house. Now save me, Messiah, cleansed of guilt and free of punishment.

Lord God, who delivered the three young men from death, out of the oven, out of the great fire, unharmed; who saved Saint Peter from the waves of the sea—Lord, free your Archpriest from his trouble.

Lord God, who promised your servants that you would be with them when they spoke in the presence of kings, and that you would prompt their speech so that they might speak more eloquently, Lord, be with me, save me from my betrayers.[1]

The great name celebrated in prophecies was Emmanuel, the Son of the Lord Most High, the Savior of Israel; in his salutation, Lady, the angel Gabriel assured you of that and you had faith in Him.

Because of that prophecy and that salutation, because of the greatness of that name—"Emmanuel, Redeemer"—Lady, grant me grace and consolation, win me the favor and blessing of your Son.

Lady, above all ladies blest, grant me your blessing; turn your wrath and your rancor away from me. Turn all this trouble against my calumniators. Help me, glorious one, mother of sinners.

*I will instruct thee and teach thee in the way which thou shalt go: I will guide thee with mine eye* (Ps. 31:8).[2] David the prophet, speaking with the help of the Holy Ghost, addresses each one of us in the 31st Psalm, 10th verse, which I have quoted above. In this verse I perceive three faculties, which some learned philosophers claim reside in the soul and belong to it. These are reason, will, and memory. And I affirm that, if these are right, they fortify the soul and prolong the life of the body, bringing to it honor, success, and good reputation.

By his right reason, one perceives what is good and distinguishes evil from it. Therefore, among the requests which he made to God, David, wishing to know God's law better, asked: *Give me*

*understanding*, etc. (Ps. 118:34). Because when a
man understands what the good is, then will he
attain the fear of the Lord, which is the beginning
of all wisdom, as our prophet says: *The fear of the
Lord is the beginning of wisdom* (Ps. 110:10). For
the fear of God produces right reason. Thus, David
follows this line of reasoning in another passage,
where he says: *A good understanding have all they
that do His commandments*, etc. (Ps. 110:10).
Similarly Solomon says in the Book of Wisdom:
*He who fears the Lord will do good.* This is the
meaning of the first sentence of our text: *I will instruct thee.*

    Once the soul is informed and instructed that
it must be saved in a clean body, man dwells on,
grows to love, and seeks after the holy love of God
and his commandments. As David says: *And I will
meditate on thy commandments which I have loved*
(Ps. 118:47). The soul also abhors and rejects the
sin of foolish love for this world, of which the
Psalmist says: *Ye that love the Lord, hate evil*, etc.
(Ps. 96:10). This is why the second sentence of the
verse now follows, saying: *And teach thee.*

    When the soul, with right reason, right will
and right memory, chooses and embraces Good Love,
that is to say the love of God, and deposits it in his
memory in order to keep it in mind, it induces the
body to do good deeds, through which man is saved.

The Apostle John speaks in the Apocalypse about the blessed, those who die doing good: *Blessed are the dead which die in the Lord; and their works do follow them* (Apoc. 14:13). And the prophet also says: *For the work of a man shall he render unto him* (Ps. 61:13). This is the conclusion of the third sentence of our text, which says: *In the way which thou shalt go, I will guide thee with mine eye.*

We must, then, acknowledge without hesitation that a right memory always remembers past deeds and that by right reason and right will the soul chooses and thereby loves the love of God, which leads the soul to be saved by good works. Because God, for the good deeds that a man does on the road to salvation, fixes His eyes upon him. This is in short the meaning of the verse with which I began above, and even though there are times when a man might remember sin and might love it and do it, such discord does not spring from right will, nor such an act from right memory; rather it derives from the frailty of human nature, which is such that man cannot escape sin. Cato says: *No one goes through life without guilt.* And Job says: *Who can bring a clean thing out of an unclean?* (Job 14:4) —as if to say, "No one, but only God." However, right reason fails man at times, because he dwells on sinful vanities. Of this kind of reason the Psalmist says: *The thoughts of men are vanity* (Ps. 93:11).

And he also says to the reckless whose reason is
clouded: *Be ye not as the horse, or as the mule, which
have no understanding* (Ps. 31:9). And I say too
that this comes from a fault of memory which is not
informed by right reason, so that it cannot love the
good nor remember it in order to do it. This happens
also because human nature is more apt and inclined
to evil than to good, to vice than to virtue: so say
the decretals.

      These are some of the reasons why books are
written on law and statutes, on morals and behavior
and other sciences; why painting and writing and
icons were first invented. Man's memory slips: so
say the decretals. To remember everything and forget
nothing is more divine than human: so say the decretals. This is why memory is a property of the soul,
which is spirit created and perfected by God, and
which lives always with God. David also says this:
*And your heart shall live that seek God* (Ps. 21:31,
68:35). But this is not a property of the human
body, which lasts for such a short time. Job says:
*Seeing his days are determined* (14:5). He also says:
*Man that is born of a woman is of few days* (14:1).
And David says: *We spend our years as a tale that
is told* (Ps. 89:9).

      Therefore, though my knowledge is meager
but my ignorance vast and profound, I realize how
many benefits the soul loses, and the body too,

thanks to a foolish attachment to worldliness, and how many evils such worldliness brings upon the soul. Thus, choosing and wishing with good will the salvation and glory of Paradise for my own soul, I wrote this little foreword as a decent warning and composed this new book, in which I have set down some of the subtle tricks of frivolous worldly love which some people employ in order to sin. If a man or woman of right reason, with the desire for salvation, reads or hears these things, he will certainly choose and act accordingly; he will be able to say, with the Psalmist: *I have chosen the way of truth,* etc. (Ps. 119:30). Even the man who has a misguided reason will not be lost. The calloused sinner will read and meditate on the evil he does or intends by wicked artifices and deceitful ways; once the scandal caused by the tricks he uses in order to seduce women and to sin becomes public, he will sharpen his memory and look to his reputation. Whoever neglects his reputation is a very cruel man: so say the decretals.

So men will prefer themselves over sin, because well-ordered charity begins with oneself: so say the decretals. They will reject and abhor the arts and evil tricks of foolish love, which makes men lose their souls and incur the wrath of God, shortening the lifespan and begetting evil reputation and dishonor as well as much harm to the body. On the other hand, because sinning is human, if anyone would like to enjoy foolish love (and I do not so advise him), he will find here means to that end. Therefore this book of mine can truly say to any man or woman, to the wise and to the foolish, to the one who perceives the good and chooses salvation and acts well, loving God, and also to the one who desires to find foolish love along his way: *I will instruct thee,* etc.

I beg and advise anyone who reads this book or hears it read, to fix in his mind the three faculties of the soul. Above all he should understand and interpret properly my intention in writing this book and the meaning of what is said, and not the ugly sound of the words, because—as it should be—the words serve the intention, not the intention the words. And God knows that my intention was not to write in order to teach people how to sin or exercise a vile tongue; it was instead to recall everyone to mindfulness of good works and to give examples of morality and counsel for salvation, so that everyone might be better informed and might better guard himself against the many artifices that some use in the service of foolish love. St. Gregory says that the arrows a man sees do him less harm, for we can protect ourselves better against what we have seen.

I composed this book also to provide lessons and examples of prosody, rhyme, and invention, for

I made the music, the poems, the rhymes, the
rhythms, and the verses precisely as the rules of art
demand. Finally, since God and the Catholic faith
are the beginning and the foundation of any good
work—as the first decretal of the Clementinae [3] says
which begins: *On the foundation of the catholic
faith*, without which mortar no enduring work, no
lasting edifice can be made, as the Apostle says—for
this reason I began my book in the name of God,
and I took the first verse of the Psalm [4] referring to
the Holy Trinity and the Catholic faith: *Whoever
wants*, the verse that says: *God the Father, God the
Son*, etc.

PRAYER OF THE ARCHPRIEST

od the Father, God the Son, God
the Holy Ghost: may He who
was born of the Virgin give us
the strength to praise Him in poems and songs, and
may He be the protection and the mantle of our
souls. May He who created sky, earth, and sea give
me His Grace and enlighten me so that I may compose a little book of songs, and may those who hear

it enjoy it. You my Lord and God, who created man, instruct and help me, your Archpriest, so that I may write this *Book of Good Love* to delight the body and profit the soul.

Gentlemen, if you wish to hear something delightful listen to my poem; do not worry, I will not tell a single lie in the contents of this book, for these things are common practice. And so that you will listen willingly, I will address you in song and narrative, for this is a pleasant manner of composition and a faultless art,[5] in which the contents are presented most attractively and the form most elegantly.

Do not think that this is a book of vain trifles or take lightly anything that I teach in it; for just as a good coin is found in a shabby purse, so wisdom is found in an ugly book. The outside of the fennel seed is blacker[6] than a kettle, but inside the seed is pure white, whiter than ermine. White flour is kept in a blackened bin; sweet white sugar can be made from worthless cane. Under the thorn one finds the rose, a noble flower; in humble letters, one finds the wisdom of a great doctor. Just as a ragged cloak hides a wine taster,[7] so under a coarse garment there is *Good Love*.

And since the beginning and root of all good is the Holy Virgin Mary, I, Juan Ruiz, Archpriest of Hita, will begin with a song of her seven joys, which runs as follows:

THE JOYS OF SAINT MARY [8]

O Mary,
Light of the day,
guide me
in all my ways.
Grant me grace and blessing
and the consolation of Jesus
that, with devotion, I may
celebrate your joys.

The first joy we read of:
in the Galilean city,
Nazareth I believe it is,
you received the tidings

Of the angel who came to you,
the holy and worthy Gabriel.
He brought you a message from God
and said, "Ave Maria."

Hearing the command,
you humbly accepted,
and then, O Virgin, you conceived
the Son that God sent.

At Bethlehem came to pass
your second joy, O Virgin;

without travail you brought
forth the Messiah.

The Scripture relates the third,
the advent of the Kings
to adore Him lying in your arms,
Him on whom you gaze.

Caspar presented myrrh,
and Melchior gave incense.
Balthazar offered gold
to Him both God and man.

The fourth blessed joy
was this: the Magdalene
saying, joy without pain,
that your Son was alive.

The fifth joy you had
when you saw your Son
ascend to Heaven and sang praises
to God to whom He went.

Mother, this was your sixth joy:
suddenly the Holy Ghost
descended upon the Apostles
in your blessed company.

Of the seventh, Holy Mother,
the whole Church sings:
with great glory you ascended
into Heaven in the flesh.


You reign with your dear Son,
our Lord Jesus Christ;
through you may we see Him
in glory never failing.


THE JOYS OF SAINT MARY


Virgin, Queen of Heaven,
Salvation of the world,
most worthy one,
hear me; so that, singing
your joys properly,
I may serve you.


Of your joy must I sing
and always beg you,
I, a sinner,
not to look, O Mary,
to my great guilt,
but to the praise.

Seven joys you had:
the first when you received
the salutation
from the angel; when you heard
"Ave Maria," you conceived
God, our Savior.

The second was perfected
when He was born of you,
without pain,
and, attended by the angels,
was quickly known
as Savior.

Your third joy came
when the star appeared
to show
the true way to the Kings:
a companion and guide
for them.

The fourth joy came
when Gabriel
told you, Mary,
that your Son was alive
and as a sign he said
that you would see Him.

The fifth brought great bliss,
when you saw your Son, the Lord,
ascend
to Heaven, to his great Father
and you remained here with desire
to go to Him.

The sixth cannot be omitted: when
the disciples came to enlightenment
fearfully—
you were there and saw,
emerging from Heaven,
the Holy Ghost.

The seventh is unequalled:
when God your Father
sent for you;
He raised you up to heaven
and made you sit with Him
as a Mother.

Lady, hearken to the sinner;
for your Son, the Savior,
came down for us
from Heaven, to abide in you;
the one you bore, O white flower,
died for us.

Do not despise us sinners,
in whose behalf you were chosen
Mother of God;
appear with us before Him,
offer Him our souls,
pray for us.

THE DISPUTATION BETWEEN
THE GREEKS AND THE ROMANS [9]

ise Cato [10] tells us that a man must
lighten the burdens of his heart
with cheerful words and pleas-
ures, for too much sadness leads to evil. Now man
cannot laugh about serious matters, and so I will
have to include some jests. Do not belittle them,
though you may criticize my structure or my style.
Pay close attention to what I say and ponder my
meaning, lest you suffer the fate of the Greek doctor

at the hands of a stupid Roman rogue, in the time
when Rome looked to Greece for knowledge.

Here is the story. Not having any Scriptures,
the Romans went to the Greeks, who had them, and
asked for theirs. But the Greeks maintained that the
Romans did not deserve the Scriptures because,
being unlettered, they could not understand them.
However, they added, taunting the Romans, if they
really wanted the Scriptures in order to study them
and live properly, the Romans would first have to
hold a disputation with the wise men of Greece and
show that they understood the Scriptures and deserved to have them.

The Romans accepted this condition and
proposed a date for the disputation. But since they
could not understand the Greek language, they spec-
ified that the disputation be conducted by signs, the
signs of learned men.

Finally, they all agreed on a date, and the
Romans departed, worried about what they should
do, since they were unlettered and could hardly
match the vast learning of the Greek doctors. But
as they worried over the problem, a citizen proposed
that they select a rogue, a low scoundrel, who would
make signs as God directed him. This advice produced good results.

They searched out a loutish knave and said
to him: "We have set a date for a disputation in sign

language with the Greeks. If you will represent us and get us out of our predicament, you can ask whatever reward you like."

Then they dressed the ruffian in expensive clothes, as if he were indeed a great philosopher, and he ascended his rostrum and declared pompously, "Now let the arrogant Greeks come, if they dare!" To the opposite rostrum climbed a Greek doctor, a very erudite and learned man, praised by all and the choice of all, the pride of the Greeks. There, before all the people, the Greek began the disputation with signs, as had been agreed. First he calmly and leisurely arose and raised his index finger; then he sat down. Scowling with rage, the ruffian rose in his turn. He raised three fingers, thumb, index, and middle, and pointed them like a harpoon at the Greek. Then he sat down, admiring his garments. The very learned Greek got up and showed his open palm, and then sat down. Growing foolish, the ruffian jumped up and shook his fist, as if challenging his opponent.

At this the Greek scholar turned to his countrymen and said, "I cannot deny it; the Romans deserve the Scriptures." And all rose, without any disagreement. Through a worthless scoundrel, Rome gained great honor.

Some asked the Greek what he and the Roman had said to each other by their signs. He an-

swered, "I declared that there is one God; the Roman replied by his sign that He was one in three
persons. I said that everything was according to His
will; he replied with great truth that all was within
His power. When I saw that they understood and
believed in the Trinity, I knew that they deserved
to be confirmed in their belief by the Scriptures."

Others asked the ruffian what he had meant
to say. He answered, "That fellow said he'd put out
my eye with his finger, and that made me angry; I
let him know—no nonsense about it; I was mad—
that right then and there I would glady poke out
both his eyes with my two fingers and knock out his
teeth with my thumb. Then he said that I'd better
watch out, because he'd give me such a slap it would
make my ears ring; but I told him I'd give him a
wallop that he would never forget. When he saw
that the fight wasn't going so well for him and that
I wasn't afraid of him, he stopped threatening."

As the proverb of the shrewd old woman
says, "There is no such a thing as a bad word, only
one that is badly interpreted." A word well read is
a word well said; reader, if you understand my book
properly, you will have a strong defense.[11] Do not
look down on the jests you may hear; the manner
of this book has to be carefully understood. You
will not find one troubador in a thousand who
knows evil for what it is and writes subtly, ele-

gantly, and interestingly about it. You will find
many magpies without finding an egg; not every
new tailor knows how to mend.[12] Do not think that
I intend to write foolishly: what Good Love [13] says
I will demonstrate rationally.

In general this work is suitable for everyone.
Those who are wise and alert will perceive its meaning. Foolish youth should beware of folly. The man
who has good luck should select the best. The teachings of Good Love are hidden; try to learn its mani-
fest signs. When you have penetrated the meaning
and understood Love's teaching, you will not ridi-
cule the book which you now belittle. Where you
are sure the book is lying, there it is speaking the
deepest truth; the false things are in the cleverest
verses. You must judge whether something is said
well or badly according to your counterpoint; praise
or reject the verses according to the counterpoint.

I, the book, am the father of all instruments;
according to the way you notate me,[14] I will speak
well or badly; dwell on what you want me to say.
If you know how to interpret me you will always
be mindful of me.

THE NATURAL DESIRE OF MEN AND BEASTS

As Aristotle rightly says, all creatures work
for two ends: to earn their bread and to mate with

a pleasing female.[15] Had I said this on my own, I would be at fault; but it is the great Philosopher who speaks; do not blame me. You ought not question what the Philosopher says, because the Philosopher and his statements are supported by the facts. It is easy to prove that the Philosopher speaks the truth: by nature, men, birds, animals, wild beasts are always on the lookout for a new companion. Men most of all.

I repeat, men most of all, more than any other creature. According to their nature, all animals mate at certain times, but a foolish man seeks a mate at all times, beyond all measure; he is always ready and willing. The embers always try to hide in their ashes, knowing that the more they are kindled, the more quickly they are consumed; man, when he sins, can see clearly that he is falling, but still he does not want to leave off, because his nature goads him on. And I, because I am a man, a sinner like everyone else, have at times had great love for women. Man is not the worse for having experimented, for having known good and evil and for having chosen the better.


THE ARCHPRIEST IN LOVE

Let me tell you how a woman once ensnared me; at the time, I had no regrets for my dalliance.

Her conversation was pleasant and her smiles were charming: she did nothing else for me, nor did I suspect any further designs. She was a lady through and through, a lady of ladies. I could not be alone with her even for an hour: in her circle, people are very careful with all men, even more careful than the Jews are with the Torah. She was expert in all types of gold and silk work, accomplished in every way, and always cheerful. She had good manners, she was calm and quiet, and she could not be won by lavish offers of money. I sent her the little song which I transcribe below [16] by a go-between whom I had carefully instructed. But the proverb is true: when a proper lady is not interested in the message, she does not deign an answer. This discreet lady said to my messenger: "I see that many women believe in you, you old windbag, and so get themselves into trouble; I will learn from their behavior as the fox learned from somebody else's head."


THE AILING LION AND HIS VISITORS

"Once, when the lion, king of the beasts, was suffering from a painful disease, all the other animals came to visit him. This cheered him and made him feel better, and the other animals rejoiced. To please him and cheer him even more, they offered to prepare a meal for him and asked which of them he chose to sup on. He selected the bull, a beast that would yield an abundance of flesh. The wolf he appointed carver, directing him to serve everyone; the wolf did so, setting aside the entrails for the lion to eat, and keeping for himself the whole huge trunk. Then the wolf asked the lion to say grace: 'My lord, we see that you are not well; hence this light meat is for you, it will do you good. The rest of us will gnaw on the trunk, which has little nourishment.'

"But the famished lion was angered by this. He raised his paw as if to bless the table and brought it down heavily on the wolf's head, to teach him a lesson, tearing away skin and an ear from the wolf's skull. Then he ordered the fox to serve the food. Fearful and clever, the sly old fox apportioned the whole trunk to the lion and the entrails to the rest of the party, including herself. The lion was pleasantly surprised by the fox's skill at carving.

" 'Who taught you, madam, to carve so well, so judiciously, so properly?'

"She replied: 'I studied the wolf's head and learned from it what I should do and what I should not.'

"So, I tell you, old woman, but no friend of mine: Do not ever come to see me with such messages or I will teach you the lion's blessing; the wise person learns from the misfortunes of others.''

As Christ says, there is nothing secret that does not eventually become known (Mark 4:22). My secret immediately got about in the public square and my lady, close confined, was kept away from me. After that I couldn't see her anymore. She did let me know that I should try to write some sad poem which she might learn and sing sadly, because I could not have her. To fulfill my lady's request, I wrote a song as sad as this sad love. The lady sang it indeed, with more sorrow, I believe, than I could have put into the song.

There is an old saying that whoever wants to get rid of his dog will find some fault with him, so that he won't have to feed him. Those who wished to keep us apart, as they did, caused a quarrel between us, spread the gossip that I boasted that she was easy game and that I treated her as if she were a whore. Angry, my lady said: "There is no cloth without flaw, nor can one find a true friend in every market place."

As the proverb says, when someone is deceived, "You make up your mind according to what people say." They made her furious, which was what they wanted. The lady said: "Lovers never give what they promise." When I sent her my go-between, the good lady, being very learned, keen and intelligent, prudent and well mannered, related this beautiful fable from Ysopet.[17]

FABLE OF THE EARTH THAT MOANED

"When a man wishes to marry a respectable lady, he gives much and promises more; but when he has won her, he gives little or nothing of what he promised. He acts like the earth, when the earth was pregnant.

"This was how the earth started to moan: she was so swollen, she was about to burst. All those who heard her were alarmed, for she screamed like a woman in labor. She complained so bitterly that the people who heard her loud moaning thought she really was pregnant, and that she must bring forth a huge dragon or monster which would devour and destroy the whole world. Shaken by the moans, the people thought of fleeing. But when the day came for her to deliver she gave birth to a mouse! What a farce! Her moans and their fears turned into laughter.

"So has it happened to many, including your master. They promise shocks of wheat but produce wisps of straw. They blind many with wind, and they go to their own destruction. Go back and tell him not to love me, because I don't love him. The man who talks much often does very little; he makes a lot of noise, but two nuts is a small thing. Very valuable things are sometimes commonplace, and lowly and cheap things are sometimes precious."

Over a trifle she became spiteful and angry. She withdrew from me; she played a trick on me. He who thinks to deceive, remains deceived; I wrote a very sad poem about this. Later, I wrote other songs as a sincere apology. I had them delivered to her, at nightfall and at dawn. But she refused them, and I thought: "This is very bad! The mallow may wither even in the best weather!"


THE VANITY OF WORLDLY THINGS


As Solomon says, and he tells the truth, all worldly things are vanities, fleeting things, which vanish with time, and, except for the love of God, they are all frivolous. When I saw my lady estranged from me, I said: "It is useless to love one who does not requite my love. It is vain to run to the door when nobody knocks." I dropped the affair because she had withdrawn from me.

God knows that I have always thought with respect of this woman, and all others I ever looked upon; I have served them faithfully, and when I could not serve them, I have not turned against them. I have always written well of a prudent woman. It would be villainous and spiteful to write vile lines about a good woman, because in a noble, beautiful, and courtly woman are contained all the good and pleasure of this world. If God, when He created man, had considered woman evil, He would not have given her to man as a companion nor formed her from him; she could hardly be so noble, if she were not meant for good. If man did not cherish woman so much, love would not trap as many as it does. No matter how saintly they may be, all men and women yearn for a companion, especially if they live alone. A proverb says all these things: A lonely bird neither sings well nor cries. There is no mast without a sail, nor do vegetables grow without the water wheel.

I, who was all alone, without any company,[18] desired to have what others had. I set my eyes on another woman, not holy, rather worldly; I was in agony over her, but another had her easily. Since I could not simply come right out and address her, just like that, I thought I might win her if I sent a friend of mine as go-between; but he played a trick on me and ate my meal himself, while I had to chew the cud. Out of my great sorrow I wrote this rustic poem. If a lady should hear it, let her not despise me, because I should be called stupider than an ass if I did not write a jolly poem on such a trick.

THE ARCHPRIEST AND FERRAND GARCÍA,
HIS MESSENGER

My eyes shall see no light
for I have lost my Cross.[19]

For my love I took a baker,
she was called a crossed Cross.
I took a path for a road
as an Andalusian does.[20]

*My eyes shall see no light*
*for I have lost my Cross.*

Thinking that I might have her
I told Ferrand García
to plead my love before her,
and be diplomatic and smooth.

*My eyes shall see no light*
*for I have lost my Cross.*

He said that it pleased him greatly
and became an intimate of the Cross.
To me she gave some bran to chew
while he ate the whitest bread.

*My eyes shall see no light*
*for I have lost my Cross.*

On my advice he promised her
certain seasoned wheat I had,
and he gave her also a rabbit,
that traitor, that false ruffian.

*My eyes shall see no light*
*for I have lost my Cross.*

May God confound that messenger
so swift and light of foot!
May God deny the rabbit hunter
who brings the game home thus.

*My eyes shall see no light*
*for I have lost my Cross.*

Whenever I saw the Cross, I always bowed
and made the sign of the Cross. But my friend was
there, himself worshipping the Cross: I was not
aware of the evil of the crossed one. I have composed
this little song about the gluttonous student from
Cockaigne; [21] I hope you will like it. Neither before
that episode nor since have I ever found, in the
whole of Spain, one who could make such a ludi-
crous puppet out of me.

he ancient astrologers say very sagely
in their books that when one is
born, they can prophesy his future. So said Ptolemy
and Plato, and many other wise men agree with
them in this: that the destiny and the character of
every living man are determined by the ascendant
and by the constellation. There are many people
who strive long and hard to become learned, spend-
ing all they have in order to go to school for years;
but they end by knowing little, because their destiny
guides them and one cannot give the lie to astrology.
To save their souls, some join an order, some become warriors, while others dedicate themselves
completely to the serving of their lords. Many of
these fail miserably: they cannot succeed either as
monks or knights, or win the lord's affection or his
money. How can this be explained? I believe that
those astrologers are right who attribute it to the
natural course of things.

To show you how true is the course indicated by horoscopes, I shall tell you of five astrologers who from clear horoscopes prophesied catastro-
phe for a boy.

There was once a Moorish King, Alcaraz by
name, to whom was born a handsome son—the

only one he ever had. He sent for his astrologers to learn the constellation and the planet of his new-born son. Among the astrologers that came to see him were five of the most learned. After they had cast his horoscope, one of the astrologers said, "He will be stoned."

The second prophesied, "He will be burned." The third said, "He will be flung from a rock." The fourth said, "He will be hanged." The fifth said, "He will die by drowning."

When the King saw how discordant the prophecies were, he placed the astrologers under guard and held them prisoner in remote places. All their prophecies he considered completely fraudulent.

Now when the prince had come of age, he asked his father the King for permission to go roaming in the mountains and hunt some game. The King was very pleased. They chose a clear day for the hunt, but once they were in the mountains a terrible storm arose; first sleet fell, and, soon after, hail. The prince's tutor recalled the prophecies of the wise astrologers who had studied his horoscope. "Sir," he said, "let us take shelter; otherwise those who foretold your future might turn out to be right." They immediately sought for shelter; but it is an infallible truth that the natural course of events, as ordained by God, cannot be changed. Because the hailstones were now pouring down, the prince spurred his horse, but as he was crossing a bridge a fierce thunderbolt struck him; the bridge was shattered, and he fell through and hung suspended by his garments from a tree on the river bank. As he hung there where all could see him, he drowned; they could do nothing to help him. Thus were all the five destinies fulfilled and the astrologers vindicated.

When the King saw how his misfortune had come to pass, he had the astrologers released from prison, compensated them generously, and ordered them to practice astrology, for now there could be no more doubt.

I believe the astrologers to be truthful according to nature. God, however, who created nature and accident, can change them and do otherwise, as I believe and as the Catholic faith teaches. Belief in nature is not evil, so long as one has a stronger belief and firmer trust in God. I will prove it briefly by an example, so that you may believe my words and have no doubts.

In his own kingdom a King certainly has the power to pass statutes and to lay down laws and decrees. He has books and papers written about them to establish punishments for transgressors. Now, it might happen that a man commits high treason; according to the statute, he should be executed. But, let us say, the councilors are on his side; because they beg the King's mercy, the offender receives a full pardon. It could also be that the offender has, at some time, done the King a great service, the memory of which, together with pity, might move the King to pardon the crime in full. Thus, although the law decreed that the man should die, the lawmaker allows an exception to the law and lets him live. He who makes the laws can also break them. So, too, the Pope can hand down decretals imposing a certain penalty on his subjects, but he can also grant dispensations and remit all punishment out of mercy or in gratitude for past service.

We see such things happen every day. But that does not mean that laws, decrees, and statutes are abolished; rather they remain a well-defined and important science. In the same manner our Lord, when He created Heaven, placed it in constellations and planets in order, and granted them certain powers and jurisdictions, while still retaining higher power for Himself alone. Thus, through fasts, almsgiving, and prayers, and through serving God in great humility, one may avoid the effects of a bad horoscope and its constellations; God's power averts the calamity. Astrologers are not, therefore, all liars; they predict according to nature in neat formulas and are, they and their science, well rounded and reliable. But they have no power to go against God. I myself am not skilled in either the theory or the practice of astrology: the astrolabe is as unfamiliar to me as to the bullock. Still, because I see their results every day, I say all this. I see also the following: many people are born under Venus, and their main aim in life is to make love to women; they think of nothing else. They struggle and work without measure, but most of them do not obtain what they most desire.

I believe I myself must have been born under this particular sign; I have always striven to serve the ladies whom I met, and I was not ungrateful for the favors they granted; but many of them, indeed, I served without reward. Although I realize that this is my sign, to serve the ladies without reward, still if I may not eat the pears off the tree, I may still enjoy its shade. The man who serves the ladies must have many noble qualities, especially vigor, sincerity, and the power of eloquence. A good man should not be reluctant to serve the ladies; if the work is hard, the pleasure is also great.

Love changes a coarse man into a refined one, makes the dumb man speak elegantly, turns a coward into a daring man and a slothful man into an active and energetic one. Love keeps youth young, takes away age from the old, makes a pitch-black man white and handsome, and makes something out of a man who is nothing. One who is in love, no matter how ugly he is—and his beloved too—can conceive of nothing more beautiful or more worthy. In the eyes of the beloved, an idiot, a fool, an imbecile, and a beggar seem good and noble men, better than all others. Therefore, any man who loses one love should acquire another. For, even though one's constellation may be the same as mine, there is a saying: constant effort overcomes ill fortune, and even the hardest pears ripen in time.

I find one fault in all-powerful love which I dare not reveal to you, my ladies. Still, so that you do not take me for a timid poet, here it is: love always speaks falsehood. As I have said, love makes what is in itself vile seem good, what isn't worth a straw seem precious. Hear me well: to seem is not to be.

If apples always tasted according to the looks and the color of the skin, there wouldn't be another fruit of equal worth; yet they rot more quickly than other fruit, although they smell good. Such is love, whose speech is resonant, making everything it says seem very good. All that makes noise is not song: do not blame me, ladies, for revealing this to you. It is said: Tell the truth and lose friends; tell lies and gain enemies. Understand the old proverb correctly and beware of your enemies' praises.

THE ARCHPRIEST IN LOVE;
THE BURGLAR AND THE HOUND

     As the sage says, it is hard and painful to change one's habits, destiny, and fortune. Habits are a second nature, certainly, which we cannot abandon until we die. Since it is a young man's habit to yearn for a sweetheart, to desire the pleasure of making love with a beloved, I found myself a new friend, a lady in a cloister.

     She was a lady of good family and high achievements. She was skilled in all feminine arts, she was wise, intelligent, and free from coarseness, and she could teach all sorts of things to ladies and other women. Her figure was elegant, her manner affectionate; she was sprightly, ladylike, pleasant, beautiful, polite and poised, gifted, gracious, and amiable in every way. Out of love for her I composed poems and songs, and sowed wild oats on Henares' shores.[23] And thus I proved the truth of the old proverb: "He who sows in the sand will not harvest his own crop."

     Expecting to win her for my congregation, I gave her gifts—not merely fine cloth and belts, stones, beads, jewels and gloves, but, besides, the songs that follow. She kept putting me off, she wanted nothing to do with my villainy; indeed, she made a fool out of me, saying: "Men are always ready to give little in order to get much. Take it all back and tell him that bargaining is ignoble. I will not throw away God and his Paradise for the sin of the world which is but the shadow of a swaying alder. I am not so stupid that I will accept gifts, for I know that, as the wise man says, one who takes must also give."

So, my experience was similar to that of the thief who was breaking into a house and found a large mastiff that began to bark. The thief, still hoping to get away with some loot, tried to appease the dog. He threw him half a loaf of bread which he had been carrying. But the hound, sensing that the bread was full of needles, said:

"Thanks, but I don't want it. Such a bad mouthful would not be healthy. For one night's bread, I could lose everything. I won't trade the delicacies and the bread I get every day for a little extra snack tonight. If I ate your tricky bread, I would probably choke, you would steal what I am guarding, and I would commit treason. But I am not going to be so unfaithful to the master who raised me by letting you steal the treasure he has left in my trust. You would get the profit and I would commit a great crime. Get out of here, thief! I don't want your confidence."

Then the mastiff started barking angrily and

pursued the thief so fiercely that he fled from the strong room.

The same thing happened to me and to my go-between with this wise lady and with another before her. My gifts were without fruit and I regretted them. I said: "The horse thinks one thing and the rider thinks another." I abandoned the lady, according to the proverb that says: "Don't brood, chin in hand, over your loss." As I say, my luck is such, because of my sign or because of my bad character, that I cannot achieve one-half of what I desire. This is why, sometimes, I fight with Love.

will tell you of the fight I had one
night, while I was pondering my affairs, angry
but without benefit of wine. A tall, handsome
man came to me; when I asked who he was, he
said: "Love, your neighbor."

In my anger, I flew out at him: "If
you are Love, you are out of place here. Liar!
hypocrite! arch-deceiver! You can't save a single person, but you can easily destroy a hundred thousand. You poison the tips of your arrows
with deceits and subtle lies; then you string your
bow. When you shoot, you aim right at your most
faithful servants, and if they fall into disgrace with
you, you cut them off from their beloved. By your
arts you drive people crazy, making them sleepless,
ruining their appetites, drying up their throats. You
have so many tricks to enslave men that finally they
abandon both body and soul. With you, no one can
tell what's coming next. Sometimes you strike
fiercely; at other times you subvert and undermine
little by little. You know that I am speaking the
truth.

"Once you have won a man, you don't care a jot about him, but just drag him along day by day in his misery. You never let your followers go, but goad them on so that, for a wretched moment of pleasure, they go a long journey. You are so malicious that when you've shot someone, there is no medicine, no balm, no plaster that can stop the hurt; and no matter how sturdy and strong a man is, no matter how much he resists, you conquer him anyhow. Volumes have been written on the sly tricks you use, the flatteries, the lies with which you weaken people, deceive them, and finally conquer them: you love most, as the fables say, to sap their strength."

## THE YOUTH WHO WANTED THREE WOMEN

"There was once a foolish youth, a very hot-blooded young man, who wanted to marry not just one woman, but three. This was his desire, but practically everybody opposed him. His father, his mother, and his elder brother argued with him at great length that for love of them he should marry only two, first the younger and then after a month, the older girl. With this condition, he agreed to marry. After the first month they told him that now his other brother ought to get married, with full ceremony, to one woman only. The married man said that they should not go through with it, because he had a wife to whom both could be married and that there was plenty for two; they should tell him this and not let him marry another.

"The good man who was the father of this foolish youth had a mill with a large and expensive millstone. Before his marriage the boy was able to stop the millstone at full speed with his foot. This amazing feat of strength he used to carry off quite easily, before his wedding. Now, after one month of marriage, he wanted to see if he could still do it. He went to the mill and tried to stop the millstone, in his usual way, but it knocked him over, his legs in the air. The fool picked himself up and swore furiously, saying: 'Oh, strong mill! I wish you were married!'

"He loved his first wife so much that he never married the other girl after all; he never tried again to stop the millstone and gave up thinking about it. So was the foolish youth tamed by your madness.

"You, Sir Love, are the father of fire, the kinsman of flame: whoever loves you, Sir Love, burns and scalds himself. Love, you burn both body and soul of any man who follows you and you consume him as completely as fire does the wood. Those who have not experienced you were born under a lucky star; they could rest without worries, they were never sad. Once they meet you, however, men lose all their peace. They find themselves in the same predicament as the frogs who asked for a king.


THE FROGS WHO ASKED JUPITER FOR A KING

"The frogs were accustomed to croak and play in a pond, completely free from all harm. However, persuaded by the devil and looking for trouble, they entreated Jupiter earnestly to give them a king. Lord Jupiter sent them a huge wooden beam, the largest he could find. As it fell into the pond, the resounding crash silenced the frogs, but before long they realized that it was not a king that could rule them. All those who could hopped on the beam and said, 'This is not a king that we would care to serve.' So they renewed their plea to Jupiter for a king.

"Annoyed by them, Jupiter sent them as king a voracious stork that went around the pond and its shore, his bill open, devouring the frogs two by two. Complaining to Jupiter, the frogs croaked, 'Lord, our Lord, help us, you who can destroy and can heal. The king you gave us at our foolish request causes us miserable evenings and worse mornings. His belly is our tomb, his bill eats us up, he devours us two by two, grabs us up and butchers us. Lord, defend us; Lord, listen to us, give us your help and free us from this plague.'

"Lord Jupiter answered them, 'You will have to keep what you asked for. I hope that the king you shouted for so loudly punishes your foolishness. You didn't care to be free and without care; now you will just have to wrangle, since that's what you wanted.'

"One should be content with enough. A man who can be his own master ought not become a slave; a man not subject to rule ought not yearn to be ruled. Freedom and liberty cannot be bought by gold. Sir Love, the same thing happens to those who struggle with you. They could be their own masters, but they become your vassals. From then on, you think of nothing but how to destroy them, swallowing them up, body and soul. They may complain about you, but it is useless: you have them tightly chained to their misery. Well, go seek those who invoke you. Leave me alone. I don't want your company; get out of here, you! All you can do is bring misery and needless pain. By day and by night, you are like a master thief: when a man thinks he is most safe, you steal his heart, and once you've stolen it, you enslave it, subjecting it to some lady who is indifferent and who torments it. The heart, disembodied, wears your chains, obsessed with a yearning for other people's possessions. You make it fly like a swallow, spinning it round and round, so that it doesn't know what ails it. Now it dwells on Susan, now on Mergelina,[24] as your goad pricks it in various ways. In a split second, you drive it miles away; under your spurs it travels all over the world. Then you leave it sad and lonely, with painful palpitations, reminding it constantly of who doesn't love it and care for it.

"Man, what do you want with me? What do I owe you, that you should persecute me so relentlessly? You tiptoe in, quiet and meek, giving no hint by look or action, and then you stab me in the heart and turn my peace into misery. I cannot catch you and even if I could I don't imagine that I would kill you, while in your arrogance you ravage me ruthlessly, night and day, whenever you get hold of me. What have I done to you? Why haven't you ever given me a break with all the ladies I have loved, and especially with the pious lady? All her promises have added up to nothing. Cursed be the miserable moment when I first laid eyes on you. The more you stay here, the madder I become. I find more and more to accuse you of, considering the harm done me by the clever tricks you are constantly weaving, enmeshed in your evil ways."

THE SIN OF CUPIDITY²⁵

"You bring all mortal sins in your train. The men you have deceived become unrestrained in their desires and ignore the commandments given by God. Cupidity is the root of all sins. It is your elder daughter, with ambition her governess. Cupidity is your overseer and standard-bearer; it subverts justice and destroys the world. Pride and anger, which cannot be restrained anywhere; avarice and lust, which burn more easily than straw; gluttony, envy, and sloth, which are as contagious as leprosy—of all these is cupidity the root and the trunk. They abide in you, sly traitor; with honey-sweet words and deceitful gestures, men make wild promises for love's sake, and to carry out these promises they covet the worst things. They covet money they have not earned in order to carry out the promises made in the heat of love. Thus cupidity has made many steal and ruin body and soul; because of their thefts, they died untimely deaths, maimed horribly and hanged.

"You are the scoundrel responsible for all this. Anyone poisoned by your cupidity is snared by the devil. Through cupidity you brought about the Sack of Troy—by means of the inscribed apple that should never have been inscribed, the apple which

Paris awarded to Venus to win her help in abducting
Helen and in becoming worthy of her. Through
wretched cupidity, the Egyptians perished, their
bodies degraded and their souls damned. Your devotees have been and are still scourged by God; they
won little of all that they lusted after. Through
cupidity, man loses the good that he has. He yearns
after more than is proper, but in the end he neither
gets what he desires nor keeps what he has. The story
of the hound is a good example of what happens to
such men."


THE HOUND AND THE MEAT

        "A hunter's hound, carrying a piece of meat
in his mouth, was wading across a river when he
caught sight of his reflection and thought that he saw
a bigger piece of meat. Wanting to have it, he
dropped the piece he was carrying. Because of a false
image and a foolish thought, the hound lost the meat
he had. His covetousness profited him nothing, for he
did not get what he was after; thinking of gain, he
only lost what he had already.
        "The same thing happens every day to the
servant   of cupidity. He expects to realize a profit
with your help, and he loses his capital. From this
evil root springs all evil: cupidity is truly a deadly

sin. Man should never abandon goods of great value,
already secure and held free and clear, for an empty
dream; he who abandons what he has strikes a very
bad bargain."


THE SIN OF PRIDE

      "Your confidence puffs you up with pride.
Because you are fearless of the consequences, you
think of buying jewels for your mistress. Therefore
you rob and steal, and suffer afterward. By your
pride you cause crimes to be committed. Precious
jewels are stolen from travelers; women are ravished
—maidens and wives, widows and nuns. For such
crimes, the law condemns men to death, and you
cannot save them from their disgraceful doom; by
your conniving, the devil carries them off. The fires
of hell burn where you set up your house.

      "Many have you destroyed through pride:
first Lucifer and his band of angels, who fell from
their heavenly thrones because of pride and ingrati-
tude. Although they had been created good by nature, they were and remain forever damned by their
pride. One could not enumerate in a thousand volumes the names of all those who have been and remain yet damned for their pride. Believe me, Sir
Love, all the battles and fights ever fought or now

being fought, all the insults, the brawls, the ugly squabbles, result from your pride; all the evil in the world accompanies you. The proud man, arrogant, without fear of God, without prudence, falls more easily than another, though he be weaker and poorer. Such was the case of the jackass and the stallion."

THE JACKASS AND THE STALLION

"A proud stallion was on his way to a duel, because his gallant master had ravished a lady. Under his handsome trappings, he felt very brave. Far ahead, he saw a wretched jackass plodding along. The stallion galloped up and made such a tremendous racket with his forelegs and hindlegs and with his rich bridle that he frightened the other animals like a clap of thunder. The jackass pulled up short in fear; that was his undoing. For the jackass, wincing under his burden, was struggling along slowly and blocking the horse's way. The stallion shoved him downhill, sneering: 'Miserable lout, find yourself a wider road.'

"Out on the field, the stallion pranced about, cocksure of victory. But his master lost. The stallion himself was wounded severely by a spear and his entrails were exposed. That finished his career. After leaving the field, he was not worth a straw—they put him to ploughing and hauling wood; sometimes he toiled at the water wheel, sometimes at the mill. Thus he paid for his master's gallantry with the lady.

"The yoke bent his neck; his nostrils became swollen and his knees badly slashed by his falling down 'to pray.' His eyes were sunken and as red as the legs of partridges. His haunches and ribs stuck out, as did his spine; his ears drooped.

"The stupid jackass, seeing him, laughed heartily, saying: 'My proud comrade, what have you gained with your pushing and shoving? Where are your jeweled bridle and your gilded saddle? Where is your pride and your fighting spirit? Now you will drag your life out in misery and shame, and your scabs will be the payment of your pride.'

"Let those who are proud and hold themselves in high esteem take note of this example and learn from it daily. Strength, age, and honor, health and vigor cannot last forever; they vanish with youth."

THE SIN OF AVARICE

"Sir Love, miser that you are, you are avarice personified: eager to take but loath to give. The waters of the Duero could not satisfy you. When-

ever I listen to you, I find myself in trouble. Dives
was damned by his nagging greed, since he would
not give even a little crumb to the poor but saintly
Lazarus. You find the sight of any poor man repulsive, whether he is big or little, and you dislike giving him even a penny out of your hoard. It does not
matter that the holy commandment orders us to
clothe the naked, to feed the hungry, to give shelter
to those in need. You are so greedy that you have
never given anybody anything, even though a hundred men might be crying for alms. What will you
do, you wretch, on the day of reckoning, when God
orders you to account for the management of your
hoard and your profits? Treasures and kingdoms—
a score of them—will be of no avail then.

"When you were poor, when you were in
need, you heaved up sighs and did penance, beseech-
ing God for health and sustenance, which you vowed
you would share with the poor. God heard your
groans and restored you to sanity, health, wealth,
and great treasure; but now, whenever you see a
poor man, you frown and act like the ailing wolf
in the glen."


THE WOLF, THE GOAT, AND THE STORK


"The wolf was having a snack on a goat,
when a bone got stuck in his throat and was choking

him. Immediately he summoned doctors and surgeons, promising to give up his evil ways. He offered wealth and treasure to whoever got the bone out. A stork flew down from the sky and, with a neat twist of her bill, removed the bone. The wolf was healed and ready to return to his snack. The stork demanded payment. The wolf said: 'What? Why, I could have broken your neck by snapping my teeth together; consider yourself paid in full that I decided not to kill you.'

"You are acting the same way. Now that you are full of bread and money—which you robbed from others—you refuse to give a little rye to the poor. But you will become dried out like the dew on the straw. It is useless to be kind to an evil man, because an ingrate never repays a good deed; the evil man spurns gratitude, saying that he has a right to all the good done him."

herever you are, there lust is too. You pant for adultery and fornication constantly, ready to sin with anyone you lay eyes on and winking in the hope of satisfying your lust. Lust drove the prophet David to send Uriah to his death in the front line: 'Go,' said David, 'bring this letter to Joab for me, and then come back.' For love of Bathsheba, Uriah's wife, David became a homicide and offended God, and so could not complete the temple in his lifetime. Instead, he had to atone greatly because of your sway. Five great cities were burned to the ground because of lust; three of them were destroyed for their own guilt, the other two for their neighbors' guilt. Fortunes may be lost even because of neighbors. I would not like you as neighbor; don't be so eager to come near me.

"The story goes that Vergil,[26] the sage, was deceived by a noblewoman, who left him dangling in the basket in which, so he thought, he was being hoisted to her chamber. But because she disgraced him and disdained his request, the great enchanter played a cruel trick on her. He enchanted all the fires in Rome so that all the tapers and fires were suddenly extinguished. Now the inhabitants of Rome could have no fire—to their harm—unless they kindled it in the genitals of the wretched woman. No other flame would last. If they tried to pass burning coals or light one taper from another, the fire would sputter out. Finally they all had to go to the noblewoman and get their flame from her as from a blazing fire. Thus did Vergil avenge himself for the shame and dishonor.

"After all this shame and disgrace, he disenchanted the fire so that it would burn again. Then, because of his desire to satisfy his lust with the lady, he performed another marvel which no one would ever have imagined. The bed of the Tiber, mighty river of the city of Rome, swollen by many tributaries, he transformed into a bed of copper which shone more brightly than lacquer. Thus does your lust ensnare the ladies. But after he had sinned with her, she felt debased and had a winding staircase built and studded with sharp blades, so that when Vergil came again, he would meet his doom. But he, divining what had been prepared for his destruction, never returned to her, nor did he desire her any longer.

"So because of lust is the world indeed mocked and mankind saddened. Of those whom you would wound, no one recovers; all the stupid fools who are addicted to your lust destroy themselves. The same thing happened to the eagle who had foolish habits."


THE EAGLE AND THE HUNTER

"The royal eagle sings on the cliffs and from her perch looks down on all the other birds. Not one of her feathers falls to the ground but the hunter who finds it values it more highly than he would silk. One hunter had feathered his well-honed arrows and darts with eagle feathers, and, while hunting according to his custom, wounded the royal eagle in the chest. The wounded eagle, looking down, realized that her own feathers had done her in, and uttered these hard words to herself: 'What killed me was born of me.'

"The wretched fool who, not caring about his own soul, submits to your folly and evil commerce, wrecks his body and damns his soul; and what kills him is born of him. Man, bird, or beast— every creature that yields to temptations of lust, immediately feels remorse. He becomes melancholic and feels debilitated. His life has been shortened. He who said this does not lie. Who could count all those ruined by lust? Who could enumerate your fornications and your evil traffic? Those who are enslaved

by your passion and your folly are carried off by the
devil if they are not careful."


## THE SIN OF ENVY

"You are sheer envy, more than all that there
can be in the whole world. Men fear you, seeing your
prodigious jealousy. Should a friend tell you gossip,
what gloom and foreboding oppress your heart.
Your pure envy nurses jealousy. You constantly
suspect that someone is flirting with your beloved,
and your jealousy makes you sad and bitter. You
feed on jealousy, not caring for anything good. From
the moment that jealousy takes root in you, you
choke with sighs and heartaches. You cannot rest
content with yourself or anyone else; your heart
pounds, you are never at ease. In your jealous suspicions, you loathe everybody, you pick quarrels, you
grow despondent, you look for trouble and find
what you deserve. You are like the fish in the net:
you start a fight but cannot finish it; your strength
fails and you cannot defend yourself. You can
neither conquer nor escape. Trapped by your sin,
you perish.
    "Out of envy, Cain murdered his brother
Abel, and so he is now inside Mongibel.[27] Out of
envy, Jacob stole the blessing from Esau, and was

cursed by him. Out of wicked envy, Jesus Christ
was betrayed, true God and man, beloved Son of
God; out of envy, He was arrested, killed, and overcome. Not a single good can be found in envy. Every
day, men vie with one another out of envy, and they
all—men and beasts—fight because of envy and jealousy. Wherever you are, jealousy thrives, produced
by envy and fostered by envious men. If your neighbor has more wheat than you have straw, you stir up
trouble for him out of envy. Trying to be better
than he is, you act as the crow did among the peacocks."

THE PEACOCK AND THE CROW

"The crow saw the peacock spreading his
tail and said enviously: 'I must see what I can do to
become that beautiful.'
"What folly! Whoever is black does violence
to himself in order to be white. First, she plucked her
whole body, her face and her brow, and dressed herself in a complete new plumage of peacock feathers.
Then, decked out in alien beauty, she strutted toward the church. (Some women act just as the crow
did.) This peacocked crow, in peacock's dress, went
a little mad when she saw herself so well turned out.
Scornful of her betters, she mixed among the pea-

cock's offspring. But the peacock was annoyed at this strange offspring, and saw through the disguise of the borrowed finery. He plucked all her feathers and threw her into the gutter; there the crow seemed even blacker than the hedgehog.

"Thus does your envy make many people act, so that they lose what they have in order to get what belongs to other people. Their bodies are bursting with envy, but they will find only evil in you. Whoever desires what is not his and wants to look like another by showing off with something not proper to him is going to lose both his own and the rest. He who believes himself to be what he is not is a fool, and goes to his ruin."

## THE SIN OF GLUTTONY

"You, Sir Love, gluttonous and greedy, bring gluttony. You wish to be the first to taste everything you see. Weakened by your lecherous habits, you are always famished, and in order to recover your strength, you act like a wild wolf. As long as I have known you, I have never seen you fast. You have breakfast in the morning, you never miss your lunch, you eat enormous snacks, and still you want a bigger dinner. If the food is available, you gorge yourself during the night. Too much food and drink increases the phlegm. You sleep with your mistress, a tumor chokes you, and the devil carries you off and roasts you in hell. Even so you urge the young man to eat well and not worry.

"Out of gluttony and greed our father Adam ate the fruit he should not have eaten and was driven out of Paradise by God that very day. And because of this, he remained in hell from the time he died. It was gluttony which destroyed many in the desert, among the best men that there were: the prophet himself tells us this. You are always ready to eat and glut yourself. By gluttony you made Lot, that noble man, drink so much that he lay with his daughters, following your lust, because abundance of wine brings abundant lust and every other evil. Gluttony causes violent death both to the body and to the miserable soul of the glutton; there are many fables and famous stories about this, but in order to get rid of you quickly, I will tell just one short tale."


THE LION AND THE HORSE


"A very stout horse was grazing in the pasture, and the lion, although he was just then coming back from a hunting trip, gazed at the horse with hungry eyes.

" 'Vassal of mine,' he said, 'come and kiss my hand.'

"The horse responded thus to the greedy lion: 'You are my lord and I am indeed your vassal, and I am willing to kiss your hand. However, I cannot come over to you because I am badly handicapped; a cursed blacksmith shod me and drove a nail so deep into my hoof that I am pierced. Come, my lord, with your blessed teeth, and remove this nail from your property.'

"The lion bent over to give him some relief; this was his undoing. The horse planted a strong, sharp kick between the lion's eyes, leaving him dead. Then, frightened, the horse started to run toward the river; he had, however, eaten large quantities of heavy herbs; he grew very tired and was taken with the vives. Thus do reckless gluttons perish.

"Eating excessively and gorging oneself, together with plenty of wine and hard drinking, destroy more men than any sword. Hippocrates often said this, while you claim that he who eats well behaves as a young man should."


THE SIN OF VAINGLORY

"You bring anger and vainglory such as the world has never seen. You display more pride and gusto than the whole of Spain; when you do not get your way, you go into a complete frenzy. Petulance and agitation are your bosom comrades. In his colossal vainglory, the powerful king of Babylon, Nebuchadnezzar, had no respect for God and no fear of Him; but God stripped him of all his power and his honor. He fell very low, to the level of beasts; he ate wild herbs, as the ox eats straw and the like; he was covered with hair like a beast and grew claws longer than those of the royal eagle.

"Rancor and murder are your servants: 'Don't you recognize what I am, the flower of youth?' You fling insults at random, and the fools slaughter each other because of you, you villain. Because of his great wrath, Samson also lost his strength when his mistress Delilah cut the hair in which that strength resided. When he had recovered it, he killed himself and many others in his rage. Because of anger, Saul, the first king the Jews had in their tradition, killed himself with a sword. Reflect, then: can I trust you? I do not think so, by my faith.

"Anyone who knows you will not trust you; anyone who sees your works will back off from you. The more a man lives with you, the less he respects you; the more he experiences you, the less he likes you."

THE LION AND HIS RAGE

"The proud lion, bursting with rage and vainglory, was cruel and noxious to all the beasts. In the end, his wrath destroyed him. Let me tell you the story: it might be profitable to you.

"In his youth, the proud lion hunted all the beasts with insolent terror. Some he would kill, others he wounded. Then old age, feebleness, and ill health caught up with him. The news spread to the running beasts, and they, rejoicing now that they were free, all came to avenge themselves on him. Even the foolish ass came, among the very first. They all set on the lion and wounded him badly. The rampaging boar dug in with his tusks, the bull and the steer gored him with their horns, while the lazy ass stamped his own seal upon him: he gave the lion a pair of fierce kicks in the forehead. Frenzied, the lion tore out his own heart and died by his own claws. Anger and vainglory paid him off badly.

"A man occupying a high position of honor and authority should not do to others what he would not wish done to himself. For he can, only too easily, lose all his power and be repaid in kind."

THE SIN OF ACCIDIE [28]

"You are the inn and the hostel of accidie; you want a good man to avoid doing anything good. Then, once you see him inactive, you provide for him a miserable life, one that begins in sin and ends in wretchedness. You yourself are never indolent. When you catch someone, you fill his mind with vicious plans and deceits, so that he revels in sin; by your dissolute arts, you destroy souls and bodies.
    "Together with accidie you bring hypocrisy. You make a show of great humility, but you are plotting secret gains; while pondering, you seem sad, keeping your eyes downcast. But when you see beautiful women, you steal sly glances like a fox. You preach a great deal but practice none of it, trying to deceive everybody with your smooth talk. You want what the wolf wanted from the fox. You, ill-trained lawyer, pay attention to this useful fable." [29]

THE CASE OF THE WOLF VERSUS THE VIXEN IN THE COURT OF SIR MONKEY, JUDGE OF BOUGIE [30]

"The vixen stole the cock from her neighbor. Seeing her, the wolf ordered her to return it,

because, he said, one ought not steal from others;
his real interest, however, was to eat the cock himself. He accused others of what he himself practiced
all the time, blaming others for what he praised in
himself, condemning in others what he himself liked
best, and saying that they should not do what he
did as a matter of course. In court, the wolf brought
his case against Mother Vixen before a renowned
sage by the name of Sir Monkey, Judge of Bougie,
a subtle and erudite man who never held court without getting results. The wolf pleaded well, in suitable, pertinent, clear, and explicit form; he had a good
lawyer, quick and keen, a greyhound, great scourge
of the vixen.

    " 'I, the wolf, institute charges against
Mother Vixen, before you, very honorable and
learned Sir Monkey, ordinary Judge of Bougie, and
appeal to law against her malfeasance. I state that
during the present month of February in the year
1263, in the reign of Our Lord Lion the Butcher,[31]
who came to our city for the purpose of making
money, she did enter the house of Sir Ram, my vassal and tenant, by way of the chimney, by night,
with thievish intent. By stealth she carried off the
cock, our herald, kidnapped him and ate him, to my
detriment, in a field. I accuse her of this before you,
a good man, and ask that you sentence her, by due
process of law, to be hanged on the gallows and die

as a thief. I offer to prove all this under penalty of retaliation.'

"After the complaint had been read in court, the vixen wisely and shrewdly said: 'Sir, little do I know, and I am poor as well; allow me an advocate who will plead for my life.'

"The judge answered: 'I have just come to this city of yours, and I am not acquainted with the people. I grant you a twenty days' deferment; get yourself a lawyer, and then come on the appointed day.'

"The judge adjourned the court, and both parties started to look for either money or gifts to give to their attorneys. The vixen already knew one who could help her. When the day assigned for the hearing had arrived, Lady Vixen came with a great lawyer, a shepherd's mastiff who wore a spiked collar. At the sight of him, the wolf was dismayed.

"This great lawyer stated for his client: 'Your honor, Sir Monkey, the wolf's statement and accusation are merely a blind, because he is the great and insatiable thief. Therefore, I take good and lawful exemption against the hearing of his claim because as an accomplished robber, he cannot make such an accusation validly. Many times, by night and by day, he has stolen and carried off sheep of mine; I myself have witnessed him cutting their throats in those fields. I recovered their bodies from

him before he could eat them. He has often been
convicted of theft, before a judge, with due process,
and has been rightly defamed. Hence, nobody should
be accused by him; he should not even be given a
hearing in your court.

" 'Further, I must bring it to the attention
of this tribunal that he has been solemnly excom-
municated by the authority of the papal legate, because he publicly maintains a concubine while he is
legally bound to his wife, Lady Wolf, who lives in
Vileburrow. His mistress is the mastiff bitch who
guards the sheep. Therefore, what he asks is not
worth a straw, and his evil words should receive no
response. Acquit Mother Vixen and let her go home.'

"Seeing that they were cornered, the wolf
and the greyhound reluctantly granted everything.
But Mother Vixen immediately said: 'Sir, let them
be held under a countercharge; I ask that they be
put to death without trial.'

"They presented all the arguments for their
case and then asked the judge to set a convenient
date for his decision. The judge fixed the date for
after Epiphany. Then Sir Monkey went home, attended by a large retinue: the litigants and the wily
lawyers went along as a sham council, trying to influence the judge. But nobody could trick him. Heeding advice of counsel, each side made offerings to the
judge—this one a salmon, that one a trout, this one

a cup, that one a basin, all offered in secret; it was as if no holds were barred.

"On the day appointed for sentencing, both parties presented themselves before the judge. The good judge said: 'Why don't you see first if you can settle this out of court, before I myself pronounce and pass sentence?'

"The lawyers tried with all their might to ascertain the judge's intention and guess at the judgment, but they simply could not make out anything. They dropped many hints, hoping to induce him to open his heart: he did bare his teeth, but without smiling; they thought he was joking, but actually he was angry. The parties and their respective counsel declared that they could not agree on a settlement; they requested a judgment. Then the learned and well-informed judge did his duty well, respecting his conscience; seated on his chair, he pronounced this judgment which he had himself written:

"'In the name of God,' said the judge, 'I, Sir Monkey, ordinary Judge of Bougie, having seen the complaint made by the wolf in which he accused Mother Vixen of theft, and having seen the defense and excuses set forth by the vixen in her answer, and having seen also the replies and replications that the wolf propounded in all his arguments, and having seen also what Mother Vixen demands for the wolf in her counterclaim and the conclusion; having seen

all the testimony and all the pleadings that there are,
and the parties insisting on a judgment and nothing
else; having personally examined all the records of
the proceedings and held a conference that was very
profitable to me, with men learned in customs and
laws; having God and not pressures or bribes before
my eyes, I find that the wolf's pleading is germane
and precise, well founded, well formed, and well
presented; I find that the vixen is partially on very
solid ground in her defense, excuses, and counterclaim. The first exception is peremptory, but the excommunication here is dilatory.

    " 'I will expound a little, because this case is
of great importance, and you, Latinless lawyers,
would do well to keep in mind what I say. The first
exception was very well pleaded, but the excommunication was somewhat out of order because the
authority ought to have been cited and it should
have been proven within nine days. Being dilatory,
it should have been clearly proven without failure
by writs, witnesses, or any valid instrument executed
by a notary public; if it had been pleaded peremptory, it would have been otherwise. When one enters
the excommunication as dilatory, a term of nine days
is mandatory. Keep this in mind—because many
lawyers forget or overlook it: an excommunication
is completely peremptory if it is entered against the
witnesses in a criminal case or against an excommuni-

cated judge to invalidate the trial; whoever handles
it otherwise errs gravely.

    " 'I find, further, that the vixen makes a pe-
tition beyond her rights, because one cannot counterclaim for an equal punishment in criminal law; I
cannot condemn or punish by exception, nor can a
lawyer present such a petition. Although an exception may be proven against the party or against a
false witness, no punishment will be imposed; his
request will be voided, and what he said considered
not worth a fig, but I can assure you that he will not
get the ordinary penalty, unless the witness is per-
jured or is seen to waver, because then the judge can
torture him, not because of the exception, but on his
own authority. In criminal cases, the judicial office
carries great weight. The plea can be voided because
of exception, and the witnesses must be indicted and
accused, but I cannot condemn or impose capital sentence on the basis of an exception, since the judge
cannot do more than apply the law.

    " 'I find, however, on the basis of the con-
fession made by the wolf before me, and on this basis
only, that the vixen's claim is proven, and I therefore silence the wolf this time. Since, because of the
wolf's confession, habit, and way of life, no doubt
can remain about the vixen's accusation, I hold that
the plea that he made and introduced should be dis-
missed, as I have already said. And since the wolf

confesses that he does exactly what he accuses her of, and it is known to me that he does so, the vixen is not required to answer to him in trial. I accept her defense and her excuse as valid. Never mind the claim that he made the confession in fear and under duress, because he was cornered; his fear was unjustified and what he said was unwise, for when a good judge presides, justice is secure. I give license to the vixen to go hunting, but I do not absolve her of the theft so easily; I order her henceforth not to steal the cock from her neighbor.'

"The vixen said that she would not take it —but then she might steal a hen. The parties did not appeal the verdict, relieved that they had not been convicted and that they did not even have to pay damages; this came about because they were not pressed for them and because the verdict was not contested. The lawyers criticized the judge, claiming that now he had really bungled the case and ruined his reputation by what he had said and brought out at this time. But Sir Monkey was not impressed. He pointed out to them that only the law and the constitution were relevant to his decision, and that his judgment complied with these: he had not introduced any irrelevant matter. And though they obviously learned much from this, the lawyers nonetheless continued to argue: once all the evidence is in and the witnesses heard in a criminal trial, a judge may not allow the parties to reach a settlement; when the summations are complete, a judgment must be handed down. The judge had a simple answer: by virtue of his special commission from the king, he had full jurisdiction over such matters. The lawyers learned much from this litigation."

THE ARCHPRIEST'S QUARREL
WITH SIR LOVE

ir Love, you behave like the wolf: you accuse others of your own crimes; you condemn them for the mud in which you wallow. You are a dangerous enemy to all who favor you, and you use your skill with words to deceive. You don't give a damn for the works of mercy and visit neither the imprisoned nor the sick. You prefer to mix with those who are strong and healthy, young and vigorous; and when you encounter beautiful women, you murmur sweet words to them.

"How splendidly you chant the hours [32] with loose young men, *cum his qui oderunt pacem* (Ps. 119:7),[33] until you complete the psaltery. You say *Ecce quam bonum* (132:1), with timbrels and basins; *In noctibus extollite* (133:2), and then you go to matins. You rouse yourself at your mistress' house and sing aloud *Domine labia mea* (50:17) and then play on the instruments, *primo dierum omnium,* and awaken her with *nostras preces ut audiat.*[34] When you hear her, your heart expands with joy; *cantate* (150:1) in the morning in the stiff cold the *laudes Aurora Lucis* [35] and you are very grateful to her. By *Miserere mei* (50:3) you win her favor.

"When the sun rises, you immediately intone prime: *Deus in nomine tuo* (53:3)—asking your procuress to take her to get water and so to complete the affair. Thus, on pretext of bring water, the procuress comes to see you. But if she is reluctant to come slinking through the alleys, she can take to the garden for red roses. If the foolish woman listens to her and follows her advice, she will get *quod Eva tristis* from *quicumque vult:* [36] withered blossoms. If your mistress is a lady who dislikes all this, your procuress knows how to wear her down; she attacks her with *Os, lingua, mens* [37] and weakens her prudence with your ardor. The lady goes to tierce and in charity *legem pone* (118:33).

   "Then you go to church to press your suit on her rather than to attend Mass or win God's mercy: your desire is for a nuptial Mass—but without *Gloria* and without chants. You are lame at the offerings, but you trot well at the end. When the Mass is over, you also pray sext and intone to the old hag who has your lover ready: *In verbum tuum* (118:81), while you tell her: *Factus sum sicut uter* (118:83) for the solemn Mass of the feast. You say: *Quomodo dilexi* (118:97) our meeting, lady; *suscipe me secundum* (118:116) in the name of my tonsure, your person is a *Lucerna pedibus meis* (118:105). She says to you: *Quam dulcia!* (118: 103) and tells you to come back at nones.

   "You go to pray the nones with the beautiful lady. You start *mirabilia* (118:129) and you continue: *Gressus meos dirige* (118:133). The lady says: *Iustus es, Domine!* (118:137), while the bell tolls nones. I have never seen a sexton who could ring the vespers bell better: he plays all the instruments like an expert. The woman that comes to your vespers may try to keep you off, but you hold her by the *virgam virtutis tuae* (109:3). *Sede a dextris meis* (109:1), you say to her when she has come; you sing *Laetatus sum* (121:1) if she lingers, or

*Illuc enim ascenderunt* (121:4) to anyone willing
to remain, and she celebrates an Easter feast with
you, a feast of six capes.[38]

"I know no pastor of souls who can intone
compline so well; the ladies come flocking—beautiful and ugly, light and dark—and cry out to you:
*converte nos* (84:5),[39] and you throw your door
open. Afterwards the secretive ones ask you: *Custodi
nos*.[40] You refuse to let them leave until the *quod
parasti;* you know how to keep them distant *ante
faciem omnium;* you make them bend in *gloriam
plebis tuae;* and if they complain about you, you
sing *Salve, regina.*" [41]

"Together with accidie, you drag along
many other evils, many other sins, caprices, and dis-
contents. You are never at ease with chaste, worthy,
and just men; rather you inflict on your devotees anguish and distress. In your service, men become liars
and perjurers; to accomplish your aims, you make
them into hardened heretics so that they have more
faith in your flatteries, poor fools, than in God's
word. Begone, I say! I do not like you, Sir Love, nor
Sigh, your son. You make me jump this way and
that, with 'Do this, do that,' and the harder I try the
more you goad me. Your empty promises are worth
nothing. You neither fear nor respect Kings or
Queens. Every month you move where you please,
from house to house, openly. Like fire, you jump

from one person to another. Many men you poison
with your glib promises, but in the end there are
very few whom you have guided properly. You
spawn more flatteries than a vineyard does leaves,
and you drive more ignorant fools crazy than a pine
tree has needles. Your false manner is that of a high-
wayman.[42] You watch from a distance and you pur-
sue the first one you sight, swooping down swiftly
on your prey—even if it is an animal hidden safely
in a covert.

"A man has a daughter whom he cherishes
with all his heart. She is a comely and beautiful lass,
sought after by many. Her father, having raised her
in luxury and kept her safe and secluded, thinks he
has something in her, but he has nothing. Like every
one else, her family expects a good marriage for her,
since this will bring honor to her parents and family.
But the girl, like a balking mule, shows her teeth,
shakes her head, and turns to wicked schemes. You
whisper your evil advice into her ear, cajoling her to
play your game: braids for her hair, comb and mirror—why, no lover could ever be worthy of her!
You turn her heart in a thousand ways every hour;
today she is betrothed to one man, tomorrow she
takes a fancy to another; sometimes wearing a tunic,
sometimes a white shirt, she gazes at herself in the
mirror, the abode of your folly.

"The more a man trusts you, the more sorrow he reaps; on men and women alike you lavish your woes. I find nothing else to praise in you, for all I get from you are sadness and sickness. You bring eternal death to the souls you strike and many enemies to the body you hit; those to whom you give most lose their reputation, as well as God and this world. You dissipate their bodies and squander their fortunes. Their souls, their bodies, and their fortunes, you swallow like Hell, reducing all your vassals to imbecility. The grand reward you promise is small and late. The giant who promises fulsomely becomes the dwarf when the time comes to make good. On the spur of the moment, you promise willingly, but when you finally do give, it is late and reluctantly. You are very good at asking.

"A noble woman you transform into a babbling fool; your heat makes a lady act like the she-wolf, who despises the handsome mate and prefers the most repulsive. Thus have many fair ladies, infatuated by you, whimsically abandoned themselves to the ugly and deformed man. They lose their good judgment and the more they trust in you the worse bargain they make. You make a good man ruin himself for an ugly woman while a very rich lady ruins herself for a stupid man. You are contented with everyone you see; one can call you 'Mr. Whim' as an insult. You are like the devil: wherever you are you make people tremble, blush, lose their wits and

their tongue, feel great pains; you blind those who
heed your praise. You resemble the hunter who sets
out his decoy, singing sweetly but deceitfully, woo-
ing the bird until the bird sets its foot into the loop
—and then he pulls it tight. While reassuring them,
you destroy them. Get out of here!"

## THE MOUSE AND THE FROG

aily your followers get what the
mouse got when he wanted to be
friendly with the mottled frog who carried
him off with her. Pay close attention to my
fable and my reason for telling it.

"The mouse had a burrow near the
river. The river rose so suddenly that it
completely surrounded his burrow and he

could not escape. The croaking frog came dancing
along. 'Dear lover,' said the frog to the mouse, 'I
want to be your friend, your beloved, and your
neighbor. I can lead you to safety right away and
put you up on the hill, which is a far safer place for
you. I am an expert swimmer, as you can easily see;
tie your foot to mine, climb on my knees, and I will
put you on the hill or in that field.'

"The frog was croaking away with lovely
arguments, but her evil heart intended something
quite different. The mouse believed her; they bound
their feet together—but not their wills. The frog,
without regard for their arrangement, dove head first
into the water. The mouse pulled upward as hard
as he could; but up or down, they were going to
their ruin.

"A hungry hawk was circling above, look-
ing for something to eat. Seeing the fight, he swooped
down on them; and with a cry, he carried off mouse
and frog to his nest. He devoured both of them without even getting full.

"So does your tricky poison work on gullible fools. Those whom you carry off, tied by your
evil yarn, all perish in your evil swarm. Once you
have trapped foolish men and women, you bind
them so tightly with your chains that they have no
fear of God or of His warning; the devil takes them

away, caught in his pincers. You destroy equally
both deceiver and deceived; they perish more miserably than did the mouse and the frog.

"An evil foe, you present yourself as a
friend. All the evil and pestilence of the world are
less than the deceitful image of the false tongue: you
say sweet words that suggest friendship and you do
evil things and desire evil. The man who mouths the
good but sins wilfully has a false heart and a lying
tongue. May God damn the body that houses such
a heart and remove from the world such a pestilen-
tial tongue!

"If a man would be good, he must not be
gullible. He must weigh well everything he is told;
when he speaks praise, he must not flatter, but be
sober and truthful. But you—under the fleece of a
sheep you hide the teeth of a wolf, and once you have
caught someone you carry him off. You kill those
whom you like most, hide everything good, and load
a heavy burden on a weak back. Believe me, I am
very happy that I owe you nothing. You raise your
interest rates daily; you make a great catch with your
miserable bait. There is much more I could say to
you, but I'd better not, or many ladies would hate
me and many foolish young men would reproach
me. So I tell you only a fraction of what I know.
Now let this be an end to it. Sir Love, go your way!"

SIR LOVE'S RESPONSE

But Sir Love answered me immediately and
gently, "My dear Archpriest, do not be angry, I beg
you. You must not slander love, whether you are
serious or merely jesting, for often just a little water
can put out a big fire. By a few evil remarks, a dear
love may be lost, and a little quarrel turned into violent hatred. For thoughtless words, a vassal may lose
his lord, while gentle speech always improves things.
Be moderate, for you have spoken very foolishly;
the man who looks for pardon should not make
threats. Now you should listen to reason. If you follow my advice no woman will turn you down.

"If you have not yet won anything from the
noblewomen and the other women you claimed to be
in love with, the fault is yours and yours alone, because you neither came to see me nor tried. You
wanted to be a master without first being a pupil;
you cannot know my ways without learning them
from me. Listen to me and heed my counsels, and
you will know how to carry them out; you will win
back your noblewoman and learn how to attract
others.

"Your love is not appropriate for all types
of women: don't go around falling for noblewomen

because it doesn't suit you; it is a hopeless love which comes from great folly. The man who pursues a vain love will always be wretched. If you read Ovid, who was an apprentice of mine, you will find in his work the fables which I taught him, with many good examples for a lover: Pamphilus and Ovid both learned from me. Whether you wish to make love to a noblewoman or to a common woman, you will have to learn many things first, if you want her to accept you as a lover.

"First you must know how to choose the woman. Select one that is beautiful, graceful, and lively.[43] She should be neither a beanstalk nor a dwarf. If you can help it, do not fall for a peasant woman, for they are dummies where love is concerned. Look for a woman with an elegant figure, a small head, blond hair (not henna), well-placed eyebrows that are long and arched. The right kind of lady has wide hips. Her eyes should be large and bright, colorful and clear, and crowned with long lashes. Her ears should be slender and tiny. Note carefully whether she has a long neck, for this is very desirable. Her nose should be small, her teeth small, very white, even, well-spaced and well-shaped. Her lips and gums should be rosy and her mouth small and shapely. Finally, her face should be clear of complexion, smooth, and free from hair. Try to choose a woman whom you can observe without her shift;

for the shape of her body will reveal all at a glance.

"Now as for the go-between, this should be some woman who is kin to you and who will be loyal to you. She should not be the lady's servant; otherwise, she would not deceive the lady and this one would know. An unsuccessful attempt is always regrettable. Make sure that your go-between is skilled and subtle in her speech; she must be able to lie with ease and to understand the lady's reactions, because the pot always boils faster with the lid on. If you have no such relative, find one of those old crones that frequent the churches and know all the back alleys—the ones with the hugh rosaries dangling from their necks. They are in on many secrets and possess magic arts [44] with which to enchant maidens' ears. They are indeed real experts, these squawking gulls; they go everywhere, in the marketplace and on the hillsides, lifting their rosaries to God and bewailing their miseries, but ah! how much wickedness these old witches know!

"Get one of those old hags that peddle herbs, going from door to door and calling themselves midwives. Hawking their powders and cosmetics and mascaras, they hypnotize and blind. Look especially for one of those black crones that consort with monks, nuns, and Beguines; they get around a good deal and are worthy of their shoe-leather. These convent-hoppers [45] know how to deal many hands.

When such women come around, few ladies can get
rid of them. Be sure to flatter your go-between so
that she won't deceive you, because these witches are
so skilled in their chants that they can easily blind
you.

"Of all the old hags, this type is the best.
Ask her not to lie to you. Show her affection, for a
good broker can pawn off many a bad animal and
a good cloak hides many rags. If she tells you that
your lady does not have large shoulders or thin arms,
you should ask immediately if she has small breasts.
Then inquire about her entire figure in order to be
sure. If your hag tells you that the lady's armpits are
sweaty and her legs short, her loins long, her hips
wide and her feet tiny and well-arched, know that
such a woman is not to be found in every marketplace. She will be wild in bed but prudent at home.
Keep her in mind—I agree with Ovid on this point.
A competent go-between searches for just such a
woman.

"There are three things which I hardly dare,
just now, to reveal to you. They are very hidden
faults which are embarassing to discuss. Few women
are entirely free of these faults, but if I should mention them, they would start giggling. Take care that
your lady be not hairy or bearded; the devil take
such a monster! And if you see that her hands are
tiny and her voice shrill, try to get rid of her.

"Summing it all up, ask your messenger whether the woman is gay, for such a one is prone to love; if she looks cold from the outside, ask whether she feels something when a man is near. If she says yes, join yourself to such a woman. She is to be served and to be loved; you will find her more pleasant than others to court. If you find such a woman and you want to have her, do all you can to serve her in word and deed. Shower her with sparkling jewels; and even if you don't have any, or don't want to part with them, make bold and generous promises. She will believe you and will do whatever you wish. Serve her zealously, for thus love will grow. Love may develop gradually, but generous service is never wasted on a good person. Untiring effort will conquer in the end. Be grateful to her for the smallest favor, show boundless appreciation, never contradict anything she may say. Go to see her often, and show yourself confident in her presence. Never let her think that you might feel shy, and above all do not neglect an opportunity. When a woman sees a lazy coward, she says to herself, "I will have to fend for myself." [46] Do not dawdle with a woman, do not wrap yourself in blankets, but show off bravely in your best outfit. Torpor brings on fear and cowardice, stupidity and vulgarity, filth and raggedness. Torpor has lost for many both my friendship and the love of a worthy woman."

## THE TWO IDLERS

"Let me tell you about two idlers who longed to take a wife. Both lusted after the same young woman and both were, indeed, elegant and handsome. One could not see out of his right eye; the other was hoarse and lame. Each hated the other; each was certain that he would win the lady. For her part, the lady thought to amuse herself at their expense, saying that she would accept as husband the one who proved himself the lazier of the two.

"Trying to gain an advantage, the cripple spoke up first: 'Lady, listen to my case. I am clearly lazier than my rival because once, to avoid the nuisance of lifting my foot high enough to reach the rung, I fell down the ladder and became permanently lame. Besides that, when I was swimming across a stream one day—a very hot day, the hottest in man's memory—I thought I would die of thirst; but I was too lazy to open my mouth and so have been hoarse ever since.'

"When the cripple had finished, the one-eyed man began: 'Lady, the laziness my rival has just described is just a trifle. Listen to mine, the likes of which you have never seen before and which no man can ever see. In April, I became infatuated with a noblewoman. I was in her presence, subdued and humble. Some filthy muck trickled out of my nose and, to avoid cleaning it, I lost my lady fair. Let me tell you more. One night I was lying in bed awake, while outside the rain was pouring down. The water began to drip right into my eye, but I was so lazy that I wouldn't even turn my head, and the constant drip-drip-drip of the rain in my eye blinded me. Lady, you must marry me for I am certainly the lazier.'

"The lady replied, 'I cannot decide which of these examples shows more laziness; the contest seems to me a draw. I can see, you stupid cripple, which of your feet is lame, and I see, you half-blind fool, how poorly you see. Find yourselves someone else to marry, for no lady could ever be satisfied by such a vulgar idler or such a vile person."

"Therefore, my friend, do not harbor faults and crudities which will displease a lady.

"If you really want to possess a lady, you must first of all make her lose her shame. Once they have thrown off their modesty, women are far friskier than men expect. Who can understand a woman's whims, her devilish arts, or the depths of her knowledge of evil? If they are desirous enough, they abandon soul, body, and reputation. The gambler who recklessly gambles away his jacket may later gamble away his trousers as well. Once the singer has sung the first song, her feet catch fire and so much the

worse for the tambourine. The weaver and the singer
are never still; their hands and their feet are constantly moving as they weave or dance. So a woman
without shame, even if you presented her with ten
Toledos, could not help following her whims.

"As I say, do not neglect your lady; like the
mill or the orchard, woman must always be worked.
They hate holidays in their private business; as the
troubadors say, they must not be neglected. These
things are certain: the mill produces as it is turned;
the orchard that is well worked yields the best apples; and the woman who is constantly courted remains ever vigorous. Keep these three things in mind
and your labor will not be fruitless."

SIR PITAS PAYAS, PAINTER FROM BRITTANY [47]

"Let me tell you the story of a man who
neglected his wife; if you think it trivial, then you
tell a better tale. Sir Pitas Payas was a Breton
painter. He married a young woman, as he liked
company. Toward the end of the first month, he
said to her, 'Madame, I wish to go to Flanders; I
will bring you many gifts.'

"She replied: 'Go with my best wishes, but
do not forget your house and your wife.'

"Sir Pitas said: 'Beautiful lady, I want to

paint a pretty picture on you so that you may avoid frivolities.'

" 'My lord,' she answered, 'do as you please.'

"Just below her navel, he painted a little lamb. Then he went off on his business. He was delayed by his work, and remained abroad two years; but his lady found a month as long as a year. She was a new bride and had not been with her husband very long. Soon she took a lover to repopulate her hostel, and the lamb was worn away to nothing.

"When she heard that Sir Pitas was on his way home, she quickly called her lover and told him to paint, as best he could, a little ram where the lamb had been. Hurriedly he painted a perfect ram, complete with horns. That very day a messenger arrived with the news that Pitas Payas would be there soon. When the painter had arrived from Flanders, he was received by his wife with coolness. They retired to a chamber, and he did not forget the sign he had painted.

" 'My lady,' said Pitas Payas, 'please show me the lamb and let us make merry.'

"And she answered, 'My lord, look for yourself and do as you like.'

"Pitas Payas looked and saw a large ram with powerful weapons. 'How is it, my lady, how can it be, that I painted a lamb but I find this?'

"Since woman is always both clever and malicious in such matters, she answered: 'Why, my lord, in two years shouldn't a small lamb turn into a ram? You should have come back sooner and you would have found the lamb.'

"Learn from this not to neglect your beloved; do not be like Pitas Payas, do not let her cast about for another man. Treat your woman with beautiful words and when she begins to yield, do not neglect her. If a man stirs up a hare and forces her out of her burrow but then doesn't chase her or catch her, he behaves like a poor hunter. Another fellow who follows her and corners her more expertly gets her. This happens to many hunters. Women mutter to themselves: 'Now this is a different fellow—more gallant and more daring than the first one you fell for. Next to him, the other is worth nothing; I will go with this one, by heaven.'

"Also, when you see someone acquainted with her, whether he is her lover or not, talk to him for her sake; if you can, give him a gift, but do not quarrel with him, because all these things may well attract a woman. For a trifle, a little gift, she will serve you faithfully and do anything you wish. For money she will do all that you ask, so give her all you can, be it little or much."

THE POWER OF MONEY

"Money can do much; it should be held in high esteem. It turns a tramp into a respected and honorable man; it makes the lame man run and the dumb man speak. Even a man without hands reaches out and grabs for money. A man may be an idiot or an ill-bred peasant, but money will make him a noble and a sage; the more money a man has, the more worthy he becomes, while the man who is penniless cannot call himself his own master. If you have money, you can have luxury, pleasure, and joy, and benefices from the Pope; you can buy Paradise and earn salvation. Piles of money bring piles of blessings.

"Over in Rome,[48] the seat of holiness, I myself observed them all curtseying and scraping before Money, and doing him solemn homage. They humble themselves as they do before the Crucifix. There, money created many priors, bishops and abbots, archbishops, doctors, patriarchs, and men of power. Money won dignities for many ignorant clerics; it turned truths into lies and lies into truths. Money created many clerics and priests, monks and nuns, consecrated religious, certifying that they had sufficient knowledge, while the poor were informed that they lacked learning. Money bought judgments and

verdicts galore, lived with crooked lawyers, and
fostered unjust suits and settlements, so that finally,
thanks to money, even absolution could be obtained.

"Money snaps heavy chains, destroys irons
and pillories, those feared prisons, but the man who
lacks money finds himself handcuffed. All over the
world, money does marvelous things. I have seen
money restore to life many who deserved to die, and
cut down many who were innocent. Many souls has
he damned, many souls has he saved. Money can destroy a poor man's house and his orchards, his furni-
ture and his estate. Its itch and scab infest the whole
earth. Where money is involved, you will always
find intrigue. Money makes knights out of stupid
farmers, counts and noblemen out of peasants. The
man who has money puts on the airs of a gentleman
and everybody kisses his hand.

"I have observed that Money always had the
best, the largest, the most costly and elegant man-
sions; castles, estates, turreted palaces served Money
and were bought by him. Money dined on exotic
delicacies, decked himself in rich and gilded clothes,
wore precious jewels, all this in leisure and pleasure,
with rare ornaments and noble mounts. I have often
heard monks in their sermons condemn money and
its temptations—and immediately afterward grant
pardons, waive penances, and offer prayers—for
money. These monks may scorn money in the public

square, but back in the cloister they hoard it in vases
and chalices. Money has more hiding places than do
thrushes or magpies. And with money they indulge
all their vices.

"Even while friars and priests protest that
they are servants of God, if they hear a rumor that
a rich man is dying and catch the sound of his silver,
they begin to haggle over which of them is to attend
him. Although friars will not take money, they give
the nod to their bursars. Immediately afterward,
their cellarers grab hold of it. (If they are supposed
to be poor, what need do they have for bursars?)
They stand about, waiting to see who will get the
largest share. The man has barely breathed his last
before they intone the paternoster—for an evil
omen! They act as the crows did who were skinning
the jackass: 'Tomorrow we will take it, because it
is rightfully ours.'

"Every woman in the world and every
noblewoman is fond of money and great wealth; I
have never known a beautiful woman who cherished
poverty. Piles of money proclaim high nobility.
Money receives high praise as judge and governor,
counselor and subtle advocate, bold and powerful,
constable and royal judge; money controls every
office. In sum, I tell you (don't take it amiss):
Money, which is the world's axis, makes a lord out
of a servant and a servant out of a lord. Everything

in the world is done for the love of money. The
world and its ways change for money; every woman,
greedy for something, is honey-tongued. She will go
out of her way for jewels and money; gifts can crack
rocks and split hard wood. Money can tear down a
thick wall and knock over a high tower. It can help
in any kind of trouble. There is no slave in fetters
whom money cannot free. But if you can't pay your
way, you won't get your horse to run.

"Money makes hard things easy. Therefore,
be generous and lavish with your old woman; do
not send her off without some profit, large or small;
I am not impressed by trifles that have no value. If
you can give her nothing at all, at least be generous
in your speech: do not offer foolish excuses. The
man who has no honey in his jar must have it in his
mouth; a trader of this sort does good business. If
you know how to play or to temper musical instruments, if you can sing well, you must use your talent
occasionally, where the woman may hear you.

"If one thing does not move the woman, you
may find help in many things together. When the
lady hears of these, she will reflect on them, and in
good time, the affair must turn out well for you.
You cannot lift a large beam with a piece of cord;
a limping beast will not run with only one 'giddap';
a crowbar alone cannot budge a heavy stone, but it
will be moved, little by little, with wedges and
sledges. Show your cleverness and your spirit;

whether she sees it or not, she will know of it in
time. She cannot be so cold-hearted that she will not
then care more for you. Do not weary of following
her, and you will conquer her obstinacy.

"She will grow fond of the man who follows her with constancy, who visits her frequently
even though she denies him entrance. Despite gossip
and slanders, she will always think of him and will
even be sad on his account. The more they tease her
or slander her, the more she suffers for his sake, and
so the more fiercely is she attached to him. Then she
can hardly wait for the hour when she will be with
him. Her devoted mother thinks that by scolding,
nagging, reproaching her, she will make her girl
quiet and chaste. Instead, these very tactics goad her
on. Her mother ought to recall her own maidenhood,
when *her* mother's reproaches only whetted her appetite; then she might be able to size up girls properly, including her own beautiful daughter. Every
daughter of woman is molded from the same clay;
what is most forbidden, that she does most willingly, that kindles her desire, that drives her mad.
But when she is ignored, she loses all interest.

"Everything that is hard becomes softened
with time. The mountain doe tires after a long flight,
so that the hunter can catch her while she is resting.
So too, the fierce lady can be worn down and softened. For each request that a man makes during the
day, she is pestered by love a hundred times during

the night; Lady Venus pleads for him endlessly, and she becomes ardent for what they both demand. Water is very soft, but even so, by dripping incessantly on the hard stone, it can wear a large hole; by constant study, the ignorant man learns a good deal. A woman solicited constantly will forget her prudence.

"Be careful not to get involved with the maidservant or court her, because this is the sure way to lose your beloved: one mistress will always be jealous of another."

SIR LOVE
ON CONDUCT
AND WINE [49]

ou must always be courteous. Above all, never drink too much wine. Wine made Lot sleep with his daughters: he was disgraced in the eyes of God and man. In the same way,

wine cost a hermit his body and his soul, a man who
had never imbibed before. The devil cleverly tempted
him to try it, to his own harm. Listen to this unusual
tale.

"There was a hermit, forty years old, who
faithfully served God in his hermitage. Never in his
life had he drunk wine; he lived a pious life, fasting
and praying. Disturbed by this, the devil pondered
how to upset the hermit's life. One day, armed with
his tricks, he went to see the hermit.

" 'God save you, good monk,' he said ever
so cordially.

"The monk, amazed, said: 'God preserve
me! Tell me what you are because I cannot make
you out. In all the years I have served God here I
have not seen any man. I will defend myself with
the Cross!'

"Though kept far off and unable to reach
his person, the devil nevertheless began to tempt the
hermit, saying: 'That body of God which you wish
to taste—let me show you how you can have it.
You know well that the true blood of God is made
from wine, and that in it the most holy sacrament
is contained; try it and see if you like it.' The devil
was casting out his net to trap the monk.

"The hermit said: 'I do not know what
wine is.'

"Eager to carry out his plan, the devil answered: 'Those wine merchants walking along the road will give you enough of it; go for it at once.'

"When he had returned, the devil said: 'Bless it and drink it, now that you have it; just taste it, and when you have drunk it you will see how grateful you are for my advice.'

"The hermit tasted, and drank the wine down. It was strong and pure, and it befuddled his wits. When the devil saw that he had succeeded in laying the foundation, he continued to build his house: 'My friend, you do not know what time it is, day or night, or how the world is ruled. Get a cock, which will tell you the hour, every day, and get some hens too, for the cock does better in their company."

"The monk heeded this evil advice. Soon he was addicted to wine, and while drunk, he would watch the cock mating with the hens. He took delight in this and, under the influence of wine, desired to indulge himself. Next came cupidity, root of all evils, and lust and pride—three mortal sins; there followed murder. These are the very sins brought on by excessive drink.

"Leaving the hermitage, he raped a woman; she screamed out but could not defend herself. After he had sinned with her, he feared disgrace and killed her, the wretch, and so damned himself.

"As the proverb says truly, there is nothing

hidden which is not discovered: his evil deeds were
quickly exposed and the monk was seized and
brought to trial. He confessed the evil he had done
because of wine. He was immediately sentenced to
die, according to the law. The miserable wretch lost
body and soul. All evil resides in excessive drink.

"Wine clouds a man's vision and shortens
his life; the man who drinks too much loses all his
strength. Wine palsies the limbs and befuddles
the brain. Drunkenness destroys everything. Wine
causes foul breath, which is very offensive; the
mouth smells evilly, but there is nothing one can do
about it. Wine burns the entrails and rots the liver.
If you want to make love to young ladies, wine is
no good for you.

"Drunkards age quickly; they lose their
color and become lean and sallow; they commit
many vile deeds and are detested by everyone. They
offend God and are lost to the world. Where wine
is abundant, wits are worth two pennies; drunkards
grunt like pigs or magpies. From wine come brawls,
fights, and murder; plenty of wine sits well only in
casks and barrels. By nature, wine is very good and
can be pleasant, if you drink it moderately; but the
man who drinks too much loses his sanity and commits all the evils and follies of the world.

"Therefore, avoid wine. When you converse with ladies, act like a gentleman, pay them

charming compliments; have a stock of elegant sayings for such occasions. Speak with sighs, your gaze
fixed on her. Do not speak too fast, but not too slow
either. Be neither impetuous nor apathetic. Give as
freely as you can, and never renege on your promises.
Nobody can understand a man who talks too fast,
but a slow speaker annoys his hearers. Great haste
borders on folly, while he who is leisurely is called
stupid. A stingy man never gets things easily; if
people see that he is always reluctant to give, he will
never get what he wants. The man who always
speaks out on the spur of the moment is judged a
liar, while the man who makes promises and carries
them out is applauded by all. In whatever you do,
in speaking and all the rest, always follow the norm.
Just as anything can be made to appear worthy if
done prudently, so anything done rashly is discred-
ited.

      "Do not play at dice or any other form of
gambling, because this is an evil source of money,
worse than the usurer's; even the Jew lends at three-
for-four a year, but the gambler doubles his ill-
gotten money in one day. Men who are all wrapped
up in their games lose their shirts at the dice tables
after losing all their money; both money and clothes
remain in the gambling house and the gamblers
scratch themselves where they do not itch. Master
Roldan [50] exposes all the evils of dice, all the tricks

and the faults of gamblers; without eating bread, dice finish off more granaries than Easter does lambs or St. John's Day geese.

"Do not associate with hoodlums or get into brawls. Do not show yourself to be coarse or evil-tongued. Do not boast about yourself or your deeds, for the man who praises himself degrades himself. Do not gossip or show yourself envious; do not be jealous of a discreet woman. If you disapprove of something, do not let her know it. Do not be covetous for her money. Never praise another woman's looks before your lady, because that will certainly irritate her; she will think you have set your heart on the other woman and such suspicion could ruin your chances. Never speak to her of another woman, but rather praise her highly; women do not want their plaything in someone else's bag. Praise her beauty, for if you do not, you will win her late, if ever.

"Never lie to her; always speak the truth. When you play with her, do not talk too much. When she speaks to you of love, be pleasant with her; women prefer the man who is silent and docile. When her neighbors are around, do not stare at her too much or make signs to her; otherwise you may ruin yourself. Many who have tried this now know better. Strike from afar, but quietly and without noise.

"Be modest and gentle as a dove, proud and
poised as a peacock. Restrain yourself: do not show
anger, peevishness, or irritation; the lover takes pride
in his self-control. Be especially careful of one thing:
when you court a woman, she must not know that
you are courting any other; otherwise all your labor
is like the shadow of the moon, or as if one were
sowing in a river or a swamp. Reflect: could you
stand it if you knew that your mistress loved Friar
Moreno? [51] Think and look into your own heart,
and you can judge her heart by that.

"Above all things praise her goodness. But
do not boast about her; that would be real stupidity
—many lose their ladies for telling tales out of
school. If she grants you any favors, keep them to
yourself. If you can keep secrets, she will do much
for you; wherever I find discretion, I share many
gifts, but never have I consorted with a gossip. Often, indeed, I have separated gossips from their ladies. If your stomach can hold plenty of food, it
should be able to keep a secret, which is much softer.
Cato, the wise Roman, tells you so in his book; he
says that secrecy is the mark of a good friend. [52] You
recognize the bramble when its thorns stick you, and
you tear it out of orchard, vineyard, and field; the
heron is known by its long neck. Preserving a trust
is worth a heap of silver in any town square. The
gossip disturbs and harms many people, and espe-

cially himself; the ladies despise him and scorn him as a busybody. And because of one blunder the whole game is lost. If a tiny mouse nibbles on a crumb of cheese, everyone cries out: 'The mice ate the cheese!' Hellfire and damnation on the man who hurts himself and others by such stupidity.

"If you ask a beautiful woman for three things, she will grant the second only if you keep the first secret. And if you are discreet about both, she'll give you the third too. Don't lose your mistress because of a clacking tongue.

"Follow my advice, and you will see that the lady who today closes the wicket in your face will throw open her door tomorrow; she who scorns you today will embrace you tomorrow. Heed the advice of a friend and flee the praise of the enemy. I could tell you much more if I had the time, but there are many other people whom I must satisfy. They are chafing at my delay, and I am not content to be idle. You yourself learn how to take advice and you will know how to advise others."

I, Juan Ruiz, Archpriest of Hita, have never found the kind of lady whom Sir Love has portrayed for you. I do not believe that I will ever find her around here, despite all my trials. And yet, even so, my heart cannot rest but must continue singing these songs.

ADVICE FROM LADY VENUS

Sir Love departed and let me sleep. When dawn came, I began to consider his counsels, and, to be quite frank, I realized that I had always lived according to his teachings. I was amazed, in thinking it all over, to realize that in all those years I had never wearied of serving the ladies, I had always kept secrets, I had never boasted: why then did I never succeed? Sighing, I turned to my heart and challenged it:

"Now, my heart, I will put you on to an attractive woman, and I declare that if I do not succeed this time, then it is clear that I never will succeed."

My heart answered: "Do it; you will succeed. And even if you do not today, try again tomorrow. What you haven't been able to get in so many years, you will get suddenly, when you least expect it."

It is indeed a true proverb which says, "Better one lively moment than a wasted day." Shrugging off my sadness and depression, I sought out—and found—a lady whom I might desire. Her figure was elegant, her manner affectionate; she was vivacious, ladylike, pleasant, beautiful, polite and poised, gifted, generous and amiable in every way.[53]

She was surely the noblest person I could hope to find. Young and very rich, she was a widow from Calatayud.[54] She was my neighbor, my death, and my salvation. In everything she did, she showed her nobility and high birth; following the custom of her class, she would leave her house only rarely.

For a go-between, I turned to Lady Venus, for she is the beginning and the end of this our earthly journey, our life and our death—Lady Venus who wears down and overcomes the most stubborn resistance, who wields sovereign power over the whole world, whose counsels prevail wherever she appears.

"My Lady Venus, spouse of Sir Love, most noble lady, I your servant salute you. You and Sir Love reign over all things. All men render you homage as their creator; kings, dukes, and counts, and all creatures fear and serve you. Fulfill my desires, grant me good fortune, be not reluctant, distant, or cold toward me. I do not ask of you anything that would be hard for you to give, but it is something I cannot accomplish by myself. Without your succor, I can neither begin nor complete it. But if you allow me this, I will be a happy man.

"I have been wounded, transfixed, utterly devastated by a shaft I bear, hidden and buried in my heart. I do not dare to show my wound. If I neglect it, it will kill me, but still I do not dare to pronounce the name of the one who wounded me. I cannot observe .nor see my wound, and so I fear still worse dangers; I fear that great evils will befall me against which all the arts of medicine are helpless. What can I do that will not in the end destroy me? Alas, what can I do? I cannot decide. My complaint is just, but I can find no help for it. And since many miseries assail me, I must seek out as many remedies as might be good for me. Sometimes many arts help, sometimes they completely fail; many live through them, and many also die. Yet if I reveal my wound—what it is, how I got it, who wounded me—I might reveal so much that in the hope of getting well I would lose the remedy itself, for as you know, sometimes the cure is worse than the disease. But if the wound and the pain are kept concealed, if I ask no help to return to health, perhaps another, graver malady will befall me and I will perish utterly. Never have I been so miserable!

"One does well to reveal his sickness and hurt to the physician or to a good friend who can provide remedies or advice which might help. Otherwise, one must surely die or, at best, live in great affliction. The fire that is covered blazes more fiercely than one which is spread and scattered about in the open. Therefore the surest and best way will be to open my heart and place it in your hands.

"Lady Sloeberry [55] lives here in this neighborhood. She surpasses easily all the other women of the city for beauty, grace, figure, and handsome features; unless love deceives me, I speak true. This young lady has wounded me with a poisoned arrow which has pierced my heart and is embedded there; my strength has left me, and my festering wound grows worse. I dare not talk of her to anyone, because she comes from a great family and noble ancestry. Her parents are of higher station and more consequence than mine, so that I do not dare to reveal my feelings toward her. Many seek her hand in marriage with pledges and gifts, but she scorns them as less than vile sticks. Grand ancestry begets great haughtiness, and great wealth begets great disdain. The daughter of a wretched swineherd, if she is rich, can choose any husband she likes out of a thousand suitors. But since I cannot have the gentle lady this way, I must win her by labor and subtle art.

"All her noble qualities drive me after her, yet because of this very nobility I dare not approach her. There is no remedy, no help for me, except you, my Lady Venus, who are my succor. In my ardent folly, I have often spoken my feelings, but she has treated me with scorn. She doesn't care a pin for me, and this makes me miserable. If she didn't live near by, I would not suffer so much. The closer you come to a blazing fire, the more you get scorched. If only I lived far away, it wouldn't be so bad.

"Alas, Lady Venus, please, please help me! You see my misery, the sufferings that afflict me; you know the perils I face, all that I must go through; and will you not answer me? Are you deaf? Listen with compassion to my terrible sorrows! Can't your eyes see how sad my face has become? Pull that flaming arrow out of my heart, and comfort my wound with ointments and peace, so that my misery and pain will not continue uncared for. Can there be a woman so cold and stonyhearted not to pity a lover thus afflicted? I insist, imploring in pain and anguish: this bitter suffering is ruining my health and my spirit. See how sallow and confused I have become; I have no strength, my eyes are sunken. Unless you help me, all my limbs will dissolve."

Lady Venus answered: "Those who endure will conquer. You have received a good deal of advice and counsel from Sir Love, my husband. He did not stay with you long because you were harsh with him, but I will fill in what he omitted. And if I happen to repeat my husband's counsels, you can be even more certain and confident, because advice that many agree upon is sound.

"The woman who is easygoing and is prone to laughter, you can be very direct with; modesty need not hold you back. Hardly one in a thousand of these will reject you; don't be concerned because, though a woman may not say much about it, love fills her head with dreams. Serve her; do not be put off. Love grows through service, for service to a good person is never lost or wasted. Even if one goes slow, all is not lost. Love never fails; ceaseless labor overcomes all things.

"Sir Love taught Ovid: there is no woman, old or young, in the whole world who cannot be won by effort and service; sooner or later, believe me, she will take pity on you. Do not fear her harsh answers; art and service will make them friendly. A boulder can be dislodged by continual digging; if the first angry wave frightened a sailor during a storm, he would never go to sea in his well-built ship. So do not be too concerned over the lady's first reaction. Attention and service will help change her mind. The high-priced merchant may swear over and over that he cannot sell his goods except for a large sum, but the shrewd buyer, if he is persistent, can bring off a good deal through a good broker.

"Now, take pains to attach yourself to her and serve her well; the dog that licks long enough will surely draw blood. Craft and skill can wear down her stiff resistance. If he is crafty, the rabbit can overcome the cow. If skill and craft can cut away the tip from a huge rock, surely a clever and subtle suitor acting swiftly and carefully will be able to move a woman. Skill clears the way for hard hearts to be softened, cities taken, walls torn down, great towers toppled, heavy weights lifted. Many swear skillfully, and skillfully commit perjury. With skill, fish are caught in the deep and men travel over the waves of the sea with dry feet. By skillful service, you will become affluent; there is, in fact, nothing which you cannot achieve by skill.

"The poor man, if he is skillful, can get by on very little work, and skill often saves the convict from his sentence. The man who was reduced to tears by poverty now sings, rich and at leisure, and long service allows the pedestrian to ride on horseback. Long service can marvelously overcome the great anger of lords who were hostile, and through faithful service, Spanish knights are victorious. So, that a woman should be conquered is not so surprising.

"But you cannot simply inherit skill, prudence, knowledge, and science, nor get the love and affection of a woman; all these things are won only by effort, constancy, and dedication.

"Even if your lady should reject you scornfully, do not stop pursuing her lest you lose what you have won. In serving her your heart will find joy; the bell cannot help ringing when it is tolled. Thus will you win your beloved: she who was your enemy will love you.

"You must frequent the places where she is wont to go. When you have the chance, entertain her with pleasant stories, speak wittily and with loving gestures, for love is fed by sweet words and clever sayings. Youth desires pleasure, and a woman desires a cheerful man for her lover. The phlegmatic and the choleric man are both despised; sulking and quarreling make enemies. But cheerfulness shows a man gracious, attractive, clever and daring, candid and urbane. Do not neglect sighs, artful ones, and don't talk too much, or she will think you a liar.

"For a trifle, a petty vice, a woman's love can be lost. She may be so annoyed that she will despise you, as has already happened to you and could happen to anyone. If, in conversing with her, you perceive that the time is ripe, then lead her on but as if you were shy. Often she herself desires what she will deny you, and then, if you keep at it, she will give you what you don't expect.

"Every woman likes experienced men, desiring them above anything else. Before such men, women have hands that are very weak and feet that are as if lame, and they allow a little and a lot, while pretending great reluctance.

"A woman would rather be coaxed a little than have to say, 'Do as you like,' as if she were a tramp. Coaxed, she feels less guilty; this has proved true for all creatures. All women have the same manner: at the outset of an affair, they are diffident, and they pretend to be displeased or unwilling. They make threats, but never strike: there is art in their coyness. Although a woman who is being courted may appear to resist a great deal, the good suitor never gives up on this account. A woman can appear very angry, but when her suitor besieges her properly, she will give way, no matter how well armed she seems. Modesty and shame hold women back from doing what they want as much as you do. However, they don't persist in their refusals; you can get what you want of them. Go to her, well armed with what you have or with what you can borrow—but do not let her know that you have borrowed. Your friend does not know what you keep hoarded; with well-chosen words you can cover up your poverty. The poor man hides his poverty and the misery of his life by a show of humor and a cheerful face; he holds back his tears. It's better thus than to display his poverty to people who would give him nothing anyway.

"Frequently, a lie helps, while the truth only hinders. A narrow, winding path is often a short cut by which one can reach the peak more quickly than by the direct way. If you see a friend of hers, be very kind, speak cordially; when the lady hears it, her heart rejoices. A flattering servant can deceive his master. Heaped-up coals and many stokers produce a bigger, warmer fire; if many praise and commend

you to her, you will have a stronger case and she
more desire.

"While they are speaking of your good qualities, the lady is debating whether or not she should
yield. You, when you realize that she is in doubt,
then you must confirm her. Unless you spur a lazy
horse, he will remain idle and worthless; a lame donkey, however reluctant, trots under the goad. So
should a man reassure a woman who is hesitant. People who are doubtful what to do can be moved by a
little prodding; if a lofty tower is shaky, it must in-
evitably topple. A woman who is in doubt is easy
to get.

"If your lovely lady has an aged mother, she
will hardly let you speak to your lady in private. Old
people are envious of the young, and they know
much because of their age. These quarrelsome old
hags are malicious when it comes to guarding their
daughters; they suspect everyone and sniff out every
affair. He who has fallen into many traps recognizes
the nets! In such a case, hire a good go-between who
knows the way and understands how things are on
both sides. She should be just as Sir Love prescribed.

"Do not handle your beloved at the very first
opportunity, nor do anything else that might
frighten her off; do not touch her roughly or handle
her without her consent. At first, give her plenty of
bait, so that she comes without fear.

"Now I have said enough; I cannot stop here any longer. As soon as you see her, start talking to her, and later you will work out many ways and occasions to see her. Time tends to all things. My friend, what more is there I can tell you on this subject? Be subtle and diligent, and you will have your lady. But I must go, I must be on my way."

Lady Venus departed, leaving me weary. Jugglers may cheer up a sick man, but they can't cure him. Rather than lessen his pain, their sweet songs increase it. The advice of Lady Venus did not dissolve my troubles; now there was nothing for it but to rely on my tongue and my words.

Friends, I am in the depths of grief; I am caught. I go to speak to the lady, relying on God's help for a favorable answer from her. I am like a man suddenly abandoned on the high seas, alone, without oars, amid the waves. Poor wretch! How can I escape? I fear that I will die. I look all about me but cannot find a harbor. My full hope, my full comfort lies in her alone who has aggrieved and fatally wounded me. I go to tell her my grief so that, hearing me speak, she might be merciful. Listening to my sorrow, she will understand my troubles; sometimes a few words bring about great happiness.

what a beautiful sight to see Lady Sloeberry walking in the square! What a figure, what grace, what an exquisite long neck! Hair, mouth, complexion, gait—how beautiful they all are! When she but raises her eyes, she wounds with the darts of love! But the place was hardly suited to amorous talk, and I suddenly began to tremble in fear. My feet and my hands could not master themselves. I lost my wits; my strength ebbed away, and the color drained from my face. I had prepared a little speech for her, but timidity in front of other people made me say something else. I hardly recognized myself; I did not know where to turn; my tongue refused to obey my will. To address a woman in the square is too public; there may be a vicious dog tied loosely behind a door. It is good to banter gently and with discretion; while in a safe place one can speak plainly.

"Lady, my niece in Toledo commends herself to you and sends you her best wishes. From what she has heard of you, she would very much like to see you and get to know you, if the occasion allows. My family wanted to marry me off to a rich young lady, Sir Penny's daughter. I told them all that I did not care for her; my body will belong only to her who wins my heart."

In an undertone, I told her that I was making small talk for the benefit of all the people watching us in the square. When I saw that they had all gone, I started to describe the ardent love that was tormenting me.

[*Two lines are missing here.*] [56]

"Let us swear that no one else shall learn of this; when friends are secretive, they are both more loyal. I love nothing in the world as I do you. For more than two years I have been pining for your love. I love you more than I love God. I do not dare to send anyone to you; in my terrible pain, I come to tell you my trouble: this urgent and anguished desire for you does not leave me, will not let go of me, will not give me peace. The more it eludes me, the more it ravages me.

"I am afraid that you are not attending to my words; it is foolish and pointless to speak long to the deaf. Believe me, I love you so much that I have no greater care; this above all else makes me very unhappy. Lady, I dare not say any more until you have answered these few words. Tell me your intentions, show me your heart."

She answered me: "All this talk is not worth a straw. Many another man thus beguiles many another Sloeberry: man is deceitful and misleads his lady friends. Do you think me foolish enough to listen to you talk? Find someone else to hoodwink with your put-on sufferings."

I said, "Now, my peevish one, let's banter. Just as the fingers of a hand are not all the same, so all men do not act and think alike. A fur coat is black and white, though made completely from rabbit fur. Sometimes the just man pays for the sinner, and many may suffer because of the mistakes of others; the guilt of evil men falls on the good, even though those that did the evil should pay the penalty. Another man's mistakes ought not afflict me. Please, permit me to speak to you in that passageway, so that all the passers-by will not see you here. Here I have said one thing to you; there I will tell you something else."

With measured steps, Lady Sloeberry entered the portico, proud and erect, calm and poised, and sat on the stone bench, casting her eyes down. I returned to the line I had originally taken:

"By your leave, lady, listen to the few words I would address to you about my death. But you think I speak falsely and frivolously, and I do not know what to do against such obstinacy. I swear before God, lady, and for this world, that everything

I have said is the honest truth; yet you remain colder than the snow in the mountains, and you are still so young that I am frightened. I run a risk in speaking to one so young: do you think that I am merely beguiling you with lies and nonsense? It is because I cannot comprehend your young heart; would you rather play ball than talk of love? Although young people might be more apt to take pleasure in playing those games, ripe age has riper brains because it is guided by time in understanding things. Long experience makes all things comprehensible, and experience and art clarify every field of knowledge; without them we would perish. Where men deal with each other, they come to know each other.

"Go now, and come back to talk another day, please, since today you don't believe me, or perhaps it's not my lucky day.

"Go now, but come back. Although you are so rigid in your attitude now, when you have heard my grief again you will understand my sorrow. Grant me this, lady, in your goodness, that you will return another day and talk with me. I will prepare my words, and I would know your desires; I do not dare to ask for more, so please come without fear. Most hearts reveal themselves in words: thus I will understand something about you and you will hear my arguments. Go, and come back for a talk, because women and men get to know each other by speaking

and become friends and companions. Even if one
does not eat or bite into an apple, its color and appearance give great joy. To speak to and look upon
such a lovely woman is a great comfort and joy for
a man."

The noble Lady Sloeberry responded as follows: "To speak wisely is an honor and no dishonor; great ladies and lowly women must give an
answer to whoever addresses them. I grant you the
right I would grant anyone: provided my honor is
safe, you can talk when I see fit. If I hear nonsense,
I will reply in kind. I will not knowingly allow you
to deceive me. I will not be alone with you, because
a woman should never dally alone in such company;
for bad reputation ensues, and that would be dishonor to me. I will speak with you some day, in the
presence of witnesses."

"Lady, I can hardly express my thanks for
the kindness which you promise. The grace you
show in your words now cannot be equalled by any
other grace. Although I trust in God that the time
will come when deeds will show who is your true
friend, I would like to speak, but I dare not—my
words might distress you."

She said: "Well, say it, and I will see what
to do."

"Lady," I said, "I want you to promise me,
in regard to our desires of love, if we can manage the

place and time to be together, as I desire, that we shall embrace each other. It is not too much to ask, for this will be enough."

Lady Sloeberry said: "It is well known that a lady is deceived by kisses. An embrace is exciting, and every woman is conquered by granting this joy. I cannot permit you this just now, but only allow you to talk. Soon my mother will pass this way from Mass; I must go or she will think that I am frivolous. There will be time for us to talk to each other this spring."

My lady went her way from our conversation. In all my life, I had never lived a happier day or been more pleased or more joyful. God was willing to be my guide and my good fortune. But I was caught in a cruel dilemma. If I pursued my lady with clever words, rumors could make the affair a public scandal and I would lose the lady—an unbearable thought. If I lay low and stayed away from her, our love would be lost; thinking that I had forgotten her, she would turn to another. Love grows with practice; not used, it diminishes. Forget your lady and she will forget you. When you pile on the wood, the fire grows; withdraw it, and the flames subside. Love and affection grow by usage. If you neglect the lady, she will pay no heed to your demands.

So many different worries assailed me on all

sides; my heart was torn by conflicting thoughts and misgivings for which I knew no remedy or art. When it has taken hold, love dispels all fears. Many times, fortune with its strength and power prevents people from reaching their goals; hence the world goes up and down. But God and great exertion can overcome fate. Fortune helps a man whom she likes, but when she is antagonistic, she can cause enormous distress. Exertion and fate usually go together, but without God's will all this cannot succeed. Knowing that nothing could help but God, I prayed that he would guide my effort and support my work so that my heart might win its desires. May he who says "Amen!" gain what he wishes.

I sought no help from brother or cousin, because when it begins to burn, the fire of love changes all hearts. Men cast off their loyalties and turn against each other; a woman can dissolve the bonds of friendship, duty, and blood. The wise man will reflect carefully and choose the better course, avoiding one that might be harmful; suspicious persons are never useful or effective as messengers. I sought out a convent-hopper, of the type Sir Love had advised, and selected the most skilled of them all; indeed, God and my good fortune assisted me! I found a real expert—an old woman who was just what I needed: experienced and skillful, a fountain of knowledge. Lady Venus could not have done more for Pamphilus than my old woman did to give me pleasure.

This Trotaconventos was an old peddler, a jewel-vender. These are the ones who lay snares and dig traps. Listen to what I am telling you: there are none more masterful than these old harlots, none who deal a better *coup de grâce*.

These old women regularly go from house to house, peddling little gifts. Nobody takes note of them; they mingle freely among the people and turn windmills with their hot air.

When this old shrew came to my house, I said to her: "Welcome, old mother! I am placing my life and my welfare into your hands. Unless you help me, I am dead. I have heard many good reports about you, all the help you give the man who comes to you with a problem. Since you have the reputation of pleasing those you serve, I have sent for you, wishing to talk to you as if I were in the confessional. Listen patiently to everything I tell you; no one but you is to know my grief and my misery."

The old woman replied: "You can trust me. Speak your heart with confidence. I will do what I can for you, and I will be loyal to you. The professional go-between must be very discreet; we harbor as many secrets as a neighborhood. If all the ladies of this city to whom we sell trinkets knew about each other, there would be no end of trouble. We arrange many marriages, that then go bad, and we sell many timbrels that make no noise."

I said to her, "I love a lady more than any other I have ever seen. She too seems to love me, unless she's making a fool out of me. To stay clear of trouble, I have been lying low until now, because I fear, as I have always feared, many things of this world. For a little trifle, a neighborhood rumor is born; and once it has started, it dies hard, no matter how false. Nourished by jealous lies, it swells up, and eventually the poor wretch finds himself ruined. Here it is, then, my dear friend. I wish you to go to her and carry messages between us in the best way you can. Be as discreet as possible in this affair, and tell her how I feel only when you know what she thinks."

She answered, "I will go to your friend's house and put such a spell on her and feed her such a potion that your wound will be healed by my art. Tell me who the lady is."

I said, "Lady Sloeberry."

She said she knew the lady well. I said, "For God's sake, woman, be on your guard against sudden disaster."

She said, "Since she has already been married, believe me she'll give in. There isn't a pack mule that won't accept the saddle. Wax which has stiffened from the cold becomes soft after it has been handled once, and then just a little warmth makes it quite pliable again. Any lady who is properly charmed will yield. My good friend, remember the old sayings: The first one to the mill gets first milling of the wheat; a belated message imitates many a man; the wise man never complains too much. Do not slacken, my friend, for another man seeks to marry the lady of your desire and wants what you want. He is a man of a good family, who comes from your region. Your pleas will have to precede his. This fellow is irritated with me because I don't press his case, but he is a miser, despite all his money. He promised me some clothes, a fur coat and a fur jacket; what he gave me is so well trimmed that it is neither. Now a present given without delay, if it is expensive enough, nullifies all laws and statutes, and is superior to the whole code. It helps many but it also hampers others. At times it produces advantage, and at times it doesn't make things any worse.

"Now this lady you are discussing is very much under my control; no one will have her except with my help. I know all her affairs and activities. She does more things at my behest than on her own account. I say no more; I have spoken enough. Remember that I live by this profession and I think of nothing else, and often I have found my services ill received and ill rewarded. If you give me something to tide me over for a while, I will talk this girl and other white-necked girls into coming to you. I know how to catch them in my sieve."

"Mother," I said, "I intend to reward you well. My house and all I own are at your disposal. For now, take this cloak and go; don't waste any time. But first, let me give you some advice. Put your whole heart into this affair. You will get help and support from me for all your efforts. Plan your words carefully so that they are discreet and appropriate. Think out what you are going to say from beginning to end. Don't say anything you may regret. Believe me, honor and dishonor rest on the outcome. If the affair ends well, then everything is fine. The sensible man is better off keeping quiet when it doesn't cause any harm; people will consider him discreet. If he speaks out when it is not fitting, he will regret it. Either plan what you are going to say or keep quiet."

The old peddler went her way, jingling her bells and carrying her jewels, the rings and the pins, in her bag. She hawked her towels by calling out: "Fine tablecloths for sale!"

Lady Sloeberry, hearing her, said, "Come in here, do not be afraid."

Entering the house, the old woman said, "Young lady, accept this ring for that blessed hand of yours. If you won't give me away, I will tell you

a story that came to my mind last night." Little by
little, she applied the spurs: "Daughter, you are always shut in at home and are growing old all alone.
Why don't you come out for a walk in the square
once in a while? Your great beauty is going to waste
inside these walls. There are many handsome young
men in this city, very charming and graceful fellows,
whose manners improve daily; you'll never find a
better group. They all are good to me in my poverty.

    "Now the one who is handsomest and who
comes from the noblest family is the young Sir Badger of the Orchard.[57] He surpasses all the others in
charm and goodness. None of his contemporaries has
become as courteous or as wealthy as he. He is gay
with those who are gay, and his elders think highly
of him. He is as gentle as a lamb and dislikes all violence. It is no mean trick for a wise man to outdo a
foolish man and keep his wits, for him to be sober
with those who are sober and foolish with those who
are foolish. The truly wise man does not become a
fool merely by conversing with a fool. I think about
this while I play my timbrel.

    "I tell you, you won't find his peer in this
whole city. He does not squander his money; in fact
he saves it. I am sure that this man must be just like
his father; you can see the ox in the new born calf,

and sons commonly resemble their fathers. This is nothing new.

"Now a man shows what he really is by his actions. Strong love or deep hate cannot be kept hidden. This man lives a wholesome and decent life. I believe he would like to marry you. If you knew him, and realized how estimable he is, you would appreciate the man I've been talking about.

"Sometimes a long speech is of little avail. As the proverb says, 'If you talk too long, you will blunder.' But from a tiny beginning a great deed springs, and often a trifle causes a heap of trouble. A short but fluent speech and a brief suit may achieve much on the spot. A tiny spark kindles a huge blazing fire; sometimes a little game ends in a big fight. It has always been my custom and my intent to promote and foster marriages, speaking as if in jest of those impulses until I can understand my clients and discern their inclinations. Now, my lady, tell me what you think. Are you pleased by my words or not? I will keep your secret, I won't give you away; speak freely and tell me everything."

The lady answered her with restraint and discretion: "Tell me, my good woman, who is this fellow? What sort of man is he, that you praise him so freely? How rich is he? I will think about all this and see if it suits me."

Trotaconventos said: "Who is he? Why,
Lady, what a wonderful opportunity God has given
you! He is Sir Badger of the Orchard, a nice young
man who lives in this neighborhood. You are sure to
like him. Believe me, child, none of your suitors can
compare with him. The day of your birth, you were
graced by good fortune which destined such a great
thing for you."

Lady Sloeberry said, "Stop all this preaching. That glib-tongued fellow has already tried to
trick me. He has often come to tempt me, but neither
he nor you can boast at my expense. The woman
who believes the lies your kind tell and the vows of
love which men make will end up wringing her
hands, clutching at her heart, and washing her face
with tears. Don't bother me any more; I have too
many other things on my mind. Such evil thoughts
don't enter my mind, and I will not listen to you
now telling me such things."

"Come now," replied the old woman, "people who see that you are a widow, living all alone,
will have no respect for you. A lonely widow is
pushed here and there like a cow in the arena. But
that good man could defend you. He could protect
you from all kinds of trouble—legal complaints, insults, disgrace, lawsuits. Many people talk of setting
all sorts of traps for you, so many that they won't
even leave the hinges on your door. My lady Sloe-

berry, take care or you may easily find yourself in the same predicament as the bustard did, when the swallow, a good counselor, was offering her sound advice."

THE BUSTARD AND THE SWALLOW

"There was once a hunter who was good at trapping birds. He sowed hemp in a good plot, from which the net maker was to make ropes and traps. The bustard was walking nearby on the path. The swallow addressed the doves and sparrows and also the bustard, saying: 'Eat up the seeds from these plots, because they are sown here for your ruin.'

"They all made fun of what she said and told her to go away, that she was just chirping nonsense. When the seeds had germinated, they saw the hunter watering the hemp, but still they were not worried. The swallow came again and told the bustard to strip off the leaves that were sprouting because the man who was watering and weeding so zealously was doing it for their eventual ruin.

"The bustard said: 'You are a stupid, crazy fool; you always start chirping nonsense about what's going to happen. I don't need your advice; get out of here, idiot! Leave me alone in this pleasant meadow.'

"The swallow flew to the hunter's house and there built her nest as well as she could. The hunter, an early riser, was very pleased by her singing and trilling. The hemp was harvested, the traps were made, and the bird trapper went out as usual to hunt. He caught the bustard and took it to the market place. The swallow said: 'Now you are done for!' Then the crossbowmen plucked her wings, leaving her no feathers except a few small ones. Because she did not accept good advice, she was ruined.

"Have a care, my lady Sloeberry, for such wicked traps. Many people conspire and connive to ruin you by playing some evil trick on you; they swear daily that they will put you in the dock and then pluck you like the bustard. But this man could protect you from all such lawsuits: he is an expert at law and litigations; and he helps and defends those who ask him. And if he doesn't defend you, I don't know who will."

The old crone kept up the refrain: "When your dear departed husband used to sit in this doorway, he provided shade for the house and he brightened the whole of it. But when there is no man in the house, it is worth little. Now, my child, though you are a widow, you are still very young; you are alone, without a husband, like a little dove. I'm sure this is the reason you are so lean and sallow: it is never good for women to live by themselves. God blesses

a house where a good man lives; such a house is filled
with mirth, pleasure, and joy. This is why I wanted
this young man for you; you would see an improve-
ment in a very few days."

The lady answered, saying, "It would
hardly be decent or proper for a widow to marry before the end of a full year of mourning; that is the
rule prescribed in mourning. If I married sooner, I
would be dishonored, and I would also lose the leg-
acy I now have. I would not have my second husband's respect, for he would think I couldn't bear
chastity for very long."

"Daughter," said the old woman, "the year
is already over. Take this man as your man and your
husband; let us go and talk to him, in private. You
have been blessed with good fortune. What good
does it do you to dress in black and go about, em-
barrassed and worried about gossip? Lady, put aside
mourning and make a fresh start. The swallow never
gave better advice. It is becoming for knights and
ladies to wear sackcloth for a deceased husband or
lord no matter how bad he was, but they should not
wear it too long or display it too much: pleasures
should be long and sorrows short."

Lady Sloeberry answered, "No more! I
would not dare do what you advise or what he
wishes. Don't sing any more of this song or try to
force too much on me the first day. So far, as you

know, I have already rejected many attractive offers
by more than a hundred suitors. If now you would
have me abandon all prudence—"

·          [*Six stanzas are missing here.*] [58]

"The wolf sat down, waiting. The fierce
rams came running hard and butted the wolf between them. He fell wounded as they ran off.

"After a long while, he picked himself up,
still shaken, and said, 'The devil sent me to meddle
in strange things. I had a good omen, God had
heeded me, I did not want to eat the bacon, and now
I have been made a fool.'

"He quit the meadow and ran as fast as he
could until he caught sight of a large band of kids
frolicking in some hollows with goats and many
horned rams. 'Now,' he said, 'the sneeze is fulfilled.'

"At the sight of the wolf, they were terrified.
Their leaders went to receive him. 'Ah, lord guardian,' said the long-beards, 'you are most welcome
among your servants! Four of us planned to come
and invite you to honor this holy festival with your
presence, celebrate Mass for us, and then feast on a
good meal. Now since God has brought you here,
please say it. Today, free from dogs or shepherds, we

are celebrating a very solemn feast with loud song. Sing loud and the choir will respond. We will offer the best kids in generous measure.'

"Believing all this, the fool started to howl, and the rams and goats to bleat loudly. The shepherds, hearing the racket, came with clubs and dogs looking for him. The wolf took to his heels, trying to escape, but the shepherds and the dogs surrounded him and gave him a bad time with clubs and rocks. He groaned, 'The devil made me say Mass in the pit.'

"He ran further on and came to a mill, where he found a sow with a litter of fat sucklings. 'Now,' he said, 'I will have a good time off her and my good omen will be fulfilled.'

"Immediately he said to the sow, 'God give you peace, good mother. I have come here to serve you and your little children. What are you doing? Just command me and I will do your wish. Then you can feed me.'

"From under the tall willow, the sow answered the wolf, speaking much to the point: 'My Lord Abbot, baptize my children with your consecrated hands so that they may die Christians. After the ceremony, I will offer them to you as a thanksgiving and a tribute. You will have no trouble in taking them and eating, and then you can rest here at your leisure in the shade.'

"The wolf bent down under the willow to

remove the suckling from beneath the sow. The sow hit him with her snout and knocked him into the water; he was washed down miserably into the mill-race. The wheel caught him and whirled him around ferociously; when he finally got out, he looked like the devil himself. He should have been satisfied with his bacon; then he would not have lost his prey or gotten into so much trouble.

"A wise man should not go looking for trouble or endanger the things he wants; rather than despise what he has, he should be content with God's gifts. Some are satisfied with two sardines in their own homes, but when they go visiting, they look for dainty dishes: they despise mutton and ask for stew, and maintain they could never eat bacon without chicken."

[*Thirty-two stanzas are missing here.*[59] *As the text resumes, Trotaconventos is trying to persuade Sir Badger not to despair.*]

on, the best remedy of all is to forget what you cannot have. Do not insist on something that cannot be, but work for what you can attain."

"Wretched me! What helpless help you are! What miserable news you have brought! Old woman, destroyer of friends! Why have you told me all this? You can never repair the terrible harm you have just done. Lousy old gossips, be damned! You go about the world cheating everybody, lying, inventing all kinds of malicious nonsense, and turning lies into the truth for stupid fools.

"Alas! my limbs have started to tremble, and I have lost all my strength, my sense, and my knowledge, my health, understanding, and life itself—all for an empty hope. Miserable, sad, foolish heart! Why do you wreck the body which is your abode? Why do you love the lady who rebuffs you? Heart of mine, you will lead a life of torment, and you are yourself to blame. Heart, why did you let yourself be trapped and held by a lady who slighted you for others? You have imprisoned yourself with

grief and sorrow, and you will suffer. Poor heart,
so neglected, so mistreated!

"Ah, eyes of mine! Why did you cast yourselves on a lady who does not care to see you or to
look upon you? My eyes, you have wished to ruin
yourselves for that sight. How you will suffer, eyes
of mine! Suffer and agonize! And tongue, luckless
miserable tongue, why do you want to speak? Why
do you want to utter words? Why do you want to
converse with a lady who has no interest in hearing
or heeding you? Poor body, so tormented, how you
will perish in misery!

"False women, treacherous and arrogant of
heart, you have no shame; you have no respect or
decency in your fickle love. May I see you destroyed
by rage and grief! Once my lady is married to another, I do not reckon this earthly life worth a pin.
My life and my death have already been decided.
Since I cannot have her, I am condemned to die."

She said, "Madman, why do you have to
lament so much? Your futile complaints will profit
nothing. Temper this grief with good sense. Wipe
away your tears and plan your next move. Necessity
is the mother of invention; if you plan, you can
avoid many troubles. Who knows, great exertion
might get you somewhere, for God and hard work
can alter fate."

I answered her, "What art, what exertion,

what prudence can heal the terrible wound brought on by such grief? If my lady takes a husband, all my hope dies and I am lost. Until her husband makes his bed in the cemetery, she will not lie with me; that would be adultery. All my pains have come to nothing, and I see only great hardship and beyond that only shame."

The good old woman said, "Ah, but it does not take long for a great grief to heal and for a great scar to disappear. After heavy rains, clear weather returns, and after dark clouds there is a bright sun and pleasant shade. Health and vitality return after a long illness, and many pleasures come after great misery. Cheer up, my friend, and take comfort. Lasting joys will replace your grief. Lady Sloeberry is yours; she will do what I tell her. She does not really want to marry anyone else; all her desire is fixed on you. If you love her very much, she loves you even more."

"Old woman, what are you saying now? You act like a mother when her child cries: she tells him stories to hush him. So you tell me the lady is mine. I think you are doing all this, mother, so that I will shake off my sadness, my misery, and my bitterness, so that I will be comforted and feel better. Are these just stories, or are you serious?"

The old woman said, "The lover is like the bird which has barely escaped the hawk's clutches:

it thinks the hunter is everywhere, ready to swoop down, and so it lives in constant fear of being carried off. Believe me, I am telling you the truth, as you will see. If you have told me the truth and really do love her, she too told me the truth: she wants what you want. Put by your misery, because you will have proof. Often things don't turn out as we expect or predict. Man cannot foretell the course of destiny, since God alone and no one else knows the future. A trifle may overturn great projects; when man despairs he loses heart. Hard work attains every possible desire; often it heaps up great riches. All our effort and our hope is precarious and uncertain. Men are encouraged by a good start to hope that things will go very well, but sometimes there might be a delay."

"Mother, can't you surmise or determine if the lady cares for me or will ever care for me? A person in love must betray herself by gestures or by sighs, or even by her words or her color."

"Friend," said the old woman, "I can see that the lady cares for you, loves you, and desires you. When I talk to her about you, I notice that her color changes and she loses her composure. If I get weary and stop talking, she urges me to go on and not to stop. If I pretend that I don't remember, then she starts me again and listens very happily. I find many signs here. Often she throws both arms around my neck and for a long time we embrace; we always talk about you, we talk of nothing else, except when somebody comes and we change the subject.

"Her lips tremble a little, she blushes and goes pale by turns, her heart thumps, beating quickly, and she presses my fingers with hers, without saying a word. Whenever I mention your name, she sighs and becomes pensive, her eyes glow, and she is all stirred up. It seems that if she were with you, she would not sleep. I recognize the scheme in many other things, and she does not deny it. As a matter of fact, she says outright that she loves you. If you just persevere, the branch [60] will bend and Lady Sloeberry will come when the old woman calls to her."

"My dear old mother, comfort of mine! My hope is already revived because of you. With your help, I am becoming more cheerful. Keep at it, stay with her constantly. Laziness undoes much; diligence and cleverness succeed. Finish your work; complete this noble deed. It would be a great shame to lose her by indolence."

"My friend, I think I can give you comfort: the lady will go wherever I wish. But, at the same time, I have received nothing but this cloak from you. If you order a good meal, you must pay well. Sometimes people do not do everything they say or carry out everything they promise. Some people are

quick to promise and slow to give, and so we have
to work and slave for empty words."

"Mother, have no fear that I intend to cheat
you, because to cheat the poor is a terrible sin. I will
not deceive you; God would not allow it! And if
I do, He will punish me for it. What we say, we
must carry out; we place our trust in the firm promise. It is a shame and a disgrace to renege on a promise which we can fulfill."

"This," said the old woman, "is very nice
talk. But still, a poor wretch is always afraid that
he will be oppressed by the powerful nobleman; the
poor and needy are ruined for mere trifles. The poor
man's rights are often trampled on; the needy, the
wretched are broken by the rich and crushed by the
haughty; they are considered as no better than dried
sardines. On every hand we see little faith and great
faithlessness, very shrewdly disguised. But one has
no power against fate; sometimes the sea is menac-
ing, but the day turns out fine. What you have
promised me I must regard as a risk; but you will
have what I promised you and you will take pleasure
in it. I will go to the lady and ask her to come discreetly to my house and there speak with you pri-
vately. Now if I can manage to bring you together
alone, I ask you to show yourself a man. Her heart
does not desire anything else, and she will easily
agree to what you want of her."

She went to the lady's house and called out, "Anybody home?" The mother answered, "Who is it?"

"Lady Branch, it's me. (Too bad I have seen you. I cannot shake off my bad luck.)"

Lady Branch replied, "What's the matter?"

"What's the matter? I do not know how to explain it. I am horribly persecuted. A huge fellow —I don't know who he is but he's bigger than that post—keeps coming after me flinging insults. He tracks me all day long as he might a doe; he chases me like the devil going after a rich man, because he wants a jewel that I've been selling. He has piles of money; I can hardly understand him."

When the sour old woman heard this, she left her with her daughter and went to the street. The clever peddler immediately turned to another subject, her old familiar tune: "May the devil carry off that old bitch. No man dares even to talk to you because of her. Well, now, my child, how are things with you? I see that you are sparkling, healthy, and lovely."

Lady Sloeberry said, "Tell me, what news do you have of him?"

The old woman answered, "What news? How should I know? He is miserable and scrawny. He is as thin as a winter chicken after Michaelmas.

A huge fire cannot hide its flames; no more can a man
deeply in love hide his feelings. I know your way of
doing things, and my heart weeps with grief. Every
time I see you, I can well understand that you are
very much loved by that man. You should see how
pale he is; his face is livid. You obsess him in everything he does.

        "And still you have no feeling or care for
him. You always turn me down, even though I plead
with you. Your rudeness toward that generous man
is destroying him, embittered and lost as he is.
Whether he's walking or standing still, he is thinking about you; he walks about staring at the ground
and sighing, clasping his hands and muttering to
himself. Damn you, when will you have pity? The
poor wretch suffers constantly. God! it was an evil
day when he saw you, you stony creature. He labors
night and day without stopping, but neither art nor
skill bring any relief. No good fruit can grow in hard
soil, and who, except a miserable wretch, sows in the
sand? His great efforts and great misery are of no
avail. How can a minnow fight against a whale?

        "First he fell in love with you because of
your looks, and then he was completely ensnared by
your speech. He is deeply in love with you for these
two reasons, but he has been badly deceived, because
you have done nothing that you promised. By talk-

ing to him, you have killed him; and even though
you are tight-lipped, I know you are as inflamed as
he is. Reveal your own wound, or you will perish
too. Your concealed fire is consuming you and making you suffer. Speak up, and say what you want.
Tell me the truth. Either let us go ahead or just drop
the whole affair; we cannot keep this business secret
if I keep coming to you every day."

Lady Sloeberry said, "This great passion is
wrecking me. The fire is not hot enough to overcome
me, but it does burn me fiercely. Fear and shame keep
me from my joy; I can find no way out of this terrible predicament."

"Daughter, put by your fear; there is no
cause to panic. There can be nothing wrong in getting together with him. In his heart, he is determined
to have you in lawful wedlock. His misery shows itself in many ways. He says to me with tears and
groans, 'Lady Sloeberry is destroying me, no one else,
and only she can save me; a dancing-girl would be
no help.'

"When I see his suffering and hear him talk
of it so pathetically, I weep too out of pity and sadness, and also to satisfy him; but I rejoice a little in
my own mind, for I see that he really loves you and
wants you without guile. I notice everything, far
more than you know, and I am convinced your love

is mutual. Your passion is tormenting and destroying both of you. Since love demands it, why do you
not come together?"

"You are asking the very thing which I desire, if only my mother would grant her permission.
But as much as we ourselves desire to please you, we
will not have the chance for pleasure and joy. I
would do many things for my lover from Hita, but
my mother guards me and never leaves me alone."

Trotaconventos said, "Oh, the hell with that
old scab! I wish the cross and holy water would
carry her off! But love is adept at breaking locks and
gates; it slips past guards as if they were dead men;
it quiets vain fears and unfounded suspicions; the
strongest locks yield before it."

Lady Sloeberry answered my old woman,
"Satisfy my heart! I have shown you my desire and
my wound. Now that you know my wishes, tell me
what to do. Do not be timid in advising me."

"To betray women is wicked and mean, a
terrible sin and disgrace. I am bound to conceal any
shameless deed you might perform, but what makes
me hesitate is my own action and my reputation.
Still if anyone should throw accusations at me, he
will have to take me at my word and take that at its
worst. Let him do all he can, let him dare what he
will: he will either shut his mouth in defeat or go
to the devil. Anyone can come to talk with me and

say the very worst, but that excellent young man,
sweet and guileless lover, will be our defense and
utterly confound him. Rumor will not be aroused,
I will see to that; there will be nobody to gossip or
tell tales. The thing itself is not shameful because
there could be many good reasons for it. It amazes
me, lady, that you hesitate over this."

"Oh, God," exclaimed the young lady, "how
many things there are which make a lover's heart
pound in fright and fear! Yearning love pulls it this
way and that; it cannot tell which is the worst of
many dangers. Different kinds of woes plague me
night and day. My heart pines for what love desires,
but I am hindered by the terrible fear that I might
be defamed. What heart so oppressed would not
grow weary? It does not know what to do; it is in
constant turmoil. It pleads, and by its pleading love's
painful wound grows worse. I have fought against
this cruel love until now, but it conquers my will;
it is much too strong for me. With such thoughts,
love has broken me; fighting with him has exhausted
me. But I rejoice in my suffering, worn out yet en-
amored. I would rather die his death than live a life
of such pain."

In a fight, the more a man curses and is
cursed, the more furious and excited he becomes; the
more sweet arguments a lady has with love, the more
Lady Venus excites and inflames her.

"Since you are not able to quench the fire, carry out the orders of your beloved lover. Daughter, your obstinacy is killing you. You will squander the pleasures of life if you do not yield. I tell you, you see your friend in your heart day and night. And he carries you in his heart. Satisfy your desires or they will kill you. This pain is destroying you as well as him; your faces, your eyes have become the color of clay. Delay and grief will kill you both. You are very much mistaken if you do not believe what I say. But certainly, daughter, I believe that you intend to neglect or thwart what you most desire. You must not think or imagine or believe this, because only death can quiet your desires.

"Remember too that some pleasures bring comfort; therefore, my daughter, come to my house sometime soon, and we will play ball and other jolly games; we will amuse ourselves and rest, and what nuts I will give you! My shop is never without fruit for lovely ladies. I have many pears and peaches, and what citrons and what apples! What chestnuts, what pine nuts, and what filberts! Those you like the best will do you most good. It is only a few steps from here to my store; come in a housedress, as if in your own house. This neighborhood is well populated, and we will go, little by little, playing and without any worries. Come to my store; there you will be as safe as you are at home, and we'll eat a

little snack. God forbid, daughter, that you should
get into trouble. We will go so quietly that no one
will notice us."

Sometimes, when they are constantly pestered, people change their minds and grant what
they should not. Only when the damage has been
done does repentance follow. A woman who is pursued is blind, and has neither wisdom nor discretion.
Woman and hare, if they are pursued, hounded, and
cornered, lose their wits, go blind, and cannot see;
it is as if they were wearing blindfolds and could
not see the nets or the traps. People then come to
laugh at the woman, and she thinks that she is truly
loved.

Lady Sloeberry agreed that she would come
and talk, eat some fruit, and play ball.

"Lady," said the old woman, "tomorrow we
will enjoy ourselves. I will come here to get you
when I see my chance."

Trotaconventos came happily to me with
the news.

"Friend," she said, "how are you? Forget
your troubles! A clever enchanter lures the snake out
of its hole. Tomorrow she will come to talk to you;
I have already arranged it. I know the truth of the
little proverb, 'The beggar who perseveres always
gets something.' Tomorrow you will need to be a
man; do not behave like a fool. Speak out and get

right to the point when I am not there. Be careful
not to miss your chance; remember the saying,
"When they give you the goat, run with the rope.'
Get what you want or you will be considered a fool.
It is better to have a blush on your face than pain
in your heart."


LADY SLOEBERRY GOES TO
THE OLD WOMAN'S SHOP AND
THE ARCHPRIEST GETS HIS DESIRES

he next day was the feast of St. James. At
noon, while men were at the table, Lady
Sloeberry came with my clever old woman and very
discreetly entered her house. I lost no time in carrying out the old hag's instructions. I found the door
closed, but the old woman had seen me.

"Hey there," she said, "what is all that
noise? Is that a man or the wind? I think it is a
man. I am right! Look, look, do you see the ugly
sinner! Is it him or not? It looks like him, I'm sure
of it. Goodness, it is Sir Badger! I recognize him,
I can smell him! That is his face and his ox-eye.
Look, see how anxious he is! He is pointing at us
like a dog! How angry he's getting! He cannot open
the lock! Now he's going to break down the door!
He's jangling it as if it were a bell! Of course, he

wants to come in. Now why don't I talk to him?

"Sir Badger, stop! Has the devil himself brought you here? Don't bash down my doors, which I earned from the priest of St. Paul's and to which you have not added even a nail. I will open the door for you. Wait, don't break it down! If you want something, just say so nice and quiet. Get away from the door! (Don't give up.) Come in, you're quite welcome. (Let's see what you're going to do.)"

"My lady Sloeberry! You, my beloved! Old woman, is this why you kept your door locked on me? What a wonderful day this is for me to find such an ambush! God and my good luck reserved this for me."

[*Thirty-two stanzas are missing here.*] [61]

"When I left the house, since you saw it was a trick, why did you dally alone with him inside? Don't throw it up to me, child, you deserve it! Now you had better be quiet about this. It will be far less trouble to conceal this little trifle than to broadcast it and so defame yourself. You will not lose a possible marriage because of this, and to me that seems better than ruining your reputation. And since you say that the harm is done, let him defend and help you for right or wrong. Daughter, when the

harm has been done one has to face it, but for the
sake of your reputation, do not make it known. If
the magpie didn't chatter more than the quail, they
would not hang it in the square nor laugh at what
it says. Learn, my dear, from the practice of the
crocodile, for all men behave like Sir Badger of the
Orchard."

     Lady Sloeberry said to her: "Ah, damned
old women! You betray us and you barter for us!
Yesterday you promised me a thousand ways, a
thousand tricks, and a thousand escapes. Today, I
am scorned: they all failed. If the birds could know
and understand how many traps are prepared for
them, they would never be caught. But by the time
they see the trap, they are already being hauled to
market. They die for a scrap of bait and have no
defense. And the fish in the water—by the time they
see the hook, the fisherman has caught them and
thrown them on the ground. A woman sees her ruin
only when she is already in grief, and is thrown out
by her father, mother, and grandparents. The man
who dishonored her leaves her without support and
she wanders about the world to her ruin. There is
no other way; she will lose both her body and soul.
This has happened to many. Since I have no other
remedy, this will happen to me too."

     Old people have wisdom and good sense,
and skill and knowledge go together with long years.

My old mistress had keen insight and offered a sound
verdict in this case.

"A wise person should not lament when
lamentation will not change anything. You must
discreetly suffer and bear up with what cannot be
remedied. One must seek out counsel, medicines, and
cures for serious sicknesses, misfortunes, and hapless
mistakes. The wise person proves himself in trouble
and grief. Anger and discord are harmful to friend-
ships and sow wicked suspicions in the soul that accepts them. Let there be peace and friendship between
you, and make grief and anger turn into pleasure.
Since you claim that your harm came through me,
I desire that your good should also come through
me. Be you his wife and he your husband, so that all
your desires may be fulfilled through me."

Lady Sloeberry and Sir Badger lived together, and their friends made merry on this occasion. If I have said anything wicked, forgive me: it
was Pamphilus and Ovid who supplied the worldly
parts of the story.

eed my good teaching, ladies; pay close attention to my words. Beware of men; be on your guard so that you won't meet the fate that once befell the ass, whom the lion left with neither ears nor heart.

The lion had been suffering from a severe headache. When he recovered and could raise his head, all the animals came to celebrate on a Sunday afternoon. The ass was there, and him they appointed jester. Fat as he was, he started to gambol and bray aloud while banging on his drum. The lion and the others were deafened. Irritated by the frolicking ass, the lion wanted to tear him apart; but he couldn't manage to catch him, and the ass ran off, beating his drum as he went. The lion felt that he had been made a fool by "longears." So he said that he would pardon the ass and asked the other animals to call him back to honor the feast, promising to grant whatever request the ass made.

The clownish vixen said that she would fetch him and went out where the ass was grazing in a meadow. She greeted him politely:

"Sir," she said, "friend, your antics pleased everyone; without you, the lot of them are not worth a pin. Your shouts and jests, your resonant drum, the sounds you made, were the best part of our feast. The lion would be very pleased if you would come back and play, safe and secure."

He believed her deceitful flatteries, and so much the worse it was for him. The singer returned dancing to the feast, and unaware of his lord's nature, he paid, poor nitwit, for playing his drum. The lion had already arranged his armed guards, and they caught Sir Ass, just as they had been instructed, and dragged him before the lion, who ripped him up the middle while the others trembled in fear for their own safety.

The lion ordered the wolf to guard the carcass with his sharp claws better than he did the sheep; but after the lion had gone a short distance away, the wolf ate the heart and the ears. When the lion came back, all ready to feast, he asked the wolf for the ass he had entrusted to his care, and found the trunk mutilated, lacking heart and ears. The lion was enraged at the wolf, but the wolf maintained that the ass had been born that way, because if he had had heart or ears, he would have seen through the lion's tricks and known what was going on. He had come back only because he lacked both.

Now, my ladies, understand the meaning of this fable: avoid foolish love; do not be entangled or caught. Hear me well: give over your hearts to the pure love of God and do not let it be soiled by foolish love. If anyone of you has been deceived, let her take care not to return to the evil a second time, not to be deprived of ears and heart; let her learn from the example of others. Women should learn wisdom from the many who have been deceived and should not desire false love or show silly joy. You have already heard that "the ass which belongs to many people is eaten by wolves." Let those who itch after this not spread evil gossip about me.

An attractive woman should guard against even a little harmful gossip, because an unripe grape can set the teeth on edge, an enormous walnut tree springs from a tiny nut, many ears from a grain of wheat. Many rumors would spread among the people about her, and there are many who afterward would scoff and sneer at her. Lady, do not be angered or annoyed if I tell you this. I beg you to examine my fables and examples closely. Give some thought to the story of Sloeberry's daughter. I tell it here as an example, not just because it happened to me.[62] Don't trust scheming old women or the words of malicious neighbors. Don't trust yourself alone near a man any more than you would near a bramble bush.

After all this, one day when I was loveless and, thus, untroubled, I saw a gracious lady sitting in her parlor. She won my heart on the spot; I had never been so taken with any woman. She had the best figure I had ever seen. She was young, rich, and virtuous, beautiful, noble, and shining with youth. God help me, I have never seen such a woman! She was elegant and vivacious, and clearly well born. She left the house seldom and was quite upright. I looked for a go-between to promote this affair, for women of her sort are the beginning of this holy pilgrimage. But I did not look for another Ferrand Garcia,[63] nor do I intend ever to send him on another errand. One is never happy in bad company; may Holy Mary protect me from a wicked messenger!

This messenger of mine was a very faithful old lady. Each day she went to talk—but nothing else. She threw herself so earnestly into this case that she seemed to live downtown instead of in the suburbs. Right at the outset, I composed these songs and the old woman took them along with other compliments.

"Lady," she said, "buy these goods from me."

"Yes, indeed," the lady said, "if you show them to me."

The old dame started to weave her spell and said, "Daughter, look here at the lovely jewel that I have brought you. It's a gift for you."

Little by little, she goads her.

"If you won't betray me, I'll tell you a little story. I know one who would rather see you every day than be lord of this city with all its treasures. Lady, don't be so shy, go out into the world for which God made you."

She charmed the lady so expertly that she outwitted her. She gave her my songs; she tied the belt around her. When she gave her the jewel, she winked and aroused her and started her on the way.

The proverb says, "A new sieve hangs for three days." This old woman, whose name is Urraca,[64] told me that she had no desire to go on being a go-between and a procuress. I answered her playfully: "Chattering magpie, don't leave the high road and take the path. Serve where you can make a profit, since you know your way. 'If you have fodder, the halter is no problem.'"

At the time, I did not remember this short proverb: "In their jests, men say cruel things." The old woman was so furious that, to my surprise, she blurted out the whole secret. After that, the lady was watched carefully, as carefully as her mother could manage; I could not see her so often any more. The man who is not discreet errs very easily. Either

think before you speak or play dumb. I learned this
with Urraca, and pass the advice on to you. Do not
reproach a person either in private or in public, once
your secret is in his care, because nothing is more
damaging than the truth. Never reproach your messenger with the name *mace;* never call her *magpie* no
matter how much she warbles; never call her *decoy,*
*blind, sledge hammer, cuirass, knocker, shoe-horn,*
*halter,* or *currycomb.* Never call her *hook, sheath,*
*rope, cover, rasp, bow rope,* or *file, guard, hone,*
*bridle, procuress, shovel, tongue,* or *fishhook.* Never
call her *bell, clapper, go-between, club, noose, leader,*
*guide,* or *walker;* do not call her *trotter* although
she trots for you.[65] If you observe all this good counsel, I know the old woman will help you. Do not
call her *spur, ladder, bumblebee, trap, cord, snare,*
*ledger,* or *gloss.* It would be a long tale to list all her
names, because she has more names and more tricks
than a fox.

  As the proverb says, "Necessity knows no
law." Goaded by Love, my lord and my king, and
feeling sorry for my lady, who, I thought, was as
unhappy as a sheep strayed from the flock, in my
great misery I had to beg my old woman to forget
her rage over my nasty reproach. The ferret pulls
the hare out of its burrow, black is made white just
by turning the fur.

  "Archpriest," she said, "one makes the old

woman trot if he needs her, and you do the same
because you have no other. You must treat this old
woman well, for she can help you; a man must often
kiss the hand he might prefer to bite off. You should
never do it again. I mean what I say. Now I will
unsay what has been said and undo what has been
done, just as caked mud crumbles when you tread
on it. I will bring everything to a happy end without much difficulty. But never call me vile or ugly
names. Call me 'Good Love,' and I will be loyal;
people are pleased by pleasing names, and good
names cost no more than bad ones."

    For the old woman's sake and to speak the
truth, I have called my book *Good Love,* and so do
I call her always. Because I treated her well, she was
a real asset to me. There is no sin without its punishment, nor good without its reward. She pulled off
a clever ruse very artfully; she passed herself off for
an imbecile by going about undressed. People stared
and said, "May God confound that stupid old
woman who commits such folly." Everywhere they
said, "Curses on anyone who believed the absurd
things the old witch said." Everyone repented of
what he had believed before. I told myself, "I never
planted a better kiss on an old woman's hand."

    In a few days, the rumors died down and the
young lady was no longer kept under guard by
mother or governess. I went back to my old woman

as to a saving branch. If you find such an old
woman, cherish her as you would your very soul.

She became a jewel peddler; as I have told
you, these women dig caves and pits. There are few
experts as sharp as these old whores; they know how
to hit their target. Listen, if you have ears! I have
also told you how these peddlers go from house to
house selling their baubles. People don't object to
them; they can stay and turn windmills with their
air. My loyal Urraca—may God preserve her for me!
—accomplished what she had promised, which is
not common.

She said, "I want to take a gamble, whatever happens, and keep things moving. Now is the
time, for they're not guarding her and they pay me
no heed as a peddler. I'll make them pay for what
they said about you; for where experienced people
do not hunt, the crows have no pleasure."

Whether she enchanted my lady or gave her
tincal or sulfur or pomegranate or poison or a
philter, she knew how to madden her quickly. As
the decoy draws the falcon, so Urraca enticed the
lady into her trap. I tell you, friend, that the proverbs are true: "An old dog does not bark in vain."

But it is part of nature that we are born and
we die. Sadly, the lady passed away just a few days
later. I can hardly speak of it. May God forgive her
soul and receive it in peace. In grief and shock, I took

to my bed, and I thought I would surely die. For two full days, I could not leave my bed. "The food was good," I said, "but the bill was too high."

### THE OLD WOMAN WHO CAME TO THE ARCHPRIEST

t was March; Spring had arrived, when an old woman came to see me and said abruptly, "A wicked boy is worth more sick than healthy." I grabbed her and started to murmur nonsense. Unsatisfied, the old woman said over and over, "Archpriest, there is more noise here than nuts."

"The devil sent me such vile old women," I said. "After they have drunk the wine, they find fault with the dregs."

I wrote some popular ballads about all this misery and grief, and all the wicked things she said to me. The ladies ought not scorn them or shun them because no lady ever hears them without a good laugh. I ask of you, my ladies, pardon in the name of courtesy. You know that I dislike being in your

bad graces, for then I would die of grief. Allow me
a bit of buffoonery among such serious matters. With
your permission, I will gladly write a great deal
about the things that have been said and done; but
one is bound to blunder once or twice in a long text,
and a courteous listener must have his pardons
handy.

## THE ARCHPRIEST AND THE MOUNTAIN GIRL [66]

The Apostle orders us to try all things,[67] so
I tried the mountains, on an absurd quest; I soon
lost my mule and could find nothing to eat. Anyone
who wants bread better than that made of wheat is
a fool. It was a day in March, the feast of Saint Emeterius,[68] when I took the road to the Loçoya Pass.
I had no protection against the snow and hail. The
man who looks for what he never lost deserves to
lose what he has. At the top of that pass, I found
myself in dire straits. I met a cowgirl near a wood
and asked her who she was.

"I am Snubnose," she said, "Snubnose the
strong who can tie men up. I guard the pass and collect the toll, but I do not bother those who pay willingly. If a man does not want to pay, I strip him on

the spot. Pay up, or you'll learn how stubble is thrashed.''

She blocked the way; it was narrow, just a path made by herders. Considering the trouble I was in, stiff with cold and weak, I said, "My friend, in a fallow field a dog barks in vain. Let me go, my friend, and I will give you some rustic jewelry, if you like. Tell me what kind is fashionable in this area. The proverb says that he who inquires does not go wrong. And for God's sake, give me some shelter; I'm dying of the cold.''

"Beggars can't be choosers," Snubnose replied. "Promise me what I want and don't provoke me. If you give me something, you need have no fear about the snow getting you wet. I'm telling you, we'd better come to terms before I take all you have.''

As the old woman says, when she wets the skein while spinning, "My friend, if you can't do any better, you'll have to die whether you like it or not.''

What with the bitter cold, my fear, and my weariness, I had to promise her an ornament and a brooch and a bag made of rabbit skin. Pleased by my answer, she hoisted me on her shoulders, to my great delight, for she carried me, and I did not have to contend with streams and slopes. I wrote the following verses about that episode.

SONG OF THE MOUNTAIN GIRL

ne morning, in the pass
of Malangosto,
a mountain girl assaulted me
on the crest of the hill.
"Poor wretch," she said, "where are you going?
What are you looking for, what do you want,
in this narrow pass?"

To her question I responded,
"I'm going to Sotosalvos."
"The devil must be chasing you,
To make you speak so boldly.
In this region,
which I keep under guard,
men do not pass scot free."

She planted herself in my path,
horrendous, wicked, and ugly.
"Yah," she said, "you scoundrel,
here I stay put
until you promise me something.
You might try to charge me,
but you won't pass through the path.

I said, "For God's sake, cowgirl,
don't ruin my excursion.
Move over and let me pass,
because I brought nothing for you."
"Then turn around," said she,
"pass through Somosierra,
because here you will not pass."


That fiendish Snubnose,
St. Julian confound her!
She flung her stick at me
and aimed her sling,
with a stone in it:
"By the Father of Truth,
you'll pay me my toll today."


The snow came down and the hail,
and Snubnose cried suddenly,
as if she were threatening me,
"Pay up or you'll see."
Said I, "For God's love, beauty,
there's something I want to tell you;
but I want to be near the fire."


"I'll bring you to my house
and I'll show you the way;
I'll make you a glowing fire,

and I'll give you bread and wine.
Aye, but promise me something
and I'll think you a nobleman.
You've had a lucky morning."

Frozen stiff and in fear,
I promised her a dress,
and for that dress I promised her
an ornament and a brooch.
Said she, "From now on, my friend,
come along with me!
Don't worry about the ice."

She grabbed my hand tightly,
lifted me up on her shoulders
like a light bag,
and carried me down the slope.
"Hey, don't you be afraid;
I'll give you a good meal
in the good old mountain way."

Quickly she transported me
to her shack and safety.
She piled oak logs for a fire;
she fed me wild rabbit,
tasty roasted partridges,
badly kneaded bread,
and savory calf meat.

And a great measure of strong wine,
heaps of cow-butter,
smoked cheese aplenty,
milk, cream, a trout.
Then she said, "Come on now,
let's finish this hard bread
and then we will wrestle."

After being there a while,
I started to thaw out;
and as I grew warmer,
I started to smile.
The shepherdess looked at me
and said, "Now, my friend, now
I think I know what's what."

Said the stubborn maid,
"Get up from there now,
come, off with the clothes,
let's have a little tumble."
She took me by the wrist
and I had to do as she wanted.
Believe me, I had a good bargain!

## THE ARCHPRIEST AND THE MOUNTAIN GIRL

Not long after that, I left her shack and went
to Segovia, but not to buy jewelry for that snub-

nosed whore. Instead, I went to see a rib of the fierce
dragon which had killed old Rando, according to the
story they tell in Moya.[69] I stayed in that city, spend-
ing all my money without finding the sweet well or
the perennial spring. When I saw that my purse was
limp, I said, "My little hut and my hearth are worth
a million." So three days later I started back to my
town, but not by way of Loçoya, for I had no trinkets. I wanted to go by way of the pass called Fuent-
fria, but being a stranger I completely missed my
way.

Down in the pine grove, I met a cowgirl who
was tending the cows near the stream. "How do you
do, fair mountain girl," I said. "Either show me the
way, or I'll have to stay with you."

"You act like an idiot, inviting yourself like
that," she said. "Don't come near me until you think
things over, or I may give you a taste of this staff;
if I catch you one with it, you won't forget it very
quickly."

As the proverb says, about looking for trouble, "The hen scratches the earth and gets herself the
pip." I tried to come near the accursed monster, and
she whacked me right behind the ears with her staff.
She toppled me down the slope and I fell stunned.
Then and there I learned how much a blow on the
ears hurts.

I cried out, "May God curse such a stork that

thus welcomes storklings to her nest outside the city!"

Grabbing me in her savage hands, the damned girl said, "Don't get so upset or angry about this little joke, for now you can take your turn, and we are good together. Let's go into the hut; Ferruzo won't hear. I'll show you the road and you'll get a good meal. Get up, Cornejo; don't look for more trouble."

When I saw that she was satisfied, I got up quickly. She took me by the hand and we went off together. It was past nones, but I was still fasting. When we reached the hut, we found nobody there; to my dismay, she urged me to play with her. "For God's sake, friend," I said, "I would rather eat. I couldn't enjoy it at all right now, hungry and stiff as I am with the cold. I never play well before eating."

She was displeased with what I said and started threatening me, but she prepared some food for both of us.

"Now," I said, "Let's see how true it is that 'you play with bread and wine, not with a new shirt.'"

I paid for my meal and left the hut.[70] I asked her to show me the path, because it was unfamiliar. She asked me to spend the night with her: a burning wick is hard to quench. But I said, "I'm in a hurry. God keep me from evil."

She got angry at me and I became frightened and cowardly. She got me out of the hut and led me to two paths which were well traveled and good for walking. I walked as fast as I could through the hills and arrived early, with the sun, at the town of Ferreros. About this curious affair, I composed a song which is not very beautiful but neither is it very vulgar. Do not speak either good or ill of the book until you understand it, because you might understand one thing while the book means something else, entirely.


THE MOUNTAIN GIRL'S SONG

> I will always remember
> that spirited mountain lass,
> Gadea of Riofrío.
>
> Quite outside the village
> that I mentioned above
> I met Gadea.
> She tends cows in the meadow.
> Said I, "May God bless you
> and that beautiful body of yours."

"Hey," answered she,
"you missed the way.
You're going all wrong."

"I go astray, lass,
in this vast wilderness;
chance sometimes means gain
and sometimes loss.
But I tell you this morning
I don't care for the way,
for I've found you, my sister,
here in this pleasant spot
on the bank of this stream."

I still laugh to recall her answer,
that angry mountain girl.
She ran down the slope
bold as she was:
"You don't know the art
of taming animals;
the devil surely gave you
such a sharp tongue.
Just let my stick catch you!"

She threw her staff at me
and caught me in the neck,
and sent me tumbling down
into the valley.

That she-devil said,
"That's how they tie up rabbits.
I'll pummel your back
if you don't stop joking!
Get out of here, you idiot!"

She lodged me and fed me
but I had to pay.
When I did not do her bidding,
she cried, "You're a cold one!
That was a bad bargain,
leaving my herdsman!
Wise up now or I'll teach you
how the hedgehog rolls himself into a ball
without water or dew."

## THE ARCHPRIEST AND THE MOUNTAIN GIRL

Monday morning, before dawn, I set off on
my journey. Near Cornejo, I met a stupid mountain
girl who was cutting a pine tree. Let me tell you
what happened. She wanted to marry me as if I were
a close friend. She asked me many things, imagining
that I was a shepherd. She abandoned her work to
listen to trifles and thought she had me by the nose,
forgetting the proverb of the old sage, who offered
this advice to his friend: "A bird in the hand is

worth two in the bush. If, ill advised, you give up
what you have, you will not get what you want;
it's easy to deceive yourself." I wrote a rustic song
about what happened there, which I have transcribed
here. That was a harsh day, although it was spring.
I crossed the pass in the morning in order to get to
bed early.

THE MOUNTAIN GIRL'S SONG

> Near the house of the Cornejo,
> the first day of the week,
> in the middle of the valley,
> I met a mountain girl
> garbed in scarlet cloth
> with a fine woolen sash.
> I said to her, "God bless you, woman!"
>
> "What are you looking for in the mountains?
> Are you lost?"
> Said I, "I'm going around,
> and I seek a mate."
> "The man who marries here
> does not err," she said.
> "You'll find good pickings.
>
> "But friend, have a care
> that you know the arts of the mountains."
> I said, "I can guard the woods;

I can ride a mare bareback;
I know how to kill a wolf;
and when I'm tracking one,
I get to it before the hounds do.

"I can punch cows
and tame a fierce bull;
I know how to make butter and cream
and how to build a churn.
I am good at decorating shoes
and playing the pipe
and riding a spry horse.

"I know how to dance
and step to every rhythm;
neither high note nor low note
can beat me, I am sure.
When I turn to wrestling,
once I get hold
I win every fall."

"You'll make a marriage here
that suits you very well.
I'd willingly marry you
if you make it worthwhile.
You'll get a good bargain."
"Tell me what you want," said I,
"and I'll give what you ask."

She: "Give me a ribbon
made out of red cloth.
Give me also a good timbrel
and six rings of tin;
a jacket for feast days
and an everyday coat;
and don't try to trick me.

"Give me earrings and a buckle
of shining tin,
and a yellow dress,
well-striped in front.
Give me boots that reach to the knee
and they'll all say,
'Menga Llorente married well!' "

I said, "I'll give you all this,
and more, if you like,
everything good and beautiful.
Invite your relations,
and let's have the wedding.
Don't forget all this.
Now I will go for what you ask."

ills and mountains are always harsh; either it's snowing or the ground is icy; it is never warm. At the top of this pass, an icy wind was blowing the hail and snow. Since one doesn't feel as cold when he is running, I trotted down the slope, saying, "If you hit the tower, the stone falls, not the falcon.[71] I am lost if God doesn't help me"

Never in my whole life had I been in such danger from the cold. I descended the pass and found at the bottom of it a strange monster, the most fantastic thing I had ever seen—a muscular shepherdess, a horrible creature to look upon. But in my fear of the weather and the bitter cold, I asked her for a day's lodging. She said she would put me up if I paid her well. I thanked God for that, and she took me to Tablada.

She had a figure and limbs that were fantastic, I tell you; she was built like a mare. Wrestling with her couldn't possibly come off well; one could hardly lay her against her will either. In his Apocalypse, St. John the Evangelist never envisioned such a prodigious creature. She could tumble with, or beat off, a whole crowd, though I cannot imagine what devil would lust after such a monster.

Her head was huge and shapeless; her hair
was short, black, and shiny as a magpie's; her eyes
sunken and red, and shortsighted. She left a foot-
print bigger than a bear's and had the ears of a year-
ling donkey. Her short, thick neck was dark and
hairy. Her nose was long, like the bill of a whimbrel;
and she could have drunk her way through a large
pool of water in a few days. She had the mouth of
a hound-dog set in a fat, dumpy face, with great long
teeth, irregular and horsy. Listen to me, anyone who
has marriage in mind! She had thick eyebrows,
blacker than the black crow, and a heavy growth
of beard around her mouth. I saw no more, but if
you dig deeper you will find many more strange
qualities, I am sure, though you would be better off
minding your own business.

In fact I did see her legs, up to the knees:
large bones, huge shanks, all scarred and burned;
ankles thicker than those of a full-grown calf. Her
wrist was broader than my hand. Her hand was covered with long, coarse hair, and was always wet. Her
loud hoarse voice would deafen anyone; her speech
was slow and harsh, hollow and graceless. Her little
finger was larger than my thumb; imagine what the
others were like! If she should ever try to delouse
you, your scalp would think her fingers were tree-
trunks. Her breasts hung down over her dress to her
waist, even though they were folded over; otherwise

they would have reached her hips. They would keep time to the guitar without lessons. Her ribs protruded so far out of her black chest that I could count them three times even from a distance.

Now I tell you that I saw nothing else; and I will say no more, for an evil-tongued young man is no good as a messenger. I wrote three songs about what she said and how ugly she looked, but I could hardly do justice to her. Two of the songs are for singing, the other is for dancing. If you don't like some of them, look, laugh, and be still.

THE MOUNTAIN GIRL'S SONG

Near Tablada
when I had left the mountains,
I met Alda
as dawn was breaking.

At the summit of the pass
I thought I would die
of the cold and the snow,
of that ice and
that terrible frost.

When I started to run downhill,
I found a mountain girl,

beautiful, sprightly,
with a ruddy complexion.

Said I to her,
"Fair one, I salute you."
And she, "You run very well;
don't stop now,
keep going."

"I am cold," I said;
"that's why I've come
to you, my beauty, to you.
I beg of your kindness,
give me lodging today."

The young girl told me,
"Friend, any man who
stops off in my shack
must marry me
and must pay me well."

I said, "I would be willing,
but I have a wife already
here in Ferreros;
Still, some of my money,
sweetheart, I will give you."

"Come along," said she.
She took me with her

and built a good fire
as was the custom
in that snowy range.

She gave me wheat bread,
grimy and black,
and gave me bad wine,
acid and watered,
and salted meat.

She gave me goat cheese
and said, "Noble sir,
open your arms
and take some of this bread
that I've set aside."

She said, "Eat, my guest,
and drink and recover,
get warm and then pay;
may you keep safe
until you come back.

"The man who gives me
the things that I request
will have a good supper
and a pleasant bed
without any bill."

"Now, if you can,
why don't you tell me
just what you want."
"You're joking," she said.
"Would I get what I ask?

"Then give me a belt,
red, good dark red,
and a pretty tunic,
with a nice collar,
cut to my size.

"A good string of beads
made of tin, and full,
and give me jewels
that are worth something,
and a fine fur.

"Give me a dress
striped for the feasts,
and give me shoes,
red, and high,
of well-crafted leather.

"With such jewels,
I tell you,
you'll be welcome;

you'll be my husband
and I will be your wife."

"My sweet mountain girl,
it happens I don't have
such presents with me now.
But I'll make you a promise
until I can return."

The ugly girl replied,
"Where there isn't any money
there isn't any bargain,
and the day will turn out sour
and the face become unhappy.

"No prudent merchant
travels without money,
and I won't be content
with the man who's empty-handed
or give him any lodging.

"You can't pay with flattery
the bill for your lodging;
it's with money that
you get what you want.
That's how it is."

THE ARCHPRIEST'S SONG OF PRAISE
TO ST. MARY OF VADO

    The Apostle James says [72] that every perfect thing and every good gift comes from God, and after I had gotten away from all that trouble, I turned in prayer to God so that He would not forget me. Near this mountain range there is an honored shrine, long revered and hallowed, called St. Mary of Vado. I went there to hold a vigil, according to the custom, and I composed the following hymn in honor of the Blessed Virgin.

To you, noble lady, abounding with mercy, Star of heaven and light of the world, humbly I offer before your majesty my soul and my body together with these poems.

THE PASSION OF OUR LORD JESUS CHRIST

> Hail, my Queen, I salute you;
> Mother of the Savior,
> holy and worthy Virgin,
> attend to this poor sinner.
>
> My soul dwells upon you
> and on your praise;

I find hope only in you
and in no one else.
O Virgin, assist me
without delay.
Intercede for me with God,
your Son and my Lord.

Though you are in great glory
and high beatitude,
I, to honor your name,
desire to do this:
to sing the sad history
of how Jesus had
to undergo prison,
pain, and anguish.

At tierce, on the Wednesday,
Christ's body
was appraised by the Jews;
at that hour, it was seen
how little valued
was your beloved Son
by Judas,
Apostle traitorous, who sold him.

The sale was made complete
for thirty silver coins,

which were due to Judas
because of the precious ointment.[73]
But they did rejoice,
the members of the council,
and paid off
the traitorous vendor.

At the hour of matins,
while Judas kissed him,
the wretched Jews—
like hounds they were
before his very face—
encircled him and
took him prisoner,
as if he were a criminal.

You stood by him
at the hour of prime,
saw him taken away
while they struck him,
saw him judged by Pilate
while they spat
on his radiant face,
the splendor of Heaven.

At the hour of tierce
was Christ judged;
Judea judged him,

that accursed people.
For this it remains
in slavery
from which it can never
be freed or delivered.

Mocking and insulting,
they led him out to die.
For his garment
they cast dice
to see who would get it.
Of your terrible sorrows,
who could say, Lady,
which is the greatest?

At the hour of sext
he was nailed to the cross:
bitter was the pain
for your dear Son;
but it was profit to the world,
for thence came light,
splendor of Heaven,
that endures forever.

At the hour of nones
he died; and it befell
that grieving for him
the sun was darkened.
When the lance pierced his side,

the earth trembled,
and blood and water flowed,
sweetness of the world.

At the hour of vespers
he was taken from the cross
and at compline
anointed was he with spices
and laid in a tomb
cut out of the rock.
Centurio was set
to guard him.

By these wounds
of the Holy Passion,
give me comfort
in my pains.
You, beloved of God,
give me your blessing
that I may be
forever your servant.

## THE PASSION OF OUR LORD JESUS CHRIST

We, who are bound
by the Law of Christ,
must always recall
his death and grieve.

The prophecies related
what things must come to pass.
First Jeremiah told
how he had to come;
then Isaiah said
that he was to be born
of a Virgin, as we know
Saint Mary to be.

Still another prophecy
from the Old Law said
the Lamb would be slain
so the flock would be saved.
Daniel said this, speaking
of Christ, our King,
and we read it also in David,
as I understand.

As the prophecies say,
so it has been fulfilled:
He came unto a holy maiden,
and was born of a Virgin—
he, whom all bless,
and who died for us all,
God and Man, whom we behold
on the sacred altar.

He came to save
the human race,

was sold by Judas
for a few poor coins,
was taken and beaten
very badly by the Jews;
our God, in whom we believe,
they struck.

They spat on that face,
the glory of Heaven,
crowned him with thorns,
sharp and cruel.
They raised him on the cross,
without a jot of pity.
For such wounds
we are grieved and in pain.

They drove the nails right through
his hands and his feet;
with vinegar and hyssop
they quenched his thirst;
the wounds which they inflicted
are sweeter than honey
for us who in him have
our hope without peer.

On the cross he died for us,
wounded and torn,

and then his side was opened
with a lance;
surely by these wounds
the world is redeemed.
May he deign to save us,
who place our faith in him.

THE BATTLE
BETWEEN SIR CARNIVAL
AND LADY LENT [74]

he season sacred to the Lord
was drawing near, so I returned to my own place to
rest for a while. It was seven
days before Lent—that time which caused fear
and dread throughout the whole world. I was at
home with Sir Thursday the Fat when a messenger
ran in, bringing me two letters. Even though it's a
long story, I will summarize for you what they contained, because after I had read the letters, I returned
them to the messenger.

"From me, Lady Lent, servant of God,

whom He has sent to every sinner, to all archpriests
and clergy without love—salvation in Jesus Christ
until Easter:

"You should know that I have been informed that, for almost a year, Sir Carnival, in
rage and fury, has been going about pillaging my
land, wreaking havoc and, what angers me most,
shedding much blood. For this reason, I order you
most solemnly under obedience and in pain of judgment, to challenge him with my credentials, in my
name and in that of Fast and Penance. Make it perfectly clear to him that in seven days I myself and
my troops shall come to do battle against him and
his arrogance. I do not believe that he will remain
in the butcher shops. After you have read this letter,
return it to the messenger to carry throughout the
land without concealing it, so that his people may
not say the message was not seen. Given in Castro
Urdiales [75] and received in Burgos."

The other letter which the messenger
brought had a large shell hanging from it like a
seal; it was the seal of the lady. This is the message
she sent to Sir Carnival: "From me, Lady Lent, Justice of the sea, Guardian of the souls that desire to be
saved, to you, gluttonous Carnival, who think of
nothing but gorging yourself, I send Fast to challenge you in my name.

"Seven days hence, you and your army shall

come to do battle with me in the field. I will fight you
without fail, until Holy Saturday, and you will not
be able to avoid death or prison."

I read both letters and understood their
meaning. I realized that the order was even stricter
for me since I had no mistress and I was not in love.
My guest and I were both upset. Sir Thursday, my
guest, got up happily from my table—for which I
am glad—and said: "I am the standard-bearer
against that wretch, and I will have to joust with
her. Every year she makes trial with me."

He thanked me heartily for the fine repast
and departed. I wrote my letters and then told Friday, "Go to Sir Carnival tomorrow and inform him
of all this so that on Tuesday he will come to the
fight forewarned."

When he had received the letters, the proud
Sir Carnival bared his teeth, though he was really
afraid. He had no desire to answer but he came, anx-
iously, leading a huge army, for he was a powerful
man. On the appointed day he was there, the defiant
Sir Carnival, surrounded on all sides with armed
men; mighty Alexander himself would have been
pleased with such a following. In his vanguard he
had ranged excellent foot soldiers: Hens and Partridges, Rabbits and Capons, Ducks domestic and
wild, and fat Geese were mustered near the embers.

They bore their lances like front-line men, huge skewers of iron and wood. For shields they had platters: at any proper feast, they are the first course. After these shield-bearers came the bowmen: salted Geese, Mutton Loins, fresh Legs of Pork, and whole Hams. And following them came the knights: Beefquarters, suckling Pigs and Kids, gamboling and squealing. Then came the squires: many Cream Cheeses that ride and spur dark red wines.

A rich train of noblemen came next: Pheasants and proud Peacocks all well garnished, their banners upright, bearing frightful weapons and fierce armor. Their weapons were well wrought, well tempered, and fine: for helmets they wore pots made of pure copper; for shields, cauldrons, pans, and kettles. Certainly the Sardines do not have an army of such value. Many Deer arrived, and the great Wild Boar who said: "Sir, you must not leave me out of this battle, because I have already set to many times with Ali.[76] I am accustomed to fighting and have always been good at it."

The Boar had hardly finished speaking when the Deer came, very swiftly. "Sir, I, your loyal servant, salute you," he said. "Am I not a hermit in order to serve you?"

The Hare came, very willing, to the muster. "Sir," she said, "I will bring a fever on that lady; I will bring on the itch and boils, so that she will not even remember the fight. She will want to have my skin when one of them breaks out on her."

Then came the Wild Ram, accompanied by Roe-deer and Doves, flaunting his courage and hurling about threats. "My Lord," said he, "if you throw the lady at me, she will do you no harm for all her fish bones."

Slow and plodding, the old, loyal Ox arrived. "Sir," he said, "I am good only for pasture or the plough; I am not fit to battle on the road or in the field. But I can serve you with my meat and my hide."

Sir Bacon came in a full pot with many a Corned Beef, Rib and Pork Loin. They were all ready for the fierce battle. But the lady knew her trade and did not show up too soon.

Since Sir Carnival is a very wealthy emperor and has lordly power over the world, the birds and animals came very humbly, but with great fear. Sir Carnival was sitting majestically at a full table on a noble dais, with jesters before him as befits a great man. A lavish feast was set before him. At his foot knelt the humble standard-bearer, one hand on the wine barrel, playing away at his trumpet. The Wine, as sergeant-at-arms, was speaking for all of them. At nightfall, long after they had all filled their bellies at the feast, they said "Goodnight" and comfortably went to sleep to rest for the battle with the lady.

That night, the Roosters were filled with fear and kept a frightened vigil without once closing their eyes. But that is not strange, since they had lost their wives. Every noise they heard made them jump with fright.

It was midnight when the Lady Lent marched into the middle of the hall and cried, "God be our strength!" The Roosters screamed and flapped their wings, and the evil tidings reached Sir Carnival. But that good man had eaten too much and drunk his fill of wine at the feast, and now he was groggy with sleep. The racket was heard through the whole camp. Drowsy, they all stumbled to the battle, mustering their troops, and no one dared to complain. The host from the sea wielded their weapons and the two armies crashed against each other crying, "Ea!"

First to wound Sir Carnival was white-necked Leek, hurting him so badly that he spat phlegm, a fearful omen. Lady Lent thought the camp was hers. Salty Sardine came in to help and wounded fat Hen by throwing herself into her bill and choking her, and then she cracked Sir Carnival's helmet. Great Dogfish charged the front line, while the Clams and the Cuttlefish guarded the flanks. The fighting was chaotic and confused, and many good heads were split open.

From the coast of Valencia came the Eels, marinated and cured, in large crowds; they struck

Sir Carnival in midchest, while Trout from Alberche
hit him in the jaw. Tuna fought like a fierce lion;
he rushed Sir Lard and hurled insults, and if it had
not been for Corned Beef, who warded off the lance,
Tuna would have wounded Sir Lard through the
heart. From the region of Bayona came many Sharks,
killing the Partridges and castrating the Capons;
from the river Henares came the Shrimp, who
pitched their tents as far as the Guadalquivir. Barbels
and other fish fought against the wild Ducks, and
Merluce cried to Pig, "Where are you? Why don't
you come out? Just show yourself and you'll get
what you deserve. Go lock yourself in the mosque,
but don't go near a church."

Catfish added to the rout, with his tough
skin barbed with hooks; he ripped into Legs and
Loins, clawing them as if he were a cat. Strange
groups of odd sizes rushed up from the sea, the
ocean, the lakes, armed with fierce bows and cross-
bows. It was a worse rout than that at Alarcos.[77]
Red Lobsters flocked from Santander, emptying
their heavy quivers and making Sir Carnival pay
heavily. The spacious meadows were becoming too
small for him.

Because the year of jubilee had been pro-
claimed and all were anxious to save their souls, all
the creatures of the sea hurried to the joust. Herrings
and Sea Breams came from Bermeo; Whale went

about with a large corps of fighters, wounding and killing the carnal hosts. The valiant Shad slew the Doves, and Dolphin shattered old Ox's teeth. Shad and Dace and noble Lamprey came from Seville and Alcántara to get their share. Everyone sharpened his weapons on Sir Carnival, and in vain did he try to loosen his belt.

Dogfish, a tough ruffian, went about madly, brandishing a mace slung from a belt, with which he banged Pig and Suckling in mid-forehead, and then ordered them salted down in Villenchón salt. Squid showed the Peacocks no quarter, nor allowed the Pheasants to fly away; the Kids and the Deer he tried to strangle. With his many arms, he can fight many opponents. There, too, were Oysters battling against Rabbits, and harsh Crabs jousting with Hare. On both sides such tremendous blows were dealt that the ditches were running with blood and scales. Conger Eel, count of Laredo, marinated and fresh, fought fiercely and wrought havoc on Sir Carnival, bearing down very hard on him. Sir Carnival was in despair, finding no comfort anywhere. Rallying his courage, he hoisted the spear; with renewed vigor, he turned against Salmon, who had just come up from Castro de Urdiales. That knight stood his ground, without flinching from the battle. They fought hard and long, and exchanged many

wounds. Had Sir Carnival been left alone, he might
have finished off Salmon, but giant Whale came at
him, embraced him, and threw him down on the
sand.

Most of Sir Carnival's army had perished;
those who could had fled. Even so, afoot, he tried
desperately to defend himself with his weak hands.
Seeing the host decimated, Wild Boar and Deer fled
into the mountains, and then most of the other animals abandoned him there, while those who remained were more dead than alive. Except for
Corned Beef and fat Sir Lard, who had turned pale
and looked like a corpse and could not fight without
a bumper of wine, so fat was he, Sir Carnival was
alone, beaten down and surrounded. The sea-host
regrouped, then spurred forward and rushed him.
But in their pity not wishing to kill him, they tied
him and his followers up and brought them bound
and under heavy guard before Lady Lent.

Lady Lent ordered that Sir Carnival be imprisoned. As for Lady Corned Beef and Sir Lard,
she sentenced them to be hanged as high as sentries
in a watchtower, and gave solemn command that no
one should cut them down. They were hanged from
a beechwood beam, while the executioner intoned,
"This is the just punishment for their deeds."

Lady Lent set Fast to guard Sir Carnival

and be his jailer, with orders that no one be allowed
to see him, except the confessor if he fell ill, and
that he should have only one meal a day.

SIR CARNIVAL'S PENANCE
ON CONFESSION
AND ABSOLUTION

oon a friar came to convert Sir
Carnival, and began preaching
to him and talking of God. Sir
Carnival must have been very
moved, because he asked, humbly
and contritely, for a penance. He
listed his sins for the friar in a letter, sealed
tight with the seals of secrecy. The friar responded
that this could not be accepted and gave him lengthy
instruction on the subject. One cannot make his confession in a letter or in writing; it must be done by
the very mouth of the contrite sinner. Neither can

one be forgiven or absolved in writing, since the holy confessor's word is needed.

While I am on the subject of penance, let me refresh your minds a little. We must believe firmly, with our hearts, that we will achieve salvation through penance. Penance is so precious, my dear friends, that we must not let it be neglected. It is good to talk much about it, and the more we practice it the more we will profit. But it is hard for me to speak of this, for the subject is a deep abyss, deeper than the sea, and I am ignorant and unlearned. I do not dare to venture into the matter except for a small part of it which I have heard discussed. This subject which I intend to take up fills me with fear; I am frightened very much of failing, with my small knowledge. You, gentlemen, must make up for my lack of wisdom. I am a very poor scholar, neither a master nor a doctor. I have learned but little and do not know enough to teach; what I tell you, then, you must understand better than I can tell it. I entrust my mistakes to your correction.

The holy Decretum discusses at length whether penance is achieved by contrition alone. Basically, it is established that confession and satisfaction are absolutely necessary. This applies when one can still speak and has enough time in his life for amendment; if such is not the case, however, one can save oneself by contrition alone, since no more is possible. He is saved as far as God is concerned, who has perfect knowledge. But the Church cannot judge such hidden things; thus it is also necessary for him to make, either by gestures or by groans, some sign showing that he has repented. This he can do by beating his breast, or lifting his hands to God, or sighing with sad and grievous moans, or, the best sign of repentance, by weeping, or at least by nodding his head. Thus he is freed from the evil realms of hell, but he must still atone for everything in purgatory. There he makes amends, purging his errors by the mercy of God, who may bring him to heaven.

Holy Church offers much solid evidence that such contrition can be full penance. By her contrite tears, St. Mary Magdalene was fully absolved from guilt and punishment. Our father St. Peter, that holy man, denied Jesus Christ in his fear and cowardice, and I read that he wept sad and bitter tears, but I find no other satisfaction in the Scriptures. King Hezekiah, condemned to death, wept contritely, his face turned to the wall, and was immediately pardoned by God whose mercy is so great that he gave the sinful man fifteen more years of life.

Many simpleminded and unlearned priests hear confessions anywhere and everywhere, dispensing full absolution to all, both their parishioners and other sinners. But they err greatly, for they do not have such rights and should not meddle where they are not allowed. "If a blindman leads a blindman, they will both fall into the pit." What power does the judge from Cartagena have in Rome? What rights has the mayor of Requena in France? "One should not turn his sickle on another man's crop." He commits injustice and does harm, and so deserves to be punished.

All important, complicated, and serious cases are reserved for the bishops, archbishops, and higher ecclesiastics, according to the law, except those that are reserved to the Pope himself. And the cases reserved to the Pope are many, according to the law; to enumerate them and describe them would take too long, longer than a pair of Manuals. To learn more about this, consult the Decretals. Now if an archbishop, anointed and consecrated, invested with pallium, staff, mitre, and pontifical robes, does not have jurisdiction in these cases, how can a simple priest make so bold?

Then there are the cases proper to the bishop and his superiors; these men hear them and have the power to grant absolution, but lower clergy are strictly forbidden this right. And these are more numerous than the cases reserved to the Pope; anyone curious to know about these should consult the

appropriate volumes, and should study them well,
glosses and texts, because only such studies can make
ignorant people learned and well prepared. Let such
a man consult the *Speculum* and its *Repertory,* the
volumes of the man of Ostia, which are a copious
collection of cases, the useful reference works by Innocent IV, the *Rosary* by Guido, the *Appendices,*
and the Decretals.[78] More than one hundred doctors
bring forth erudite arguments and subtle reasons,
in whole tomes or in short articles, and end up with
differing opinions. So do not blame me if I avoid
the subject. But you, my simple clergymen, do not
make this mistake: Do not confess my parishioner,
do not sit in judgment where you have no power,
and do not get yourself into trouble over another
man's sinner. Unless you have a commission from
the prelate or permission from his parish priest, you
cannot grant him forgiveness. Be careful not to absolve or impose penance outside your own domain.

    Ordinarily, this is the principle. However,
at the moment of death or in an emergency, when
the sinner cannot receive help from any other source,
you can hear and absolve him whether he is your
parishioner or not. In such time of danger, when
death stalks, you are Pope and Archbishop for
everybody; all their power is vested in you; dire
necessity takes care of everything. But even in such
cases, you must see to it that they should have their

own priest to confess them before they die if they possibly can do so. This is for their own benefit. Also, when you have an emergency, you should insist that, if he does not die, then when he has recuperated, he should go and wash off those serious sins of which you absolved him, at the river or at the spring. The Pope is obviously the perennial spring, for he is the vicar general of the whole world; and the others are the rivers, that is, those who have pontifical office—bishops, archbishops, patriarchs, and cardinals.

Now the friar I mentioned was an intimate confidant of the Pope. Because of the emergency, he absolved the imprisoned Sir Carnival of all his sins. After hearing Carnival's confession, the good friar assigned this penance: for each of his sins, he was to eat a particular food each day, and nothing else. So he would be pardoned.

"On Sunday, for your mortal cupidity, you will eat nothing but boiled chick peas with oil; you will go to church, without dawdling along in the streets or looking on the world and desiring evil things.

"On Monday, for your great pride, you will eat not salmon or trout but vetches. You will attend the Hours and will not attempt any tumbling or start a brawl as you usually do.

"On Tuesday, for your great avarice, I order

you to eat porridge, but only in small servings; you can eat one-half or two-thirds of a loaf of bread, and the rest you will keep for the poor.

"On Wednesday, you will eat a little spinach, just a little, for your craven lust. You did not spare wives or nuns, for you were prone to making grand promises to satiate your lust.

"On Thursday, you will have salted lentils for supper, to pay for the deadly rage and the perjury you committed by your lies. Be devout at your prayers, and when the lentils begin to taste good, you must stop eating them.

"On Friday, for your excessive gluttony, you will have nothing cooked, just bread and water; and you will scourge your flesh with the holy discipline. By God's mercy, you will be free soon.

"On Saturday, you must eat only beans, nothing else; for your great envy, you will not eat fish.

"Although you may suffer during this period, you will be able to save your sinful soul. Meanwhile, visit all the cemeteries and go to church, reciting the psalms and assisting very religiously at the holy ceremonies. With the help of God, you will profit from your penance."

With the penance assigned, Sir Carnival recited the prayer of confession, saying "Mea culpa" with great devotion. Then the friar gave him absolution, blessed him, and departed. Wretched Carnival remained locked up, weak and ailing from the battle, badly wounded and feeling quite sick, afflicted and sorely tried, and without the company of any Christian soul.

OF ASH WEDNESDAY AND LENT

When the task was completed, the lady ordered her tent pulled up and the camp moved, for she goes about everywhere commanding that penance be done and putting an end to strife. On Ash Wednesday, the first day of Lent, she leaves nothing unpurified in whatever house she enters; no basket large or small, no dish, basin or jar, but she has it scoured in a clean sink. She has her cleaning women scrub and scour the deep dishes, pans, jars, and cauldrons, barrels and containers—every item in the house—including skewers and platters, pots and lids. The houses themselves she renovates, replastering the walls and doing some of them over completely, while she simply paints others. No corner she peers into, but the dirt disappears from it. Everybody likes her except Sir Carnival.

On this day she provides for the body, and so too on this day she provides for the soul: she calls sweetly to all Christians to go to church with a purified conscience. She marks a cross of palm ashes on the foreheads of those who come to church with good will, telling them to know themselves and bear in mind that they are but dust and unto dust shall they return. This holy sign she makes on the devout Christian so that he may be holy and worthy during Lent. And to the unworthy sinner she assigns a light penance, bending the tough oak with her sweet wood.[79]

Now while she was doing these things, the ailing Sir Carnival recovered; little by little, he was able to get out of his bed, thinking the while how he might manage things so that he would be able to laugh again. On Palm Sunday, he said to Sir Fast: "Sir, let us go to Mass, you and I; you will hear Mass and I will recite the Psalms, and we will listen to the Passion being read, since we have nothing else to do."

Sir Fast replied that this pleased him. By now, Sir Carnival was quite recovered, but he pretended to be still weak. They went to the church, but not for what he had suggested; when he got there, he unsaid what he had said at home. He ran from the church to the Ghetto, where he was gladly received in the butcher shop. It was Passover time. They got on well together, and he had a good day of it. Then on Monday morning, Rabbi Acelin lent him a nag on which to make his escape. Quickly he

crossed the border in Medellín [80] while the lambs
were saying, "Baaa! Our end is nigh!" Rams and
kids, tups and sheep bleated aloud: "If Sir Carnival
carries us off into the city, many of us will lose our
skins, as you will too."

The rascal quickly attacked and plundered
the meadows of Medellín, of Cáceres, of Trujillo,
and the Vera of Plasencia as far as Valdemorillo and
all the Serena. In three days, he covered the fields of
Alcudia and all Calatrava, the fields of Hazálvaro,
and entered Valsaín. He seemed to be flying on the
Rabbi's nag, which hurried along out of fear. When
the bulls saw him coming, they humped their backs;
the oxen and cattle tolled their bells, and the calves
and heifers cried out for help, "Mooo, maaaa, cow-
herds and dogs, come and help!"

He sent letters to the areas he could not
reach, while he remained in those mountains and up-
lands. Furious as he was against Lady Lent, he did
not dare attack her alone. This was the text and
gloss of his letter:

"From us, Sir Carnival, grand plunderer of
all things, to you, lean, weak, vile, and scabrous
Lent, not health but a leech, for you are dried up
and full of phlegm. You know well that we are
your mortal enemy. We are sending Lunch, our
friend, to tell you, for our part, that we will be with
you on the fourth day, which will be Sunday. You

came in the dark of night, like a thief, while we were
asleep and peaceful. But now, you will not be able
to defend yourself even in a castle or behind a wall,
nor will you save your old skin."

The gloss of the letter went to everyone:
"We, powerful Sir Carnival, by the grace of God,
to all Christians, Moors, and Jews, send greetings
and abundance of flesh, from us to you. You know
well, friends, how, confound it! seven weeks ago we
were challenged by treacherous Lent and the sea,
while I was in disgrace; while we were asleep, we
were defeated by her. Therefore we order that, after
reading our letter, you challenge her before she
leaves; make sure she does not escape, because she
deceives all the world. Send your challenge to her
by Lady Snack. Send also Lunch, who is more ver-
satile, and have them tell her that on Sunday, before
dawn, we will come to fight with her, making a
great noise; unless she is stone deaf, she will hear
our call. After you have read our letter, make a copy
of it and give it to Sir Lunch, who carries our orders;
he must not delay but go swiftly and secretly. Given
in Valdevacas, our beloved place."

The letters were written in fresh blood.
Wherever they were read, the people made merry
and said to Lady Lent, "Where will you run and
hide, you wretch?"

Lady Lent, who had not yet received the

letters, was very disturbed by these remarks. And after she received them and read them, she said, pallid and with sallow cheeks, "Would that God had defended me from the evil things I hear."

Now everyone should keep in mind this proverb: "Pardon your enemy and die at his hands." If you do not destroy your enemy when you have the chance to do so, he will destroy you if he is clever. The natural scientists say that all females, not only cows, are weak of heart, without the strength needed for a fight, like sticks in the sand—except for the hairy ones, who are like she-boars. Being a weak female, Lady Lent was frightened by thoughts of battle, prison, or death; she had made a vow to go to Jerusalem and was very anxious to get overseas. Now as you know, she had already set the day for the battle, and so was no longer bound to fight with one she had already defeated. When the set period had expired, she could leave without dishonor. Moreover, it was already Spring, and the fish would not come from the sea to her aid. Besides, a thin stick of a female cannot do battle alone. For all these reasons, she decided not to wait. On Good Friday, she donned pilgrim dress, a large round hat decked with sea shells, a staff covered with images, with the holy palm on it, and a little wallet and beads to carry with her. She wore round, well-soled shoes, and covered her shoulders with a great cloak.

Like all good pilgrims who make proper provision, she brought along well-kneaded loaves and breads. Under her arm, she carried an excellent hollow of squash, redder than a jay's bill, that holds more than two quarts; no pilgrim would ever set forth without this.

Thus disguised, on that Saturday night she jumped from the walls, saying, "You guards, I wager you cannot catch me, for an old sparrow cannot be caught in any net." Very quickly, she left the streets behind her, saying, "You, proud Carnival, I think you will not find me." That same night, she arrived in Roncesvalles. Let her go, and God go with her through the mountains and the valleys.

I t was Holy Saturday, near the
end of April. The sun was high
in the sky, shining all over, and
a great noise was made throughout the whole
world about the arrival of two emperors on
earth. These two were Sir Love and Sir Carnival. Rushing out to receive them came all
those who had waited so long. The birds
and the trees gave promise of a good season
to come, and especially happy were those who
understand what love is. The butchers and
the rabbis with their knives welcomed Sir
Carnival; the tripe vendors came out to him, playing
their timbrels, and the hillsides were covered with
hunters. The shepherd awaited him at the wayside,
playing his pipe and his flute. The chief shepherd
meanwhile played the zither for dancing, while his
boy played the reed-pipe. From the pass there appeared a red sign, with a figure in the middle which
looked like a lamb; many sheep, together with tups
and short-fleeced kids, were dancing around the sign.
Nearby were sturdy rams, herds of cattle and bulls—

more numerous than the Moors in Granada—and so many dark brown and tawny oxen that Darius could hardly have bought them for all his wealth.

Sir Carnival rode in on a very rich wagon, covered with furs and trimmed with leather. That good emperor was appropriately arrayed in shirt sleeves and tunic, his robe tucked in at the belt. In his hand he bore a great sharp axe with which to slaughter all the animals he met; with a keen-edged knife, he slit the throats of the beasts that he caught and proceeded to bone them. Girding his waist was a white apron spattered with blood. He gave the fat ram a bad time, making him bleat "B" natural in doubles and fifths. His head was bound with a coif so that his hair would not fly, and the tunic he wore was white with long tails. Nobody rode the cart with him.

If he saw a hare escaping, he quickly set the hounds on her. Hounds there were a-plenty around him, and other dogs too: herd dogs, hunters, blood-hounds, and mastiffs which eat huge amounts of bread, and many night-hunters that can catch all sorts of rabbits. He had with him ropes for the cows, scales and weights, chopping blocks, hooks, tables of all sizes, kettles, troughs for his tripe vendors, and bitches, with puppies, tied by a chain. The herds from Castile and the shepherds from Soria welcomed him in their villages with long speeches, tolling the

bells while singing *Gloria:* no one could recall a
similar jubilation. The emperor rested in the butcher
shops while villages and granges came to do him
homage; with great pride, he told stories of bravery
and started to perform knightly exploits. He slaugh-
tered, slit, and boned animals, giving freely to all,
Castilians or Englishmen. Everyone gave him
money, and some gave tournois coins, so that he
recouped all the losses of the past months.

THE RECEPTION GIVEN SIR LOVE BY CLERGY AND
LAITY, FRIARS AND NUNS, LADIES AND JUGGLERS

It was the solemn feast of Easter. The sun
was rising bright and splendid. Men and birds and
all the lovely flowers emerged to greet Sir Love with
song. The birds, large and small, jays and nightin-
gales, buntings and parrots, welcomed him, singing
sweetly in harmony, and the best birds rejoiced the
most. The trees with their variegated leaves and colorful blossoms welcomed him, and the men and
women welcomed him with great affection. Out
came the drums and other instruments—the Moorish
guitar with its shrill voice and strident notes, the
pot-bellied lute which plays the tune for the dance,
and with these the Spanish guitar.[81] The loud rebec
with its high tone was there, as well as the Orabin

playing his zither; with them, a huge psaltery
(which was taller than La Mota [82]) and the plucked
viol were dancing. The half qanum, the harp, and
the Moorish rebec made merry in a French-style concert, while the flute, taller than a boulder, joined
them, as did the taboret; without it, the flute is not
worth a straw. The bow viol gave forth sweet
rhythms, sometimes soothing and sometimes lively,
with dulcet, full, clear, well-tuned sounds that glad-
den and please everyone. The full qanum came out
together with the timbrel, whose brass jingles make
such sweet sounds; the organs recited chansons and
motets, with the lowly jester intermingling. The
flageolet, the Moorish flute, the swollen oboe, the
hurdy-gurdy, and the zither were found in this
feast; the French bagpipe played in tune with them
and the whining bandore added its sound. Tubas
and trumpets came out along with kettledrums.
Such exultation had not been seen in many years,
nor such great and widespread feasting; the hills and
the farm lands teemed with jugglers.

The roads were crowded with mammoth
processions—numberless friars who go about granting indulgences, clergymen accompanied by their
clerks; even the Abbot of Bordones [83] was in the
procession. There were also the Order of Cistercians,
the Order of St. Benedict, the Order of Cluny with
its holy abbot—I could not record how many orders

were there. These sang loudly, *Venite, exultemus.*[84]
There was the Order of Santiago along with the
Hospitalers, the Order of Calatrava and of Alcan-
tara and of Buenaval. And on this feast, the holy
abbots were singing only *Te, Amorem, laudamus,*[85]
and nothing else. Next came the Preachers of St.
Paul; St. Francis was not there, but the Friars Minor
were. Augustinian friars too, and their cantors, cellarers, and priors, intoning *Exultemus et laetemur!* [86]
with the Trinitarians and the Carmelites, and those
of St. Eulalia. To avoid strife, Sir Love ordered
them all to say, sing, and shout, *Benedictus qui
venit!* [87] and all answered, *Amen!* The Friars of St.
Anthony were in this group as well as many good
knights mounted on many bad horses; the squires
came out in their short tunics; all the city sang *Alleluia.* Nuns of every order, white and black, Cistercians, Dominicans, Franciscans—all came out singing and chanting the hymns of compline, *Mane
nobiscum Domine.*[88]

    From the east, I saw a banner coming,
white, shining, as high as a peak. In the midst of it
was the image of a lady all embroidered in gold; her
vestments were certainly not poor. On her head she
wore a noble crown, made of precious stones and
ornamented with love, and her hands were full of
rich gifts. Paris or Barcelona could not have ran-
somed that banner. Only after some time could I see

who was carrying the banner, it was such a glowing sight. He smiled on everyone. The whole kingdom of France could not pay for the raiment he wore; priceless too was his Spanish horse. Together with that great emperor came many bands, and leading them all were the archpriests and the ladies; after them, the rest of the people in the great procession already described. The whole valley resounded with their shouts.

When the sprightly Sir Love had arrived, they all knelt down and kissed his hand; anyone who did not was considered a knave. After this ceremony, a bitter quarrel arose over who was to give him lodging. The parish clergy wanted this advantage for themselves, but the monks and the friars were bitterly opposed, for they wanted him to lodge with them. The monks and friars argued:

"Sir, we shall give you famous monasteries, richly painted dining halls with tables all laid out, large dormitories full of beds. Do not accept the clergy's hospitality this time; they do not have quarters suitable for so great a festival. Their little houses are hardly proper for a great lord. Besides, a clergyman takes with an open hand but gives very unwillingly. They thoroughly fleece anyone who approaches them, and they do not have the means to please you in anything. A great lord must needs have a great palace and a great estate; it is not proper for him to lodge in a cubbyhole."

"Sir," replied the clergymen, "why go dress yourself in wool? A single monk could eat up all the monastery's profits. Their guest halls are unhealthy for you; they have huge wine flasks but small bells. They will never please you as they promised; instead, they will give you beds without blankets and tablecloths without food. They have huge pots but little meat, and plenty of water but little saffron."

"Sir, be *our* guest!" said the knights. "No, no!" cried the squires. "They will give you loaded dice and you will lose all your money. They are quick to plunder but slow to do battle. They spread a large tapis, and they set the tables all gilded like those of gamblers. They are the first in line to collect their wages, but many of them are the last to reach the front."

The nuns said, "Ignore all of them; accept our services. Sir, you would get no leisure from them. They are all poor miserable wretches who bicker and fight all the time. Come along with us, sir, and try on our hair shirt."

But all the others argued against this, crying that the nuns were false to their lovers, and calling them kin of the crow, procrastinators and deceivers, who fulfilled their promises grudgingly if at all. Their whole practice, they said, was to prepare some concoctions, to lisp beautiful little words which were nothing but ornaments: too many fools had been taken in by their loving gestures, their false smiles, and their guile.

Now for my part, the lord Sir Love, if he would only believe me, should have accepted the nuns' invitation. He would have all the leisure and pleasure in the world and never regret entering their dormitories. However, because a great lord should never take sides, he was hesitant to accept an invitation that would cause a fight. He thanked them profusely and expressed his great pleasure, promising favors to all, and first to me. Since my lord still had no lodging, when the dispute had died down I knelt before him and his retinue and asked this special grace:

"Sir, you have brought me up from my childhood; whatever good I know I learned from you. You have been my master and my guide; now be my guest on this solemn feast."

Such was his condescension that he granted my request and came to my house. The whole procession accompanied him there with loud song; I could not remember when I had had such a good walk. Most of the people then went home, although their instruments were left in my house. My lord

Sir Love attended to everything when he saw how
small the house was for so many servants. He said,
"I command that my tent be pitched in that
meadow, so that if someone in love should come, at
night or by day, he can stay there. I want to please
all of you."

After he had eaten, the pavilion was laid
out. The whole was perfect beyond imagining; indeed, I am sure it must have been sent by the angels,
for no mortal man could ever have made it. Let me
now describe the pavilion, even though the telling
might make you late for supper. It is a long story,
but it should not be omitted; and people will often
forgo supper for a good poem.

The center pole was pure white, an eight-
sided beam of ivory, the finest in all the world,
studded with stones and so bright that its gleam il-
lumined the whole pavilion. At the top of the pole
was a gem, a ruby I believe, which glowed like fire,
with a splendor that made the sun superfluous. The
guys of the pavilion were woven of pure silk. (I am
trying to be brief in order not to detain you; if I
tried to describe it in detail, there would not be
enough paper in all Toledo for my task.) The in-
terior workmanship was so elaborate that if I could
describe it, I would certainly deserve a drink.

Imagine immediately beyond the entrance,
to the right, a stately, well-carved table. In front of

this table blazes a great fire. Three men sit, very close to each other, eating at the table. The three knights sit eating at that same table, near the fire, each one quite separate; they could not reach each other with a long pole, and even so the thinnest coin could not be wedged between them.

The first knight eats new parsnips.[89] He is the man who feeds carrots to the stable animals and fodder to the oxen, who makes the days short and the mornings chilly. He eats new walnuts and roasted chestnuts; he has the wheat sown and the hay cut, the fatted pigs butchered and the herds brought in, while old wives recount their tales around the hearth.

The second knight eats all sorts of salt meat at his part of the table, which is clouded with fog. He is the one who presses new oil, does not disdain the coals, and blows on his hands sometimes because of the frost. This knight eats cabbage soup and is very busy decanting the wine and throwing in it handfuls of gypsum. Both of these men wear overcoats and warm tunics.

Behind the second is the other knight, with two heads. This two-headed man looks in two directions. He eats many helpings of fricasseed chicken. He has the tuns sealed, and when they have been filled through a funnel, he has elder blossoms thrown in to keep the wine dry. He has his laborers build

corrals, repair the mangers, and clean out the cess-
pools, seal up the granaries, and fill the straw ricks.
He would rather have a fur coat on his shoulders
than a suit of armor.

At another great table sit three more
knights, also close to each other, but none saying a
word to the others. Here too one could not reach the
other with the longest beam, yet not even a hair of
milady's head could be slipped between them.[90] The
first of them is a dwarf, who is sometimes morose
and irritable, sometimes gay and sprightly. He grows
new grass in the old meadow, dispatches winter and
ushers in spring. He is especially anxious that the
vines be pruned, the scions grafted, and the shoots
tied. He orders vineyards planted in order to have
abundant grapes, for a small horn of wine cannot
satisfy him.

The second of these knights sends diggers
to the vineyards and orders the farmers to plant
many cuttings while the grafters turn the pale grapes
into dark ones; then he makes men, birds, and animals fall in love. This one has three devils tied to
his chain. One he sends to vex the ladies, making
them itch where they are most modest, after which
the wild oats are sure to shoot. The second devil
shakes up the priests. Archpriests and nuns speak
of love to each other, and because of this license, they
neglect their vows and speak nonsense. You will

sooner see a white crow than that these will cease
their silliness, male and female going about as if they
were nuts. And wherever they are, the devils join
them and play their evil tricks. The third devil he
sends to the jackasses; this devil enters their heads,
as well as another place, and so all summer long they
bray and bray, after going out of their minds in
March. This can be confirmed.

The third nobleman abounds with flowers,
and the winds he blows cause the wheat and the rye
to grow. He props up the branches that produce
good oil, while his thunder frightens off the timid
boys.

Next, there are three aristocrats dancing,
and the point of a spear could not get between them.
Between the first and the second there is a large field,
and the second cannot touch the third in any way.
The first of these, who ripens the grains and fruits,
lunches on ram's liver with rhubarb; the cocks shun
him because he would gobble them up, while for his
supper he often has barbels and trout. He prefers a
cool house and avoids the sun because the summer
heat makes his head ache. He walks about more
sprightly than a peacock in the woods, and seeks out
the grass and the breeze in the depth of the forest.
The second one carries a sickle in his hand and gathers the crops all over the district. He eats new figs
and harvests the rice. His voice has turned hoarse

from eating too many sour grapes. He grafts various
barks on the trees, he eats up the honey, he sweats
freely and drinks the cold spring water, and his
hands are always stained with cherries.

The third man carries the rye, spreading
wheat and the other grains in the farmyard, shaking
the fruit from the trees while the gadfly stings the
donkey. He eats small quail and draws barrels of
cold water from the ice wells; the horsefly makes the
beasts lower their heads and drag their noses on the
ground.

Three farmers are coming, on the same road.
The first one waits for the second while the third
waits for the second on the borderline. But the one
who approaches does not reach the one that waits.
The first is eating the ripe grapes and the figs that
have ripened on the trees. Threshing and winnow-
ing, he separates the chaff; he brings with him au-
tumn with its sicknesses and troubles. The second
man coats and tightens the tuns, manures the fallow
fields, and shakes the walnut trees. Then he gathers
the grapes from his bowers, clears the fields and
fences in the pastures. The third laborer presses the
good wines, fills all the tuns like a good cellarer, and
has the seed spread on the land while winter draws
near, just as at the beginning.

The vision left me so amazed that I thought
I was dreaming, but it was the truth. I asked my lord

254 / THE BOOK OF GOOD LOVE          (1298)

to explain it to me so that I would understand what
it was and what it was not. My lord, Sir Love, being
a learned man, clarified the whole thing in one short
stanza, by which the reader shall be instructed. This
was his brief answer:

"The dining table, the other table, the dance,
and the road are the four seasons of the solar year;
the men are the months, and it is true that they approach and do not reach each other, and they await
each other at the border."

Other strange things I saw in the pavilion,
almost unbelievable; but I do not want to delay you
or trouble you, so I will say no more of the pavilion.
After his pavilion had been prepared, my lord came
to sleep in it for a short time; when he arose, he did
not find his retinue there because most of them had
gone to stay with Sir Carnival. Seeing him at leisure,
I, his pupil, made bold to ask him about former days
and how it was that he never came to see me and
where he had been. He answered me with a sigh and
as if in grief:

uring the winter I visited Seville and all Andalusia, without neglecting any city; there every notable person humbles himself before me, and I had a perfectly good time. At the beginning of Lent I went to Toledo, expecting to have a good time and to be merry and joyful; but I found great holiness there and this made me keep quiet because few received me or called me. I lived in a palace that was painted red, where many ladies, pinched with long fasting, came to see me. With many Paternosters and other continual prayers, they drove me out of the city through the Visagra gates. I didn't stop trying but went to a monastery where I found many nuns in the cloisters and in the cemetery, reciting the Psalms, and I knew I could never stand that misery. I thought I might find some way to get by all that in some other monastery, but I could find none; with prayers and alms and much fasting, they avoided me as if I were contaminated. They spoke of charity, but they did not show me any. I could see their faces, but not what they said. By waiting, one can get a good bargain, but it is foolish to remain where one is not welcome.

"I was going through the city wretched and lost while the ladies and other women kept drowning me out with their yammering of Ave Marias.

Seeing how badly off I was there, I left in rage, putting behind me all that misery, vexation and pain, and went to spend Lent in the city of Castro,[91] where they were glad to see me and my followers. There I found some who called me stepfather. Now that Carnival has arrived I want to get rid of this misery and turn the Catholic Lent over to Saint Quiteria; [92] I want to go to Alcalá and stay there for the fair; then I will travel through the land and provide many people with gossip."

The following morning before dawn, Love left with his followers and went his way, leaving me worried but content, according to the custom of this master of mine. Always, wherever he is, he brings heartaches, but also great pleasure, for his devotee. He seeks only joy, pleasure, and ease, and does not care to be the guest of a sad or an angry man.

THE ARCHPRIEST SEEKS SOLACE

On the first Sunday after Easter I saw the churches and altars full of joy, with weddings and songs; there were great feasts and great banquets as the priests and jugglers went from wedding to wedding. Those that had been single were getting married, and I saw them accompanied by ladies. I tried to procure some such joy for myself, for a lonely man has many worries. I summoned Trotaconventos, my expert old woman. She came quickly, with eagerness and joy. I asked her to find me some good woman, because to be alone, without company, is a painful life. She told me that she knew a sprightly widow, very rich, very young, and very proud. "Archpriest, you will fall in love with her. Tomorrow I will go to her, and if we succeed in winning her, our work will have been worthwhile."

By my old woman's hand, I sent her a little gift, along with the songs which I present to you here; the old woman did not convince her and I did not seduce her, so if I did not exert myself, I also did not get much out of it. My old woman did everything she could, but she could not make the catch, tie and secure the knot; she came back to me, sad and grieved at heart, saying, "Do not keep returning where you are not welcome."

THE ARCHPRIEST IN LOVE
WITH A LADY WHOM HE SAW PRAYING

Soon came the feast of St. Mark, a solemn day, which holy Church celebrates with a solemn procession, one of the greatest of the year, deservedly praised by all Christians; before the day was over,

I found myself involved in an adventure. I saw a very beautiful lady, praying very devoutly before an image of the Virgin; I begged my old woman to take pity on me and to do a kind deed on my behalf. She did as I asked, but with great discretion, saying, "I would not like to pay dearly for this, as I did with the Moorish woman, who gave me a peck of trouble. Still, a loyal friend is ready for good and for evil."

She went on my errand, taking pains for my sake; and feigning to be a jewel peddler, as they all do, she got into the house. No one answered and nobody—man, cat, or dog—saw my old woman. She told the lady why she had come, saying:

"Lady, buy my bolsters and my borders."

The good lady said, "I understand, Urraca, your evil schemes, all of them."

"Daughter," said the old woman, "dare I speak?"

Said the lady, "Urraca, why not?"

"Lady, I do not suggest that you marry. A widow is better off free than badly married. It is better to have some secret solace, for a good friend is better than a bad husband. Daughter, the one I would bring you, the one I would send to you, is very sprightly and courteous, the most elegant man around."

Whether the good messenger obtained anything or not, she came to me very happy and told me immediately, "If you send the wolf you expect meat." These were the verses that my procuress brought to me:

"The dove spoke in the kingdom of Rhodes, saying: 'Aren't you afraid, you women, to change your love and take new lovers?' "

This is the reason women do marry men, it seems.

Once the lady was married to another man, she broke off from me and I from her, in order not to commit sin shamelessly or perhaps because she was too cautious. A man cannot be friendly with every married woman.

THE ARCHPRIEST
AND THE NUN

gain being alone, without a sweetheart, I sent for my old woman and she said, "What now?" Then she laughed, saying: "Greetings, my good sir. Here comes good love, as good as a trusted friend could hope to find."

She said: "My friend, listen to me a little. Take my advice and bestow your love on a nun.

She will not marry you or expose you; you will love
each other for a very long time. I have had experience with nuns, for I was among them for more than
ten years. Their lovers are happy; they are not anxious. Who could relate all the delicacies, the expensive gifts, the many precious and rare electuaries they
give! [93] Among the many they present you with are
candied citron, preserved quince, and nut electuary,
and others too, even more expensive; each day they
send each other cheaper ones made of carrots. They
have cumin seed from Alexandria with fine traga-
canth, candied citron *abbatis* [94] with fine ginger, roseate honey, candied fruits, cinnamon and almonds,
together with a fresh roseate sweet, which I should
have mentioned earlier. They have sugar-coated almonds, candied sugar with storax, clove carnations
with marigold, very fine sandalwood, with satyrion,
which is a precious and noble gift for one who goes
with women. You must know that there is a great
abundance of sugar—spongy, in lumps, in crystals,
and plenty of the roseate sugar; there is sugar for
confitures and of the violet type, and many other
kinds which I have forgotten. Montpellier, Alexandria, and renowned Valencia do not have so many
electuaries and of so many varieties; still, the lady
who is most proud gives the most precious ones because these nuns devote all their ingenuity to feats of
love. Let me tell you something else that I learned
there: when they have Toro wine, they don't serve

cheap wine. When I left them I lost all these luxu-
ries. The man who does not love a nun is a fool.

"Besides all these nice things, they are well-
mannered, very discreet, talented, and quite pleasant.
As for love-making, even their scullery maids know
more about that and are better at it than aristocratic
dames. These nuns are the very picture of perfect
beauty; they are generous and forthright, noblewomen by nature, excellent lovers, with a love that
is constant and steady. They are thoughtful, respon-
sive, and very discreet in this regard. Every pleasure
you can imagine, all the tricks of making love, the
keenest joys and most delectable kind of play—these
nuns are more skilled at than anyone else. Try them
just once and you will want to remain with them."

"Trotaconventos," I said, "listen. How can
I get in there when I do not know the door?"

She answered, "Let me look after that. If I
can make a hamper, I can also make a basket."

She went off to see a nun whom she had once
served. As she told me later, the nun said: "What
brings you here? How are you, my dear friend?
What are you doing now?"

"Just so-so, lady," said the old woman.
"Nothing extraordinary! Since leaving you, I have
been serving an archpriest, young and wealthy, and
I live by his help. Daily I advise him to serve you;
lady, please do not drive him away from the convent."

Lady Garoça [95] said, "Did he send you to me?"

She said, "No, lady; I came on my own. I would like you to have the same good things you did for me while I was your servant. Really, I have never seen better."

But this good lady was wise. She led a good life and was not frivolous. She said, "If I took foolish advice, I would get the same as the orchard farmer got from the snake."


THE ORCHARD FARMER AND THE SNAKE

"There was once an orchard farmer, simple and without guile. As he went through his orchard during a severe storm in the month of January, he saw a little snake lying half dead under a pear tree. With all the snow, wind, and ice, the snake was stiff with cold. The farmer, a kindhearted man, was struck with pity for the motionless snake and wanted to bring it back to life. He wrapped the snake in his tunic, brought it home, and laid it by the warm fire of the hearth. The snake was revived by the great heat and before the farmer could catch it, crawled into a hole in the kitchen. Each day, the good man gave the snake bread and milk, and some of whatever food he himself ate. With all this comfort and nourishment, the little snake gradually grew into a large serpent.

"When summer came with its heat and there was no more danger of wind or of ice, the serpent crept out of his hole and in his villainy began to spread poison throughout the house. The orchard farmer said, 'Get out of this place! Do not spread poison here!' Angered, the serpent coiled himself around the farmer, squeezing and choking him cruelly and without mercy.

"The evil one is happy when he can return poison for honey and pain for favor to friend and neighbor, deception for charity and good treatment. Thus you are doing to me. You were in trouble, poor, in bad repute, and without any friend to protect you; I helped you a little. I was your mistress for a long time, and now you advise me to throw away my soul."

"Lady," replied the old woman, "why am I reviled? When I bring a gift, I am treated well; today because I came empty-handed, I am insulted. I am like the old hound that does not catch anything."


THE HOUND AND THE MASTER

"The hare-hound, a good valiant dog and good runner, had swift, light feet when he was

young; he had good tusks, a good mouth, and good
teeth, and when he saw a hare he could catch it easily.
He always brought his master something and never
returned from the hunt without prey. His master
patted him and praised the hound to all his neighbors. But with all his hard work, the hound soon
grew old and lost his teeth and the strength of his
legs. When his master went hunting and a rabbit appeared, he would catch it, but he could not hold on
to it and it would escape into the ditch. The hunter
beat the hound with a stick. The hound moaned,
complaining, 'What an evil world! When I was
young they shouted "Hey! Hey!" But now that I
am old, they despise me and scorn me. In my youth
the quarry never escaped from me; I brought it to
my master, dead or alive, and he would praise me.
Now that I am old, he despises me. Since I can no
longer bring him game, he does not praise me nor
whistle to me.'

"The many good gifts of youth must com-
pensate for weakness, a malady of old age. A man is
not less worthy because he is old; the wisdom of an
old man is not easily swayed. To like a youth and
his freshness and to despise and slight him when he
has grown old is stupid and blameworthy, a villainous evil. One should praise an old man for his youth.
But the greedy world is like this: when love gives
fruit, they continue loving, but when it does not give

anything and it does not serve, love dies out. Men do not care for friends that give no profit. A person is praised as long as he can give; when I gave much I was praised, but now that I cannot give anything I am despised and reviled. No mention or gratitude for past service. Nobody remembers the former profit; if you serve an evil man, you will always be a beggar. An evil man does not give anything to his servants, and the poor old man hardly finds a friend. My lady, the same thing is happening to me at your hands: I served you well and still do, but because I came without a gift you are angry and insult me, as you have done."

"Old woman," said the lady, "it was not my fault. I was insulted by what you told me. As for what I said, I repented, for I realize that your intention is good. But I am afraid that I might be deceived. I would not like to do as the village mouse with the city mouse, when he went shopping. Let me tell you the story and we will stop quarrelling."


THE GUADALAJARA MOUSE
AND THE MONFERRANDO MOUSE


"A Guadalajara mouse got up early one Monday and went to Monferrando to the market. A noble looking mouse received him in his hole, in-

vited him to eat, and served him a bean. They dined
at a poor table, but their manners put a good face
on it; good will makes up for scanty food, and a
warm welcome compensates for humble dishes. The
Guadalajara mouse was pleased by the good intention. After they had eaten their dinner, the city
mouse invited the Monferrando mouse to come on
Tuesday to see his market and to be his guest in turn.
The country mouse went with him to his house, and
he gave him plenty of cheese, much unsalted bacon
fat and bread, without counting or weighing; the
country mouse considered himself very lucky. The
tablecloths were of good linen, as they consisted of a
white bag full of flour; the mouse enjoyed being
there. His host did him much honor, adding to all
his joy and happiness with many pleasant services.
The rich table was heaped with good food and a
great variety of dishes, one better than the other; and
there was good will besides—which a guest wants
most of all, because joy with good food soothes
everyone.

"While they were happily eating, halfway
through their meal, there were great noises at the hall
door. The lady of the house was opening it and entering. Hearing her footsteps, the mice were stricken
with fear and ran off. The city mouse sped to his
hole, while his confused guest scurried back and forth
without finding a safe hiding place. Finally, he

stopped in the darkness near the wall. When the door
was closed again and the terror gone, the country
mouse was feverish and trembling; his host tried to
soothe him, saying: 'Now, my friend, rejoice and eat
whatever you like. This is good food and it tastes
like honey.'

   "But the country mouse said, 'There is poison in it. When one has to fear for his life, honey
tastes like gall. If you find it so tasty, eat it yourself.
Nothing is sweet to the frightened man; fear will
kill appetite. The man in fear of death finds even
honey without taste, and everything is bitter in a
dangerous life. I would rather nibble at beans in
peace and safety than enjoy a thousand delicacies if I
have to be chased and worried. Delicacies turn sour
with fear; the peril of death poisons everything. The
longer I stay here, the more I perish of the fear I had.
When I reflect on it, I realize that if the cat had
found me, alone, I would have been caught and had
a bad time. You have a large house but there are
many guests; you feast abundantly, and you are deceived by these things. My poverty, in a safe hut, is
good, because man has a heavy foot and the cat
scratches badly. A poor but contented man is rich
and rich enough, while the wealth of a frightened
man is poverty; he is always worried, in fear and
sadness, but a happy poverty is true perfection.'

   "So, I would rather have salted sardines in

the convent, serving God together with the other honored ladies, than lose my soul amid roasted partridges and then be mocked like other lost women."

The old woman said, "Lady, you are acting foolishly in passing up pleasure and looking for hardship. You are making the same choice the cock made. I will tell you the story; do not take it amiss."

THE SAPPHIRE IN THE MANURE HEAP

"A stupid cock, strutting on a manure heap, was digging in it one cold morning and found a sapphire that had fallen there, a very fine stone. Bewildered, the cock said foolishly:

" 'I would rather have a grain of wheat or a bunch of grapes than you, or a hundred like you, in my hand.'

"The sapphire replied, 'Listen, you hillbilly, if you knew me you could be happy. If I might be found by the right person, if the man who values me could have me, what is now smeared with manure would be resplendent. You do not know or appreciate my true worth.'

"Now, many people read a book and hold it in their hands, but they do not know what they read or how to understand it; they have something precious and much sought, but they do not respect it properly. Whoever receives a fortune from God and does not want to take it, who does not desire to be worthy or learned or to advance, deserves to suffer misery and worries and vexation; he deserves the same fate as the cock digging in the manure.

"You, Lady Garoça, are like him. You would rather drink water from a jug in the convent than from silver cups as the bride of this young man, who would make you young again. In the convent you eat sardines and shrimp, cabbages and all sorts of garbage and tough dogfish, and meanwhile you pass up your lover's partridges and capons. You women without men are lost. You pass your lives with bad food, salted sardines, and coarse tunics. And then you can refuse the trouts, the hens, the pleated shirts, the Malines cloth of your friend!"

Lady Garoça said, "I will say no more today. Let me think about what you have told me. Come back tomorrow for my answer. I will give it to you then. I shall do willingly what seems to me best."

The next day, the old woman returned to the convent and found the nun sitting in choir. "Hey, hey, lady," she said, "what a dreary litany! Every day I find you amid this noise. I find you either singing or reading, or bickering and quarreling with each other; never yet have I found you playing or laughing. My master speaks the truth, from what

I can see. Ten geese in the swamp make more noise and utter more words without reason than one hundred oxen at pasture. Leave all this, lady, and hear my message. Mass is over, let us go to the parlor."

The nun is always glad to go from the choir to the parlor; the friar is always glad to go from terce to the refectory. The nun desires to hear news of her lover; the gluttonous friar wishes to get to the table.

The old woman said, "My lady, let me tell you a little story. I hope I don't have the same luck with you as the ass with the little dog, when he saw the dog playing with his lady on the rug. I will tell you the story; I hope it makes you laugh."

THE ASS AND THE LITTLE DOG

"A little dog was playing with his mistress, kissing and licking her hands, barking and wagging his tail for her; in everything he did, he showed he liked her very much. He would stand on his hind legs before her and her friends, and they all took great pleasure in his tricks and gave him part of whatever they ate. The ass observed all this every day, and, stupid as he was, he started to think about the matter. The foolish donkey said to himself, 'I do

more good to my lady and all her people than a thousand of those dogs. I carry loads of wood on my back
for her; I haul from the mill the flour they eat. Now
I too will stand on my hind legs and flatter the lady
like that dog that is under her fur coat.'

"Braying loudly, he ran out of the stable
and charged at them like a mad jackass. Leaping and
clowning around, he came to the dais where the lady
was sitting and put both his hooves up on her shoulders. She started to scream for help and the farm
hands rushed up, beating him furiously with sticks
and clubs until the sticks broke on his back.

"One should not act rashly or say or think
what is not proper for him. No wise man would
dare do what God and nature have forbidden. A fool
who thinks that he is speaking properly and that his
actions are useful and pleasing, will talk idiotically
and annoy and irritate people. Sometimes it is very
profitable to stay silent. Now, my lady, since you
became so annoyed with what I said in all good faith
yesterday and got angry with me, I do not dare ask
what you thought. But I beg you to tell me what
you have decided."

The lady said, "Old woman, you arose early
this morning to come here and tell me stories. As for
what you said yesterday, I cannot consent to what
you asked, because I should not enter such a wicked

affair as this is. That is what Mother Fox said when
the surgeon wanted to pluck her heart out with his
hands! Let me tell you this story, right now, and
then I will give you the answer, as plain as I can
make it.''

## THE FOX THAT ATE THE HENS IN THE VILLAGE

"In a village encircled by a high wall, there
was once a sly fox that had the habit of breaking in
at night, after the gates had been shut, and of eating
the hens from house to house. Provoked by this out-
rage, the villagers closed up their gates, windows,
and holes. When the fox realized that she was
penned in, she said, 'Now it looks as if I may have to
pay for my chicken dinners.'

"Playing dead, the fox stretched herself out
at the village gates, rigid and disfigured, her mouth
open, her paws clenched. The passers-by-said, 'Look
at that night-prowler!'

"A shoemaker came by very early. 'That's
a fine-looking tail,' he said, 'and worth good money.
Out of that, I can make a shoe horn to ease the shoes
on.' He cut it, but she, still as a lamb, did not make
a move.

"Then came the barber, returning from a
blood-letting. 'That tusk of hers would be fine for

someone with toothache or a sore jaw.' He pulled her tooth, but she lay quiet, without a whimper.

"An old woman came; the fox had eaten one of her hens. The old woman said, 'Her eye would make a good charm for girls who are bewitched or who are going through their pains.' She removed the fox's eye, but that wretch did not dare move a muscle.

"Then the physician came down the street. He said, 'This fox's ears would be very good in cases of poisoning or for earache.' He cut them off, but she lay quieter than a sheep. Then the master said, 'The heart of the fox is very useful for people who have palpitations.'

"But the fox cried, 'Hell, take the devil's pulse!' and jumping up, she ran off down the moat. 'One can suffer all sorts of pains, but nobody is willing to have his heart torn out and die, for then there is no use crying over spilt milk.'

"People must be wise and prudent in choosing any course of action, so that there will be some way out for them. Before doing something that he might get caught at and blamed for, one has to have an escape prepared. When a lady is dishonored by a man, she is despised and rejected by him, and she incurs both the wrath of God and the mockery of the world; she loses her honor, her name, and her life. What you are urging on me would lead to the ruin of my soul and my body, to death and ill fame. I do not want to do it. Go away right now or I will pay you as you deserve!"

Frightened by this violent outburst, the old woman said, "Lady, calm yourself, do not strike me! After all, you can get as much advantage from me as the lion got, while asleep, from the mouse."

## THE LION AND THE MOUSE

"Up in the cold mountains, the lion was asleep in the thicket where he had his underground lair. Some nimble mice, playing there, woke up the lion with their noise. Seizing one of them, the lion was about to kill him, but the trembling mouse soothed him thus: 'Sir, do not kill me. I can hardly fill your stomach, and my death would bring you no glory. What honor can the great and mighty lion win by killing a poor, wretched little creature? This would be dishonor and shame, not glorious victory. To conquer a mouse is a paltry prize. Even though everyone regards victory as honorable, to overcome the weak is evil and sinful; a victor is honored according to the merit of the vanquished. The harder the fight the greater the glory.'

"Persuaded by this speech, the lion released the little mouse. Free, the mouse thanked him over and over and said he would gladly do everything in his power to serve him. Then the mouse returned to his hole, and the lion went hunting. Prowling through the mountains, the lion stumbled and fell into a huge net from which he could not get free. He was completely ensnared and unable to move. His roaring complaints were heard by the little mouse, who came quickly and said:

"Sir, I carry a sharp knife. With these teeth of mine I will gnaw, and little by little I will chew a hole big enough for your paws. Then you can free your strong arms and easily pull the net apart and break through it. My small teeth will set you free. You spared my life, and now you will be saved by me.'

"You who are rich and powerful, do not despise the poor and the weak, or chase them off; even the man who has nothing can do something, and the helpless man can be of some use. A small, worthless thing can be of great advantage and bring great profit; people without power, money, or title should at least have skills, good sense, art and knowledge."

Now this pleased the lady a good deal.

"Old woman," she said, "have no fear, you are safe. A lady should not be rash, but I am very much afraid of being cruelly deceived. I would not like these fine words and sweet flatteries to become bitter gall for me, as the evil words and crooked advise of the fox were to the crow."

THE FOX AND THE CROW

"One day the hungry fox spotted the black crow perched on a branch, holding a big piece of cheese in his mouth. She started to flatter him artfully:

" 'O beautiful crow! You are as white and as graceful as the swan, so beautiful and shiny! You sing more sweetly than any other bird; come, sing a song for me now, and I will sing twenty. Ah, your song surpasses the songs of the bunting, the parrot, the thrush, the nightingale, and the jay. If you would only sing for me now, this would ease my burden more quickly than anything else.'

"The crow really believed that his croaking was more pleasing to the world than any other melody; he believed that his crowing tongue made people happier than any troubador could. He started to sing and to modulate his voice; the cheese fell from his mouth. In a flash, the fox ate it, and the crow was left to mourn the loss.

"Flattery, vainglory, and deceitful smiles bring needless sorrow and grief and pain. Many think that the vineyard keeper guards the vineyards when it is only the scarecrow on his pole. To heed sweet flattery is dangerous, because the sweetness usually turns bitter. To sin in this way is not proper for a religious; an unchaste nun is like a rotten orange."

"My lady," said the old woman, "dismiss that fear. Do not avoid the man who loves you. Every woman fears the same thing you do, and you nuns are frightened as easily as the hares."

## THE HARES

Hares were running about in the forest, when they heard a little noise that made them flee in fear. It was the sound of breakers in the swamp, but the timid hares crowded all together. Looking all around, they could not calm themselves; in their great fear they thought of hiding. While they debated this, they saw the frightened frogs scampering into the water. One of the hares said: " 'Let us hope. We are not the only ones that have a stupid fear—look how even the frogs are

hiding without reason; we hares and those frogs
have a ridiculous fear. Let us not lose our heads. We
are afraid of things that are not fearful; we are timid
and ready to run. One should not give in to needless
fear.'

      "When his speech was over, he started to
run; this was reason enough for them to flee.

      "If one wants to live well, he should be
afraid only to the point of not losing his head for
fear of dying. If you lack courage and daring, fear
is very dangerous; in any struggle, only hope and
valor prevail. The cowards die in flight, shouting
'Run!' while those who are brave live, crying, 'Hit
them hard!'

      "Now this is exactly what happens to you,
my lady, and to all convent-bound nuns. Because of
one wretched woman's disgrace, you are certain that
you will all go the same way. No, you must preserve
your confidence and abandon this vain fear. Give
this good man love, and appreciate his noble love.
Even if you refuse to do more, at least speak to him
as you would to a common country lad; dismiss your
fear and say to him, 'God bless you!' "

      "Old woman," said the lady, "you are like
the devil who supplied his friend with bad advice
and a bad end, bringing him to the gallows where
he abandoned him. Listen to the fable and do not
seek my harm and disgrace."

THE ROBBER WHO SIGNED A CONTRACT
WITH THE DEVIL

"In a city without law there were once many
thieves. Hearing about all the complaints and
bans, the king sent his judges, his royal constables,
and his executioners, so that from then on a thief
would be hanged for stealing four pennies. One of
the thieves thought to himself, 'Since I have already
lost my ears for theft, I consider myself almost a
groom for the gallows-bride. If the constable catches
me in one more robbery, he will marry me to the
scaffold.'

"Now before that groom-to-be could repent,
the devil, in order not to lose him, came to him and
proposed that he sign over his soul by deed, after
which he could safely steal all he wanted. The thief
signed the deed and granted him his soul, and the
devil promised never to abandon him, just as he always deludes his friends. The thief went to a bank
and stole a large hoard of gold, but he was arrested
and put in irons. He called on his evil friend for help.
The devil came and said:

" 'You see, I am prepared. Have no fear, be
brave, for you will not die for this. When they bring
you to trial, today or tomorrow, take the judge aside
and talk to him. Put your hand inside your coat and

give him whatever you find there. My friend, you will get off scot-free.'

"On the next day, when the prisoners were brought to trial, the thief called the judge aside and spoke to him, and putting his hand in his bosom, he pulled out a magnificent, expensive gold cup. He gave this to the judge as a gift without anyone's knowledge. The judge immediately declared: 'Gentlemen, I do not believe that this rascal should die. You have arrested him without cause, and so I acquit him and dismiss the case. You constables, turn him loose.'

"The thief was set free without any sentence, and for a long time he pursued his villainous trade. Many times he was apprehended, but he always escaped by means of bribes, so that finally even the devil was annoyed. The next time the thief was caught, he called on his evil friend as usual. The devil came and said:

" 'What is this daily invocation? Do just as you always do, don't worry, trust me. Tomorrow you will present your gift and get out through my art.'

"The thief called the judge aside, as always, but when he put his hand in his bosom, he found an evil omen; he pulled out a long rope and handed it to the judge. The judge said, 'I sentence him to be hanged.'

"While they were leading him to the gallows, he saw the devil perched on a high tower and cried, 'Why don't you help me?'

"The devil answered, 'Don't hesitate, just keep going. Keep walking and talking as you are, my friend; I will be with you as soon as I get a friar together with his nun, who's always nagging me, "Bring him, bring him!" Deceive the deceivers and do ill to the man who does it to you. Meanwhile, friend, go along with your bailiff.'

"Near the foot of the scaffold, the thief began to scream, 'Friend, help me, help me! They are going to hang me!'

"But the devil answered, 'Come on, do you think I'll let them? I will help you as always. Don't worry; let yourself be hoisted up. Be bold and let them hang you, and then put both your feet on my shoulders and I will support you just as I have supported other friends on similar rides.'

"The executioners, then, strung up the thief, and, thinking he was dead, they all went away, leaving the two wicked companions in their peculiar predicament. The two villains chatted with each other, the devil complaining, 'Ay, what a heavy burden you are! Your burglaries and thefts have cost me dearly'; and the hanged man saying, 'Your damnable evil works brought me to this end; that's why you're holding my weight.'

"Then the devil spoke again and said, 'Friend, look and tell me what you see, no matter what it is.'

"The thief looked down, and said, 'I see nothing but those ill-shod feet of yours. I see too a great heap of old shoes with cracked soles, and torn old clothes; and I see your hands bristling with hooks from which hang many cats, both male and female.'

"The devil answered: 'All that you have seen, and twice that, which you could not see, I have worn out chasing after you. I cannot bear you any more; now you must take what you deserve. These hooks are my arts, and the cats are the many souls I have caught. My feet are bloody from going after them day and night.'

"And saying this, he pulled himself away and jumped down, leaving his comrade swinging high on the gallows.

"Anyone who believes the devil is caught on his hook and will shortly come to great evil and a bad end. If you trust in the devil or consort with an evil friend, sooner or later you get your just desert; he is a false friend and brings every kind of trouble. The world is full of rags. During good times, a man has many cronies, self-styled kinfolk, and friends who are not friends. But when they see him having a hard time, they will not spend two words in his behalf. Bad returns come from bad friends; they give no more help than a villain would, but they are quick with their lying excuses, their flatteries, and their promises. May God protect you, my friends, from such friends!

"The man who gives bad advice is not a 'friend'; indeed, he is really an enemy. Don't invite to your table the one who deserts you in bad days, nor come to the defense, in public, of the person who would, in private, do you mortal harm."

"Lady," said the old woman, "you know many fables, but my advice is not really what you make it out to be. All I wish is that you speak to him and that you come to an understanding with him when I bring you together."

"I tell you," cried the lady, "you would do what the devil did to his comrade, the thief. You would leave me alone with him, you would close the door on us, and so I would be disgraced by remaining in his company."

"What a heart of stone!" the old woman said. "Lady, let me reassure you, you need have no fear. I swear on your hands that I will not leave you; if I do, may the perjury fall on my head."

The lady said, "Old woman, it is not customary for a lady to broach the subject of love; the most she can do is look at him keenly—and that is a sure sign."

"Yes, lady," she replied, "but you cannot learn anything from a bird that is mute."

Lady Garoça said, "God bless you; tell me what that archpriest looks like. Describe his features, just as they are, and do not put me off with jokes now that I have asked this seriously."


PORTRAIT OF THE ARCHPRIEST [96]


"Lady," replied the old woman, "I see him often. He is big and husky, with strong limbs; his head is not small, he has bushy black hair and strong jaws, a stout neck, and big ears. His eyebrows are black as coals and well spaced; his gait is firm, like the peacock's, his step quiet and measured. His nose is long, and this is a flaw. He has healthy red gums and a mouth that is not too small, with regular lips, rather full and red as coral. His voice is very deep. He has broad shoulders and strong wrists. His eyes are small.

"He is somewhat dark in complexion, barrel-chested, with muscular arms, shapely legs, and small feet. Lady, this is all I can describe, but for his sake I embrace you. He is energetic, bold, and youthful; he knows how to play the instruments and is expert in the arts of the jongleur. He is a merry lady's man, and, by my slippers! you could not find his equal anywhere."

My old woman kept coaching the lady:
"You know the proverb of the man who went to
the fairgrounds: 'God brings bargains right to your
door.' Love, ladies, love such a man as I have described! You nuns are so prudent but so full of desire and so beautiful, and the lusty clergymen want
the haughty ones. Fish and frogs all wish to swim,
and the hungry man is not choosy about his bread."

Lady Garoça answered, "I must have time to
think about this."

"What!" said the old woman. "Love cannot be lazy. Let me go and tell him. Ah, ah! How
grateful he will be! I will have him come to this hall
tomorrow."

The lady said, "Old woman! God save me
from your wiles! Go and tell him to come tomorrow in the presence of my good friends. He must
speak good words to me, no jokes or stories, and tell
him I don't want to hear any of your tales."

My old woman came to me happy and joyful. Without even a "God bless you," my covent-
trotter said: "When you send the wolf, by my faith,
you look for meat. This is how a good messenger
handles an affair. Friend, God bless you! Rest; be
happy! She said you should go tomorrow, but not
alone, and speak to her, but be careful not to tell her
tall stories because nuns are not pleased by a tale-
spinning priest. Tell her only what is appropriate;
plan today what you will say tomorrow. Go to

Mass early, make the nun fall in love, and then come back."

I answered, "Trotaconventos, my friend, I beg you, bring her this letter before I speak to her; if she does not seem unfriendly in her reply, the words will lead to action."

She brought her my letter at the first Mass, and my beautiful verse received a favorable answer. The nun had more skill in fencing than I did, but the good speech bore good fruit. In the name of God I went to Mass in the morning and saw the nun praying: she was sprightly, with her long heron neck, her fresh color of pomegranate. What a waste that she should be a nun!

"Holy Mary help me! I wring my hands! Who put a black habit and veil on that white rose? A beautiful woman should have children and grand-children rather than a black veil like that or a hun-dred habits. Although it is a sin against God for a lady's man to make love to a nun, oh, God! if I could only be that sinner and expiate the fault later!"

She looked on me with eyes that glowed like fire. I sighed for them. My heart said, "There she is!" I went to the lady, she spoke to me and I to her; I fell in love with her and she with me.

The lady accepted me as her faithful servant, and I was an obedient and royal lover; she did me great good in God's eyes by her clean love; while she lived, God was my guide. She prayed often to God for me; she helped me greatly with her fasts. Her clean life took delight in God,[97] and she was never inclined to the folly of the world. Nuns are good at this type of love and for praying to God and doing charitable works; but as far as sensual love is concerned they are dangerous, hypocrites, idlers and gossips.

Such was my luck that just two months later my good lady died and I was plunged into grief anew. But the sons of men must die. May God pardon them their sins. In my misery, I composed this threnody; it was not very well polished because of my grief and sorrow. Anyone who practices good love should improve it, for errors and badly made things should welcome emendation.


THE ARCHPRIEST AND THE MOORESS

To forget my grief and sorrow, I asked my old woman to try to find a mistress for me. She spoke to a Mooress, who did not want to listen to her. She acted wisely, and I wrote many songs.

Trotaconventos said to the Mooress on my behalf: "Hello, my friend! How long is it since I saw you last? Nobody can get to see you. Why are you this way? A new love greets you."

The Mooress said, "I don't know." [98]

"Daughter, a man from Alcalá sends you many greetings and a robe together with this note. God is with you, because this man is very well to do. Accept it, my child."

The Mooress said, "No, by Allah."

"Daughter, may the Creator give you peace and health! Do not disdain it, for I could not carry more. I bring you a good gift; speak to me kindly; do not send me away without an answer."

The Mooress said, "Be quiet."

When the old woman saw that she could not accomplish anything there, she said, "I see that I have wasted my words; since you will not say anything else to me, I will go away."

The Mooress nodded and said, "Go away."


INSTRUMENTS FOR WHICH MOORISH SONGS ARE NOT SUITED


Afterwards I composed many songs for dancing and marching, for Jews and Moors and lovers, to be arranged for instruments and popular tunes; if you do not know the melody, listen to the singers. I also composed some songs of the sort that blind men sing, and some for the students who go carousing at night, and for many others who beg

from door to door, some of them playful and farci-
cal. I could not write them all on ten full sheets.

　　　Certain instruments are more appropriate for
some songs than for others. In order that they be
well matched, I will indicate here, out of those that
I have tried, which ones are most suitable. The bow
viol is not suited to Arabic songs; neither is the
guitar or the hurdy-gurdy. The zither and the bagpipe do not favor childish verses; these favor the
tavern and the ribald dances. The flute, the bandore,
the pipe, and the country flute are more suited for
students' songs than for Arabic things; if they must
play them, they do so with shame, and anyone who
forces them should be fined.

THE DEATH OF TROTACONVENTOS;
THE ARCHPRIEST'S COMPLAINT;
HE REVILES AND CURSES DEATH

philosopher says, in his famous
book, that sadness and misery dull
the wits. In my great grief, I cannot
speak now, because Trotaconventos can no longer go
about on her trots. Cursed day on which my old
woman died! She died serving me. How miserable I

am! I do not know how to say it, but many good doors, that once were open to me, were closed then.

Oh, Death! Would that you might die, and be wretched! You killed my old woman! You should have killed me first! You are the enemy of the world, without peer; there is no one who does not fear your bitter name. Death! When you strike someone, there is no defense. You carry off the good man and the evil, the nobleman and the slave; you make them all equal and you take them all at one price; you make no allowances for popes or kings. You have no respect for lordship, for family or friendship; you are the foe of the whole world. You have no courtesy, no love, no pity, but only misery, sadness, and cruel grief. No one can hide from you, no one can escape, no one can fight successfully against you. Your miserable coming cannot be foreseen, and when you come you will not wait for anyone! You snatch away the soul that lived in the body and leave the lonely corpse to the worms in the grave. A man can never know the crooked road you take. Death, I tremble to talk about you!

You are so detested by all that no matter how well liked a man was while still alive, once you have come on your evil visit, all avoid him immediately, like a rotten carcass. Those that took pleasure in and looked for his company while he was alive, detest him now that he is dead, as something horri-

ble; relatives and friends all hate him; they all flee
from him, as if he were a spider. Your coming,
Death, makes all creatures loathsome: beloved children are loathsome to their parents, desired and
honored lovers to their mistresses, loving husbands
to their faithful wives. You make the rich man lie
in great poverty, without a penny left from all his
wealth. The man who, while living, was noble and
good becomes, when he is dead, filthy and detestable.

     In the whole world, there is no book, no
writing, no paper, no wise or foolish man that
speaks well of you; except for the black raven that
battens on you, nothing in the world gets any benefit
from you. Each day you tell the raven that tomorrow you will make it fat; man does not know when
or where you will strike. If a man can do some good,
he ought rather do it today than wait for you and
your friend tomorrow.[99] Gentlemen, do not try to
make friends with the raven! Fear its threats; do
not heed its call. The good you can do today, do it,
without putting it off. Believe that tomorrow you
will die, for life is only a game of chance. Life and
health change rapidly; in a moment, they can be
lost, when one least expects it. The good you will
do tomorrow is only a naked word, which you must
dress with deeds before Death comes. One who per-
sists in an unlucky game loses more than he gains;
he expects to dispel his bad luck, but instead he rolls

the deuce. Friends, concentrate on doing good deeds,
because when Death comes, it conquers everything.

There are many who think only of winning
when they cry, "Double or nothing!" Bad luck
comes; the dice roll wrong. Man amasses treasures
to enjoy them, I suppose, and then Death comes and
reduces everything to dust. He loses speech and understanding: he cannot take either his great treasures
or his estate with him; he cannot even make a will.
An evil wind scatters his hoard of treasures.

When his relatives hear of his death, they
gather together, to get it all. When they ask the doctor about the illness, if he says that the patient will
recover, they are all provoked against him. Those
who were closest to him, brothers and sisters, cannot
wait for the moment when the bells toll. His kinfolk
value the inheritance far more than family ties or
white beards. When the soul of the wealthy sinner
has departed from the body, they leave him there on
the ground, alone; they are all afraid of him. They
steal everything, going first for the most valuable,
and each thinks himself badly off if he gets less than
anyone else.

They think it enough to bury him
promptly. Because they are afraid that the strong-
boxes might be opened, they do not want to waste
time by going to a long Mass. In return for all his

treasures they give him a pitiful dowry. They will give nothing to the poor in the name of God; they will sing no Mass, offer no prayers, nor carry out any of their duties. All the new heirs do by way of a service is sing praises to the money! They bury him gladly, but once they have the money, they attend the Mass for his soul reluctantly and late, if at all, because they have already gotten what they were after: they carry off his goods as Satan carries off his soul. If he has left a young wife who is rich or attractive, other people begin to make plans for her, even before the Mass is over; she will marry either a richer man or a lusty young fellow. She completes hardly a month of mourning; it makes her too sad to wear black. The poor wretch saved, without knowing for whom. And though this happens all the time, there is no man who makes a proper will until he can see Death coming.

Death! I urge my heart to indict you further! You bring comfort and strength to no man, but only worms to feast on him when he is dead. You have a fault like that of the cress: eating too much of it gives one a headache. Just so, at the very moment when it looms above one, your evil club strikes with full force and conquers even the strong man, and no medicine is of any use, for your fury takes him away. Those eyes that were so beautiful you blind suddenly and fix them on the ceiling, making them useless. As speech fades, the voice becomes hoarse. In you dwell all evil, grief, and spite.

Hearing and smell, touch and taste—all the five senses you ravage. No one can insult you as harshly as you yourself are insulted by the very dwelling-place you choose.[100] You destroy all sense of shame, you deface beauty, you deprave charm, you vitiate courtesy, you dissipate strength, you turn wisdom into madness and contaminate sweet things with your bitterness. You pollute freshness, you tarnish gold, you undo what was well done, you sadden joy, you despoil cleanness, you revile courtesy. Death! you destroy life and hate love. You are pleasing to no one, but many there are who please you— those who kill and those who do evil things. Your club undoes everything well made; there is nothing ever born that your net does not catch. You are the enemy of good and the lover of evil; you have the same nature as gout, illness, and pain. The place where you are is worse off, and the only good place is where you come rarely.

Your regular abode is the pit of Hell; you are the prime evil and Hell is the second! You live in a wicked house and depopulate the world, telling everybody: "I alone destroy everyone!" Death, the infernal place is made for you! If men could live forever in this world, they would not fear you or your

evil abode; human flesh would not tremble at your
coming. You depopulate cities and populate cemeteries; you replenish graves and destroy empires. The
saints sang the Psalms for fear of you; except for
God, all dread your pains and your miseries. You,
Death, have deprived Heaven and its thrones of inhabitants! You soiled those that were all cleanliness;
you turned the angels into devils and rebels; now
they pay your wages many times over.

You killed the very Lord that created you.
You gave pain to Jesus Christ, Man and God. You
frightened and terrified him whom Heaven and Earth
fear. Hell fears him but you did not! His flesh feared
you, and he trembled before you. His human nature
was saddened by fear of you, though his divine nature was not afraid. But you did not realize this;
you did not look at it and did not perceive it. However, he perceived you and looked at you! His cruel
death gave you a fright; he destroyed Hell, your
crowd, and you. You killed him for an hour, but he
killed you forever. When he conquered you, then
you recognized him. If you frightened him, he
frightened you more. You gave pain to him, but you
were pained a thousandfold; by dying he gave us
life, he to whom you gave death. The cross on which
you put him freed us from bondage.

The blessed whom you held in your evil
dwelling received life through Christ's death; your

house was depopulated through his holy death: by killing him, you wanted to populate it, but it was made barren by him! He freed from your pains our father Adam, our mother Eve, their children Shem, Ham, and Japheth, the patriarchs, the good Abraham, Isaac, and Jacob, and Daniel too. He freed St. John the Baptist and many patriarchs whom you kept in pain in your evil dungeons; he freed the holy Moses, whom you held in your clutches, together with many prophets and saints whom you had captured. I could not tell which ones were kept or how many were left oppressed in your hell. He freed all the chosen saints, but left with you those wicked lost souls that belong to you. He took those that were his with him to Paradise, where they have life, looking on all the glory they desire. May he bring us with him, he who accepted death for us; may he guard us from your abode, so that you will not laugh at us. Those evil lost souls that he left in your power, you torment in the fire of hell; you make them suffer the eternal flames, which they will not escape in all eternity. May God who protected us before and does not need to protect himself, protect us from your ambush, because no matter how long we live, no matter how late, it must come, that fury of yours that weeds the whole world.

You, Death, are so barren of good that one cannot express one tenth of your evil. I commend myself to God, for I know no other remedy that could defend me from your fatal coming.

Implacable Death! Would that you could destroy only yourself! What did you have against me? Where is my faithful old woman? You killed her, Death! Jesus Christ paid for her with his sacred blood and bought salvation for her.

Ah, my Trotaconventos, my truly loyal one! Many followed you when you were alive, but now you are lying alone. Where have they brought you? I do not know anything for sure. The man who starts on that road never returns to tell of it. I am sure that you are sitting in Paradise! You must surely be together with the martyrs! In the world you always suffered martyrdom for God's sake. Who snatched you away from me, old woman, that endured so much for my sake? I call on God's grace to grant you his glory, for there has not been in the memory of man a more loyal messenger. I must write an epitaph, putting into it all my grief, so that though I cannot see you, I can at least see your sad story. I will give alms in your honor, and I will pray for you; I will have Masses sung and offerings made. May God, my Trotaconventos, give you his blessing; may he who saved the world grant you salvation.

Ladies, do not mock me or call me foolish. If she had served you, you too would mourn her!

You would weep for her and for her subtle hook which brought down all it chased after. No woman, high or low, cloistered or guarded, could resist her when she swooped. I do not know anyone, man or woman, who would not mourn and grieve inordinately, having lost such a person as she was.

Grieving, I composed a small epitaph for her. My sadness made me a hoarse singer. All you who hear it, in the name of God our Lord, offer a loving prayer for the old woman.

URRACA'S EPITAPH

I AM URRACA, WHO LIE BENEATH THIS STONE. WHEN I WAS IN THE WORLD, I WAS CAREFREE AND HAPPY. I MADE MANY MATCHES SUCCESSFULLY AND AVOIDED TROUBLE. IN ONE MOMENT, I FELL UNDER THE EARTH FROM THE HEIGHT. DEATH CAUGHT ME UNSUSPECTING IN ITS NETS. RELATIVES AND FRIENDS, YOU CANNOT HELP ME HERE. RATHER, LIVE WELL, DO NOT OFFEND GOD, FOR YOU WILL ALL DIE, JUST AS I DIED. MAY GOD BLESS THE MAN WHO COMES HERE AND SAYS A PATERNOSTER FOR ME, A SINNER; GOD GRANT HIM LOVE AND JOY WITH HIS BELOVED. AND IF HE WILL NOT PRAY, LET HIM AT LEAST NOT SPEAK ILL OF THE DEAD.

THE CHRISTIAN'S ARMOR
AGAINST THE DEVIL,
THE WORLD, AND THE FLESH

Gentlemen, I urge you, keep your minds fixed on the good. Do not believe in any truce with your enemy, because he can hardly wait for the chance to drag you off with him. If you catch me lying to you, consider me worthless. We know well that we cannot avoid death because our enemy is strong by nature, and we cannot elude him through good luck; each one of us must wear his armor. If tomorrow any of us had to take the field and fight with some enemy, we would look for weapons to arm ourselves; nobody likes to meet such danger unarmed. Now if we do this for men, who are alive, as we are, much more should we do against all those powerful enemies that seek to enslave us and say, "You must go to Hell forever!"

You have already heard about the deadly sins. They do battle with us every day and, after having assaulted our bodies, wish to kill our souls. We must be well provided with weapons against them. Also fighting against us are three other principal enemies: the Flesh, the Devil, and the World. Of these are born the deadly sins; from these three proceed all the rest. We must find weapons with

which we can conquer them. Let me tell you what
weapons to take up: the works of mercy, that is,
good deeds; the gifts of the Holy Spirit which enlighten us; the works of piety, the practice of the
virtues, and the seven sacraments, by which we overcome these enemies.[101]

Baptism, the gift of the Holy Spirit and of
good Wisdom, resists great Cupidity. We must keep
hands off what is not ours; we must not say, "I
would like this." The virtue is Justice, which judges
our folly. We must clothe the naked poor, in the
pious hope that God, for whose sake we do this,
will grant us good fortune. Wearing such a coat of
mail, we can conquer Cupidity which wounds us;
God will defend us against excessive desires.

We must overcome excessive Pride and speak
humbly; it is proper that we fear the Majesty of
God. Strike home with the virtue of Temperance,
the strong sword of prudence and modesty. Show
compassion and shelter the poor, certain that works
of piety are rewarded by God. Do not steal your
neighbor's goods, do not violate women, or do any
violence. Pride is rooted out by Confirmation.

Against Avarice we need Piety; we must give
alms to the poor, and have pity on their sufferings;
the virtue is natural justice, judging in humility; this
is the mace with which you must strike Avarice un-

sparingly. With the sacrament of Holy Orders and with strong Faith that is refined and clearer than crystal, arranging for the marriage of poor orphans, we will conquer Avarice with the wealth of the spirit.

Lust we can check easily: we can avoid it by chastity and conscientiousness, and Fortitude will help us. Certainly we can destroy it with this brassard. By using for cuisses and jambs the holy sacrament of Matrimony that God made in Paradise, by aiding in marrying the very poor, and by giving drink to the thirsty, we will win the struggle against Lust.

Anger is a foe that dispatches many. With the gift of Understanding and with becoming charity, by realizing anger's great harm, and by doing good, with patience, we will have a good helmet to fight with. With the virtue of Hope and abounding patience, by tending the sick and doing Penance, by detesting insults and living in peace—with all this we will conquer Anger and win God's favor.

Gluttony is a great sin which ruins many. Fast and abstinence can free us from it, and Knowledge, knowing how to observe courtesy, and eating just so much so that we can save some for the poor. Also, we must pray to God in the Holy Sacrifice, that is, the sacrament and service of the Eucharist, with faith in this commemoration, and we must fight in His service; with this armor, we can conquer the vice of Gluttony.

Envy killed many of the prophets. Against this foe, which wounds us with its darts, we must take up the strong shield of Good Counsel, with scenes depicted on it and framed by these letters. With the sacrament of Extreme Unction, by burying the dead and having compassion and charity for God's sake, we could not err, nor harm the simple or insult the poor. With these weapons of God, we will beat off Envy.

Against that dangerous Accidie, we must be very well armed. Of the seven sins, this is the most subtle and deceptive. It gives birth each day wherever the devil is and produces more evil offspring than does a rabid bitch. Against her and her offspring, to avoid being overcome, we must make pilgrimages, chant the hours, and meditate on thoughts that arise from good deeds, so that God will not find us empty of holy works. Out of all our good desires and good deeds, we must fashion a spear shaft, and with the iron of good works, performed with unflagging zeal, destroy our vices. Fighting with these weapons, we could conquer them.

Against the three major evils, so that they do not form an alliance, let us strike: the World with charity, the Flesh with fasting, and the Devil with

fortitude; thus will all three of them be overcome
and none of them left, neither parents nor children.
All the other sins, both mortal and venial, are begot-
ten from these like rivers from the perennial springs.
These are the source and the sum of all evils. May
God protect us from the wickedness of these parents
and their children and grandchildren! May God
assist us, granting us such courage and strength that
we can conquer these vices and win the field, so that
on the Day of Judgment we will be invited and Jesus
Christ will say to us, "Come to me, ye blessed!"

THE QUALITIES
OF SMALL WOMEN

entlemen, I want to cut my lec-
ture short, because I have always
been fond of a short sermon, a short woman, and a
short speech; what is brief and well said remains
in the heart. The man who talks too much is
laughed at; the man who laughs too much is crazy.
A small woman has great and abounding love; I
have exchanged large women for small ones, but I

never give away small for large. Neither the small
ones nor the large ones regret the exchange.

Love has requested that I speak about small
women and their noble qualities, and I will do so
immediately. I will tell you such things about small
women that you will think I am joking. They are
as cold as snow and burn better than the fire: they
are cold outside, but are burning with love. In bed
they are a solace—jolly, romping, and laughing.
About the house they are prudent, accomplished,
poised, always pleasing. You will discover many
other features if you look for them.

A little zircon has great splendor, just as a
tiny lump of sugar has great sweetness. In a small
woman there is abundant love. A few words suffice
for the man of good understanding. The acorn of
good pepper, though small, is hotter and gives off
more heat than a walnut; it is the same with a small
woman who accepts love: there is no pleasure in the
world which one cannot experience with her. Just
as a little rose abounds with color, a tiny goldpiece
has great price and worth, and a little balsam has a
strong perfume, so a small woman is full of love.
Just as a little ruby has outstanding qualities—color,
power and value, nobility and brightness—so a
small woman has great beauty, attractiveness and
grace, love and loyalty.

The bunting and the nightingale are small, but they sing more sweetly than the larger birds; a woman is no worse for being small. In her love, she is sweeter than flowers or sugar. The parrot and the oriole, small birds, are both of them sweet singers; they are gifted, beautiful, worthy, good singers, and such is the small woman in her love.

The small woman has no peer. She is an earthly paradise and a consolation, a solace and a joy, a pleasure and a blessing; and she is even better in deeds than in looks. I have always preferred a small woman to a great big one: it makes good sense to avoid a huge evil! Of the evils available, one should choose the least, as the sage says, and therefore, of the women, the smallest is the best!

SIR  FERRET,  SERVANT  OF  THE  ARCHPRIEST

At the end of February and the beginning of March, the devil, father of evil, had his lap full of abbots and was preying merrily on the women. Since I no longer had my lady messenger, I took on a boy to be my messenger. His name was Ferret, a fine young fellow—I have never seen one better—except for some fourteen details! He was a liar, a drunkard, a thief, and a gossip, a gambler, a brawler, and a conjurer; he was gluttonous, quarrelsome, violent, and dirty, superstitious, stupid, and lazy. Such was my squire! Two days of the week he fasted strictly; that is to say, this sinner ate nothing because he had nothing to eat! Unable to eat, he fasted with grief; my messenger fasted always on those two days.

The common proverb says, however, "It is better to struggle with a stupid jackass than to travel alone and carry fagots on your shoulders." Out of sheer necessity, I engaged him as a messenger.

I said to him, "Ferret, my boy, find me another lady."

He answered, "Sir, I will search, even if the world should crumble, and I will bring her to you without too much fuss. Sometimes even an old mongrel has a good joint to eat."

He could read little, and that slowly and badly. He said, "Give me a poem and you will see how well I do. Sir, you'll see—I don't want to praise myself—but when I start something I follow it through."

I gave the Godforsaken man these poems. He went off and began reading them aloud to the lady—right in the town square! She said, "Get out of here, you beast! He did not send you to me and I do not want your message!"

THE ARCHPRIEST ON THE MEANING OF HIS BOOK

Because the Virgin Mary, as I said before, is the beginning and the end of all good, and this is my conviction, I wrote four songs for her. With these I will put a period to my book, but without ending it.

This book has good qualities, whatever part of it is read, because if a man with an ugly wife or a woman with an impotent husband should read it, they would devote themselves immediately to the service of God. They would wish to go to Mass and to make offerings, to provide bread and food for the poor, to give alms and to say prayers. This is how one serves God, as you gentlemen can well see. Now if anyone who hears my book knows how to compose poetry, let him add to it and revise it if he wishes. It should go from hand to hand, to anyone who wants it. Like girls playing ball, whoever can catch it should. Since it is about *Good Love* let it be borrowed freely; do not contradict its name and do not pass it on to get rid of it; do not take money for it, by selling or renting it, because if it is bought, *Good Love* provides neither pleasure nor taste.

The text I have composed is small, but I do not think that the *glossa* is small. As a matter of

fact, it is quite massive, because each story has another meaning on a different level, beyond that which
is stated in the pleasant narrative. In sacred matters,
it resembles a huge lectionary, but in folly and pleas-
antries it resembles a small breviary. So I will stop
here and close my writing table. Let it be a little
tale, a source of pleasure, an electuary.

  Gentlemen, I have served you with my little
learning. In order to amuse you all, I have spoken
in the manner of a jongleur. Now I ask of you this
in recompense: that when you go on a pilgrimage,
in the name of God, you say a paternoster and an
Ave Maria for me.

  This book was composed in the year 1343,[102]
because of the many injuries and wrongs that many
men and many women do to each other with their
wiles, and also to show the common folk fables and
interesting verses.

## THE JOYS OF THE VIRGIN MARY

> Glorious Mother of God,
> Holy Mary, Virgin,
> daughter and faithful spouse
> of your Son, the Messiah,
> you, O Lady,
> grant me now

your grace at every hour,
so that I may serve you forever.

Yearning to serve you,
I, a sinner, therefore
offer you as a service
your joys, which I sing.
The first one
was the angel,
true messenger to you
from the Holy Spirit.

You conceived your Creator.
This was your second joy,
when you gave birth to him, Mother;
without pain he came into the world.

.   .   .   .   .   .   .   .   .   .

As you were born,
so you remained,
Virgin of purity.

The third joy was the star
that guided with its light
the Kings from their own lands,
with their rich treasure;
they offered praise
and they worshipped

and gave to your Son
frankincense, myrrh, and gold.

Your fourth joy was this,
that you received the message
from the sister of Martha,
that your dear Son,
was risen from the dead;
the Light of the world,
whom you saw die on the cross,
where they had put him.

When he ascended to Heaven
you had your fifth joy.
And your sixth, you enjoyed
when he sent the Paraclete.
The seventh
was even better,
when your Son came for you
and you were assumed into Heaven.

I beg your mercy, O glorious one,
always and ever
be merciful to me,
pleased and content with my efforts.
When Jesus comes to judge
and to pass judgment,

help me, I pray,
and be my Advocate.


THE JOYS OF THE VIRGIN MARY

Let us all bless
the Holy Virgin,
and tell of her joys
and her life, as
it was, as we find
tradition tells
of that life.

In her twelfth year
this young maiden
was saluted
by a holy angel of God

.    .    .    .    .    .

.    .    .    .    .    .

the beautiful Virgin.

She gave birth to a Son,
what joy so great!
to this young Boy,
in her thirteenth year.
Soon the Kings came

to give rare gifts
and to adore Him.

Thirty-three years
she passed with Christ.
When he was risen,
her fourth joy she had.
The fifth she had when
she saw him,
Jesus, ascending to Heaven.

The sixth joy
she had when,
the disciples being gathered
together with her,
God sent them
the Paraclete
to enlighten them.

After the death
of her Son, the Messiah,
the Virgin lived
nine years more.
She was taken to Heaven.
What great joy
on that day!

Seven were the joys

and fifty-four the years
that, we know,
were granted to her.
Keep us always
from evil and harm,
O gracious Virgin!

You Christians, all,
you must rejoice
·   ·   ·   ·   ·   ·   ·
on this day:
to save us, he was born
of Saint Mary,
and to help us.


ALMS FOR THE STUDENTS

Gentlemen, give alms to the student
that comes begging to you.

Give me alms or bread,
and I will pray for you
that God may save you;
give me alms, in God's name!

The good which you do for God's sake,
the alms that you give me,

these will help you
when you depart this world.

When you render to God the account
of your capital and interest,
to have given alms for God's sake
will protect you from harm.

For the dish of food you give,
may you receive a hundred from God,
and may you enter Paradise;
I pray he may grant that!

Remember, your good deeds
will never be lost;
they may protect you
from Hell, that evil place.


ANOTHER STUDENTS' SONG

Gentlemen, give alms to us,
two poor students.

The Lord of Paradise
loved us Christians so much,
that he accepted death for us
and was killed by the Jews,

Our Lord died
in order to be our Savior;
give to us for love of him.
May he save us all!

Remember his story,
give for God's sake, in his memory,
and may he give you his glory;
give us alms for God's sake.

Now, as long as you live,
always give for his love,
and so you will escape
from the roaring pit of Hell.[103]

SONG OF THE BLIND MEN

Good and honored men,
we beg you to help us;
to these miserable blind men
give your alms.
We are wretched paupers,
we must live by begging.

Of the goods of this world
we have no portion.
We pass our painful life
in great affliction;

blind are we, as moles,
we see nothing of the world.

O Lady St. Mary,
grant your benediction
to him who is the first
to give us some food today;
give happiness to his body
and salvation to his soul.

St. Mary Magdalene,
pray to the true God for
whoever gives us a good gift,
a penny or more,
to make a tastier supper
for us and our company.

He who today gives us first
a penny or some crusts,
may he have, in all he undertakes,
a good beginning from St. Julian.
May God grant completely
all that he would ask.

May God, the heavenly Father,
guard his sons and his family
from blindness such as this,
and keep them from this sorrow;

and may St. Anthony ward off harm
from his cattle and his flocks.

To the man who gave us his penny,
out of love for the Savior,
O God grant him your grace,
grant your glory and your love;
protect him from the guile
of the deceitful devil.

You, with the blessed angel,
Lord St. Michael,
be you the advocate
of the man or the woman
that has given us some bread;
we offer it to you on his behalf.

When you weigh the souls,
keep those in your right hand
that give suppers and food
to us and to our guides;
their sins and their evils
throw on the left side.

Lord, we beg for your mercy
with both our hands;
the alms which we offer to you,
take them in your hands;

give Paradise to the souls
of those who gave us to eat.


ANOTHER SONG OF THE BLIND MEN

Christians, friends of God,
we beg you to succor,
in the name of God,
these blind beggars,
with your pennies and your bread.

Unless you give to us,
we will have nothing else
with which to break our fast;
to earn we are unable,
with these wretched bodies,
blind, poor and miserable as we are.

Give us your charity,
and may God
for whom you do it,
guard the sight of your eyes;
may you see the joy and pleasure
of the children you love so much.

May you never see sorrow,
and may God let you raise them

to be rich and healthy,
and to great prosperity;
may God not give them blindness,
may he guard them from poverty.

May he give them much bread and wine,
to give to poor wretches;
treasures and money,
to give to poor pilgrims;
cloth and garments,
to give to the blind cripples.

Your beloved daughters
may you see well married
to noble husbands,
to honored rich men,
to refined merchants
and to rich burghers.

Your mothers and fathers-in-law,
your sons and daughters-in-law,

.    .    .    .    .    .    .    .    .

.    .    .    .    .    .    .    .    .

the living and the dead,
may they be forgiven by God.

May he grant you a fine reward,
forgiveness for your sins.

May the angel receive
this offering in his hands.
Lord, listen to us sinners,
for the sake of our benefactors.

Please accept this song
and listen to our prayer,
which we, the poor, offer to you
for them who gave us to eat
and for him who wanted to give.
May God, who suffered death for us,
give you the holy Paradise.
Amen.[104]

## THE Ave Maria OF THE VIRGIN MARY

*Ave Maria,* glorious,
precious, holy Virgin,
how merciful you are,
at all times!

*Gratia plena,* without stain,
our advocate:
by your grace, Lady,
do this miracle
extraordinary.
In your goodness, now,

protect me always
from disgraceful death
that I may praise you, O beauteous one,
by night and day.

*Dominus tecum*, star
resplendent,
consolation of the afflicted,
vision ever glorious,
refulgent,
without stain of sin.
By your precious joys,
I beg you, O virtuous one,
to protect me, O pure rose,
from folly.

*Benedicta tu*, noble
beyond compare;
a virgin, you conceived,
praised by the angels
on high;
by the Son whom you bore,
by the grace which you received,
O blessed flower and rose!
protect me, compassionate one,
and guide me.

*In mulieribus*, chosen,
Holy Mother,

refuge of Christians,
Queen of the Saints;
and your Father
is beyond doubt your Son.
Virgin, my surety,
from malicious people,
cruel, wicked, proud,
keep me safe!

*Et benedictus fructus,* haven
and salvation
of the human race,
you relieved our misery
and our damnation;
through our malignant evil,
that unclean devil
with his deceitful toils
would cast us into
the ruinous dungeon.

*Ventris tui,* holy flower
without blemish:
by your great holiness
preserve me from error,
so that my life always follows
the path of goodness;
and may I find a place
with the saints, most gracious

miracle of sweetness,
O Maria!

SONG OF PRAISE TO THE VIRGIN

Many miracles the Virgin ever pure performs,
protecting those who are vexed by grief and
    misery.
The man who praises your image
you never do forget,
and, overlooking his sin,
you save him from misery.

With your true love, you succor the innocent
and you free your servant easily.
Your patronage, assuredly,
cannot fail him;
the full measure of your goodness
protects him from evil ways.

Queen and Virgin, my strength! in wretched
    terror I dwell,
I implore you to save me from disaster.
Since I sing to you, Lady,
protect me from harm,
from death and danger,
for your Son, the Holy Jesus.

I am grievously troubled being in this city; [105]
may your aid and vigilance free me and defend me.
Since I commend myself to you,
do not look on me with scorn;
your wondrous goodness
I will always praise and serve.

I commend myself to you, Holy Virgin Mary,
dispel my trouble, save and guide me.
Guard me always,
compassionate Holy Virgin,
by your mercy, which is so great
that I could not describe it.


SONG OF PRAISE FOR SAINT MARY

Holy Virgin, chosen,
beloved Mother of God,
glorified in Heaven,
salvation and life of the world.

Salvation and life of the world,
vanquisher of death,
abounding with perfect grace,
salvation of the afflicted:
from this misery which I endure

in a dungeon, undeserving,
deign to liberate me—
be my advocate.

Be my advocate,
reckoning not of my evil
or my true deserts,
but only of your bounty;
because I confess, in all truth,
that I am an erring sinner;
grant me your assistance
by your virginity.

By your virginity
which is beyond compare,
as you were never equalled
in deed or in intention,
so full of blessing:
although I am not worthy
may you decide, O Lady,
to grant my petition.

To grant my petition
as you granted to others;
from a temptation so fierce,
in which I suffer now,
guard me, by your hand
for you clearly have the power.

You have ever granted aid
to those whom you wished.


SONG OF PRAISE FOR THE VIRGIN

I desire to follow
you, flower of flowers!
And always relate
and sing your praises,
without ceasing
to serve you,
best among the best!

A great trust
I place in you, Lady,
and my hope
ever abides in you:
from tribulation,
make haste to come
and deliver me now!

Holy Virgin!
Troubled I endure
so much pain,
tormented by sorrow,

I am beset by fear,
by the grief I foresee.
Horrible devil!

Star of the sea!
Haven of peace!
From grief and pain
and from my sadness
come to deliver me
and comfort me,
Lady, from Heaven.

Your perfect mercy
never fails;
it always heals
troubles and gives us life;
never does man perish
never is he saddened,
if he does not forget you!

I endure great evil
wrongly, undeserving,
so great a torment
that I think I will die.
You must help me,
for I see no other
that can guide me to harbor.

SONG OF PRAISE FOR THE VIRGIN

> I rest my hope in you,
> Holy Virgin Mary!
> In such a worthy lady,
> one has reason to trust.

[*One folio is missing here.*]

SONG AGAINST FORTUNE

> My miserable fortune,
> cruel and vexing
> evil and wretched—
> why are you so angry,
> so noxious to me,
> so false a friend?
>
> I cannot write down,
> I cannot describe
> the acute torture
> you make me suffer!
> Can I desire to live
> amid so harsh a storm?
>
> Until today
> you kept constant your will

to make me miserable.
Be generous now
and grant me joy,
content and pleasure!

If you will remove from me
vexation and cares,
and my great tribulation
you will turn into joy,
and so will assist me,
then you will do a good deed.

But if you are obstinate
and do not give respite
but only deepen my grief,
all my cares
could, very quickly,
be brought to an end.

n Talavera, on the first day of
April, a letter did arrive
from Archbishop Don Gil,
a letter containing a just de-
cree, but one such that, if it did please one, it distressed more than two thousand others. The archpriest who brought the decree must have done so
more reluctantly than willingly. He summoned a
capitular meeting, which quickly convened—for
they expected something far more pleasant. The
archpriest addressed them as follows:

"If this distresses you, it distresses me quite
as much. Wretched old man that I am! For what
have I grown old? To see what I see now and have
seen before?"

The tears streaming down his face, he
went on: "The Pope sends us this order, I must tell
you, whether I like it or not, and you can be sure
that I tell it to you with anger in my heart."

A letter had come that decreed the following: No cleric or married man in the whole of Talavera could have a mistress, whether she be herself

married or a spinster; if he had, he was to be ex-
communicated.

This message saddened all the clerics. Some
of them became bitter. They agreed to meet another
day and decide what to do. When they had all gathered in the chapel, the Dean arose to express his
grief and declared:

"My friends, I propose that all of us here
appeal to the King of Castile, against the Pope.
Even though we are clerics, we are still his subjects,
we serve him well, and we have always been loyal
to him. Besides, the King understands that we are
all made of flesh: I tell you, he will take pity on our
troubles! What, am I to discard Orabuena, whom I
took up last year? To throw her out would do me
serious harm. In the first place, I presented her at the
outset with twelve measures of cloth; and besides,
by my tonsure, she had a bath only last night! I
would renounce all my benefices, my high office, and
my stipends, rather than let my Orabuena be insulted like this! I trust that many others will follow
my lead."

He called to witness the Apostles and all
that is holy. With tears in his eyes and great grief,
he said, *"Nobis enim dimittere est, quoniam
suave!"* [106]

The next to speak was the Bursar, a loyal

member of this group, who said: "Friends, if these
things should come to pass and you expect hard
days, I expect even worse. I am deeply pained by
your misfortunes, but also by mine and those of my
Teresa. I will leave Talavera! I would move to
Oropesa before putting her out of my house! Bian-
cofiore was never so loyal to her Florio, nor is Tris-
tan now to all his loves—which might well quench
their ardors. If I let her go, my miseries would never
leave me. They used to say that if a dog was cornered and feeling the fury of death, he would bite
his master in the face. If only I could have that
Archbishop in such a corner! I would hit him so
hard that he would not see next August!"

      After him spoke the cantor, Sancho Muñoz:
"I don't know what that Archbishop has against
us. He wants to denounce us for what God has forgiven. Therefore, I want to appeal against this letter.
Don't despair! For if I now keep, or ever kept, a
maidservant in the house, that is no reason for the
Archbishop to be angry. She is neither my kin nor
my relative. She was an orphan, and I brought her
up! And I'm not telling a lie. To support an orphan
or a widow is a work of mercy—that's the absolute
truth! If the Archbishop looks on this as evil, then
let us give up good works and turn to wicked ones!"

*[There is apparently a lacuna in the text.]* [107]

"I understand that the canon Don Gonzalo takes their jewelry, while his neighbors say that he receives her at night, although I have forbidden him to."

But, to make a long story short, the priests and other clerics appealed, first composing very good pleas and then arranging, for the future, certain powers of attorney.

THIS IS THE BOOK OF THE ARCHPRIEST OF HITA [108]
WHICH HE COMPOSED
WHILE IN PRISON
BY THE ORDER OF THE CARDINAL
DON GIL, ARCHBISHOP OF TOLEDO.

*Laus tibi Xriste, quoniam liber explicit iste.*
*Alfonsus Paratinensis.*

# ΠOTES AΠD
# BIBLIOGRAPHY

## NOTES TO THE INTRODUCTION

1. Ruiz' work has no title in the MSS. The present title, which has come to be accepted by editors and scholars, was provided in 1898 by Ramón Menéndez Pidal, "Título que el Arcipreste de Hita dió al libro de sus poesías," *Revista de Archivos, Bibliotecas y Museos* 2 (1898): 106–9.

2. The verse translation by Elisha Kane (New York, 1933), rollicking and freely illustrated but often inaccurate or misleading, was originally pri-

vately printed and hard to come by. Kane's work has recently been reprinted, with introduction by J. E. Keller, but without the illustrations (Chapel Hill, 1968). Keller's introduction, generally bland and unhelpful, is at times inaccurate and at times wrongheaded (as when he raises Brenan to the status of major scholar-critic of Spanish literature).

3. Throughout, we use the numeration of the Latin Vulgate text and the translation from the King James version.

4. Numbers in parentheses indicate stanza numbers.

5. Edited by G. Cohen, La "comédie Latine" en France au XII siècle (Paris, 1931), 2: 167–223.

6. "Zur Auffassung der Kunst des Arcipreste de Hita," Zeitschrift für romanische Philologie 54 (1934): 237–70.

7. Recherches sur le "Libro de buen amor" de Juan Ruiz, Archiprêtre de Hita (Paris, 1938), p. 244.

8. María Rosa Lida de Malkiel, Two Spanish Masterpieces: The "Book of Good Love" and the "Celestina" (Urbana, Ill., 1961), p. 44.

9. Ibid., p. 27.

10. Ibid., p. 8.

11. The descriptions are from Lida de Malkiel, Two Spanish Masterpieces, pp. 45, 47–48, and

from Otis H. Green, *Spain and the Western Tradition* (Madison, 1963) 1: 46 f, 53.

12. Green, p. 33, says that Ruiz "felt instinctively that art is play."

13. The survival of three MSS (the *Poema de Mío Cid* has come down in a single MS) itself indicates that the *Libro* enjoyed a continued popularity in the centuries immediately following its composition. The *Libro* was translated into Portuguese at the end of the fourteenth century; during the fifteenth and sixteenth centuries, it was mentioned and quoted often. For example, at the beginning of the fifteenth century, the work was quoted extensively by the Archpriest of Talavera and in the sixteenth century by the Spanish Humanist Álvaro Gómez de Castro. The *Libro* seems to have faded from view during the seventeenth and eighteenth centuries, until the first edition was published by Tomás Antonio Sánchez in his *Colección de poesías castellanas anteriores al siglo XV* (Madrid, 1779–90), 4 vols.

14. The thirteen passages are: 1–10; 75; 90–92; 452; 575; 910–49; 983–84; 1007; 1015–20; 1318–31; 1472; 1655; 1660–1709.

15. Lecoy, *Recherches;* Chiarini, *Libro de Buen Amor* (Milan, 1964). It should be added that Juan Corominas, in his edition of the *Libro* (Madrid, 1967), disagrees with Chiarini and maintains that there were two versions.

16. See Lecoy, *Recherches*, p. 330.

17. See Lida de Malkiel, *Two Spanish Master-pieces*, pp. 20 ff.

18. Lecoy, *Recherches*; Otto Tacke, "Kritische Untersuchung der einzelnen Fabeln des 'Libro de Buen Amor,'" *Romanische Forschungen* 31 (1912): 550–705; Arthur F. Whittem, *The sources of the fables in Juan Ruiz's "Libro de Buen Amor"* (Cambridge, Mass., 1908).

## NOTES TO THE TRANSLATION

1. Apparently, the first prayer breaks off here, and a separate prayer to the Virgin begins in the next verse. Neither prayer is complete.

2. We have indicated in parentheses the Vulgate references for all Biblical citations here. José María Aguado, *Glosario sobre Juan Ruiz* (Madrid, 1929) and Giorgio Chiarini's edition of the *Libro de Buen Amor* (Milan, 1964) contain full notes on references to the Bible and to medieval hymns and ecclesiastical documents.

3. The reference is to the Decretals of Pope Clement V (1305–14) promulgated after the Council of Vienne of 1311–12.

4. This is not actually a psalm but the beginning of the *Symbolum Athanasianum*, as Castro Guisa-

sola has shown, *Revista de Filología Española* 16 (1929): 72–73: "Quicumque vult salvus esse, ante omnia opus est ut teneat catholicam fidem. . . . Fides autem catholica haec est, ut unum Deum in Trinitate, et Trinitatem in unitate veneremur. . . . Ita Deus Pater, Deus Filius, Deus Spiritus Sanctus. . . ."

5. We have rendered *saber sin pecado* as "faultless art," but it could mean either "without blemish" or "without sin."

6. *axenuz* means "fennel seed," which is, of course, not black; the meaning seems dubious.

7. This seems to be a popular proverb. It is not clear whether *bevedor* means a drunkard or a particular type of cellarer (as in F. Sacchetti, *Trecento Novelle*, ed. V. Pernicone [Florence, 1946], Novella LXXXII).

8. On the metrical problems of this song and of others in the work, see Chiarini's Introduction.

9. This story appears to follow Livy (iii. 31), the account of the Roman legation to Athens. See E. François, "Una sugestión," *Revista de Estudios Clásicos* 2 (1946): 11–16. For the meaning of this episode, see Leo Spitzer, "Zur Auffassung der Kunst des Arcipreste de Hita," *Zeitschrift für romanische Philologie* 54 (1934): 237–70.

10. In the Gayoso MS, the copyist cites the text of

*Disticha Catonis* i. 18: "Interpone tuis interdum gaudia curis."

11. Despite Chiarini's insistence on the reading *dueña garrida* ("choice maiden") and his scathing attack on Reckert and Hart, we have adopted the reading *buena guarida*, "strong defense" (literally, a "good hideaway") as proposed by S. Reckert, ". . . avras dueña garrida," *Revista de Filología Española* 37 (1953): 227–37.

12. On "magpies" and "tailors," see G. Sobejano, *Homenaje a D. Alonso* (Madrid, 1963), 3: 434–35.

13. For a history of the expression *buen amor*, see G. B. Gybbon-Monypenny, "Lo que buen amor dize con rrazon te lo pruevo," *Bulletin of Hispanic Studies* 38 (1961): 13–24.

14. We have translated the verb *puntar* and its derivative *punto* as "notate," "dwell on," and "point"; the meaning is somewhat obscure.

15. According to Erasmo Buceta, "La 'Política' de Aristoteles, fuente de unos versos del 'Libro de buen amor,'" *Revista de Filología Española* 12 (1925): 56–60, this is actually an adaptation of Aristotle *Politics* i. 1, 3 and is used ironically.

16. Here and elsewhere in the text there are references to songs which are not preserved in the MSS. See stanzas 92, 122, 915, 918, 947, and 1319.

17. *Ysopet* probably does not refer to the Isopet

of Marie de France, but to any collection of fables so titled by antonomasia.

18. *E yo, como estava solo, syn compañia:* the motif and the formula are common in this poem (see stanzas 743, 757, 1317, and 1331) and in medieval literature generally. The formula occurs in Dante (*Inferno* xxiii. 1: "Taciti, soli, sanza compagnia") and in Chaucer several times: *The Knight's Tale,* I, 2779; *The Miller's Tale,* I, 3204; *Melibee,* VII, 1560—always in the same rhythm: "Allone, withouten any compaignye." In the last instance, Prudence quotes from "Pamphilles," but as F. N. Robinson, *The Works of Geoffrey Chaucer* (Cambridge, Mass., 1957), p. 681, notes: "Not from Pamphilus. Skeat compares Ovid, *Tristia,* i, 9, 5 f." Robinson's note provides references to other examples, French and English, of this formula.

19. We have tried to preserve the pun on *Cruz,* the name of the girl and *cruz,* "cross."

20. *Andalusian* must refer to a proverbial dullard.

21. The meaning seems to be that the "gluttonous student" is a freeloader. The English "Cockaigne" seems appropriate in its meaning of the land of plenty and in its overtones of the Spanish *cucaña* or cuckoo (see Italian *cuccare,* to be deceived as by a cuckoo.)

22. On the horoscope and its medieval Latin

sources, see F. Castro Guisasola, "El horóscopo del hijo del rey Alcaraz . . . ," *Revista de Filología Española* 10 (1923) : 396–98, and J. P. W. Crawford, "El horóscopo . . . ," *Revista* 12 (1925) : 184–90.

23. *Henares:* the biblical quotation "to sow wild oats" is adapted here, using the Henares River near Madrid, on whose shores it was useless to sow, perhaps because of frequent flooding.

24. *Mergelina,* according to Cejador, is a popular figure in ballads.

25. *The Seven Sins.* Ruiz is fairly free in schematizing the capital sins. Here, he lists *cobdiçia* (217), *sobervia* (230), *avarizia* (246), *luxuria* (257), *enbidia* (276), *gula* (291), *vanagloria* (304), and *açidia* (317), which is linked to *ypocresia* (319). In stanzas 1163–69, he gives them as follows: *cobdiçia, sobervia, avariçia, luxuria, yra, gula, envidia.* Describing the Armor of the Christian (1586–99), he cites the following sins: *cobdiçia, sobervia, avariçia, loxuria, yra, gula,* and *enbidia,* for which he provides specific antidotes in the Seven Works of Mercy, the Seven Gifts of the Spirit, the Seven Virtues, and the Seven Sacraments; following them is *açidia* (1600), which, he says, "Es de los siete pecados más sotil é engañosa" and is the mother of the seven sins: "Contra ésta é sus fijos . . ." (1601). María Rosa Lida de Malkiel has argued, about the first group,

that Ruiz was following literary precedent (cited in Chiarini, p. 46) in presenting greed twice, first under cupidity, then under avarice. But in stanza 219, Ruiz specifies that from *cobdiçia* come "sobervia e ira . . . , / avarizia e loxuria . . . , / gula, envidia, açidia. . . ." What is curious about this passage is that he includes *ira* and omits *vanagloria,* while in his lengthy discourse he omits *ira* and includes *vanagloria* (304); it is significant also that he makes *açidia* and *ypocresia* both the offspring of *cobdiçia* and the result of all seven preceding sins, including *cobdiçia.* In effect, Ruiz has four schemata of the sins, each slightly different from the others. If he seems unable to make up his mind, it remains true that he is largely following tradition, since the general order of the sins is fairly common among Church writers, while the specific emphases are varied. Only in one respect does he differ substantially from tradition—in not giving pride the first place, as the foundation of all the other sins. Dante, in the *Purgatorio,* lists pride, envy, wrath, sloth, avarice, glottony, and lust, in descending importance; the order is the same as that found in Aquinas' *Quaestiones disputatae: De malo* (VIII. i), but Aquinas has them also in three other arrangements (see *Summa* i–ii. Q. 84. art. 4) and apparently regards their sequence as unimportant. C. H. Grandgent, *La Divina Commedia* (Boston, 1933), pp. 6,

321, notes that Aquinas prefers *inanis gloria* to *superbia* as a designation for pride. But Aquinas concurs with the view of Cyprian and Gregory that pride is the foundation of all sin. The number of sins varied. Cyprian (*De mortalitate* iv) listed eight, as did Cassian (*De coenobiorum institutis* v–xii: "De octo principalibus vitiis"), Columban, and Alcuin. Gregory (see *Moralia in Job* XXXI. xvii, xlv) listed seven—lust, gluttony, avarice, sadness, wrath, envy, and vainglory, plus pride, the mother of vices; his sadness, unlike that of Cassian, would appear to be the familiar *açidia*. See also Robert Ricard, "Les péchés capitaux dans le *Libro de Buen Amor*," *Les Lettres Romanes* 20: 5–37.

26. For typical stories of Vergil in the Middle Ages, see Domenico Comparetti, *Virgil in the Middle Ages*, trans. E. F. Benecke (London, 1895), and John W. Spargo, *Virgil the Necromancer* (Cambridge, Mass., 1934). Spargo (p. 354) says that the two legends of the copper bed of the Tiber and of the dagger-studded staircase are perhaps original with Ruiz (see also F. Lecoy, *Recherches sur le 'Libro de buen amor' de Juan Ruiz, Archiprêtre de Hita* [Paris, 1938], pp. 170–71).

27. *Mongibel:* Mongibello, here obviously used to represent Hell, is an ancient name for Mt. Etna, the volcano of Sicily.

28. The sin *açidia* cannot be translated merely as

sloth; it is rather the medieval *accidie,* paralysis of the will which degenerates into sadness and a life of evil. The Archpriest here seems to break the pattern of his discourse. Instead of an ordinary fable, the Archpriest gives us here a fable in the form of a lengthy legal parody which exemplifies the way in which a mind turned to evil ensnares those afflicted by accidie. Then follows the liturgical parody of the hypocritical cleric, who is another example of the perverse nature of accidie.

29. The *abogado de fuero* handled cases based on common law, in which knowledge of Latin was not necessary as it was in Roman law. Since modern legal practice does not observe such distinctions, we have translated it as "ill-trained lawyer."

30. Bougie (Bugía) is a city on the northern coast of Africa. The allusion could be to the traditional perfidy of the Moors, and also to the Italian *bugia,* a lie or falsehood. On the satire of legal processes in this fable, see M. Eizaga y Gondra, *Un proceso en el Libro de buen amor* (Bilbao, 1942).

31. In their editions of the *Libro,* both J. Cejador y Frauca ([Madrid, 1913], I: 121–24) and Juan Corominas ([Madrid, 1967], pp. 152–54) see in Lion the Butcher Alfonso XI, who went to Alcalá in 1343 (and before that) to obtain more levies. However, the Salamanca MS, the only source for this

passage, reads *era de mill e trezientos en el ano pri-mero,* or the era of 1301 (A.D. 1263: the Spanish *era* was reckoned according to the Caesarian, which preceded the Christian era by thirty-eight years. See note 102). Corominas corrects the manuscript to read "era of 1381," and Cejador adds thirty-eight years instead of subtracting. The allusion to 1263 is obscure.

32. Stanzas 374–87 are a complex parody of the canonical hours, in which the lover's activities are described by very compact allusions to familiar verses and phrases from the liturgy. The allusions are generally so compact as to be untranslatable. We have retained the Latin phrases, with Vulgate Psalm references in parentheses, and with brief identifications of other elements in the notes. The reader interested in detailed analysis of the allusions and the action should consult Otis Green, "Juan Ruiz's Parody of the Canonical Hours," *Hispanic Review* 26 (1958): 12–34.

33. The allusions here are to compline, the evening prayer of the liturgy.

34. *Domine labia mea* is the versicle at the beginning of matins. *Primo dierum omnium* and *nostras preces ut audiat* are from St. Gregory's hymn, sung at matins.

35. From a matins hymn sung at Easter.

36. *Quod Eva tristis* is from the hymn sung at lauds; *quicumque vult* is from the *Symbolum Athanasianum* used only on major feasts.

37. From the second strophe of the hymn at tierce.

38. "Feast of six capes," i.e., a Pontifical Mass.

39. *Converte nos* alludes to the versicle in compline before the psalms.

40. *Custodi nos* alludes to the versicle in compline after the psalms.

41. The phrases here are from the Canticle of Simeon (Luke 2:29–32), *Nunc dimittis,* sung at the end of compline and followed by the *Salve Regina.*

42. *golhin:* a kind of thief. Here the Archpriest seems to switch to imagery of hunting.

43. D. Alonso, "La bella de Juan Ruiz toda problemas," *Ínsula* 6, no. 80 (1952): 3–11, argues against the widespread view that Ruiz' description of the beautiful woman is not conventional.

44. *lagrimas de Moysen:* literally, the "tears of Moses." It has been conjectured that this refers to a magic pool (attributed to Moses) or to the beads of the rosary or to a manual of magical arts.

45. H. Petriconi, "Trotaconventos, Celestina, Gerarda," *Die neueren Sprachen* 32 (1924): 232–39, argues that Trotaconventos remains a type and never achieves any dimensions as a character; A. Miró Quesada Garland, "La Trotaconventos," *Le-*

*tras 9* (Lima, Peru, 1943) : 408–14, finds her source in the old woman of *Pamphilus,* who was in turn derived from Ovid's Dipsas. Earlier, A. Bonilla y San Martín, "Antecedentes del tipo celestinesco en la literatura latina," *Revue Hispanique* 15 (1906) : 372–86, affirmed that the type of go-between was created in Spanish literature by Ruiz independently of classical sources and was adopted later, with the help of classical authors, by the author of *Celestina.*

46. *tomaré mi dardo!* means, literally, "I will get my arrow." The meaning is quite obscure; we take it to refer to some means of defending herself.

47. L. G. Moffatt, in "Pitas Payas," *South Atlantic Studies for Sturgis E. Leavitt* (Washington, 1953), pp. 29–37, after comparing several versions of the story of Pitas Payas, concludes that the Ruiz version is chronologically the first and that it was probably derived from French oral tradition, beginning a half-century or so before Ruiz. Our translation of this fabliau does not attempt to render the flavor of the broken Spanish spoken by both Pitas Payas and his wife, who are Bretons.

48. *Rome* is here meant figuratively; at the time, the Papal court was in Avignon. For the source of this episode, see E. K. Kane, "A note on the supposed foreign residence of the Archpriest of Hita," *Modern Language Notes* 46 (1931) : 472–73.

49. J. A. Chapman, "A Suggested Interpretation

of Stanzas 528 to 549 . . . ," *Romanische For-schungen* 73 (1961): 29–39, compares this episode to others in which one particular thing leads to ruin. Particularly in stanzas 156–59, 163, 400, 402–5, 420 (where it is love that leads to ruin), in 490–91, 494, 495, 498–500, 510 (money), and in 1546, 1548–49 (death), Chapman finds numerous stylistic similarities with the story of the hermit. However, since Sir Love narrates this story, Chapman concludes that the episode must be taken ironically.

50. The author of a handbook of games, *Libro alfonsí de las Tafurerías*, written in 1277 at the request of Alfonso X.

51. *Friar Moreno* seems to mean simply an attractive young man; cf. *morena*, which means a lusty dark-haired young woman.

52. A marginal note in the Salamanca MS gives the text of *Disticha Catonis* ii. 22: "consilium arcanum tacito committe sodali."

53. This stanza (581) is almost identical to stanza 169.

54. *Calatayud:* a city northeast of Madrid.

55. The implications of "sloeberry" have been much discussed—by Cejador, Spitzer, Lecoy, and by W. Kellermann, "Zur Charakteristik des Libro del Arcipreste de Hita," *Zeitschrift für romanische Philologie* 67 (1951): 236, and U. Leo, *Zur dichterischen Originalität des Arcipreste de Hita* (Frank-

furt, 1958)—and will no doubt continue to be discussed, as Chiarini says. María Rosa Lida de Malkiel argues effectively in "Nuevas notas para la interpretación del *Libro de buen amor*," *Nueva Revista de Filología Hispánica* 13 (1959): 56 ff., that any interpretation must begin with the passage in Quiñones de Benavente: "también la doncella es como endrina, / Que apenas le han tocado / Cuando el dedo le dejan señalado."

56. The first two lines of stanza 660 are missing from all the MSS. Stanzas 660–91 are missing from the Salamanca MS because two folios are missing there; they are supplied by the Gayoso MS.

57. *Don Melón*, here "Sir Badger," is usually translated as "Melon." The name of *Don Melón*, like that of *Doña Endrina*, has caused much scholarly discussion. The common view is that *Melón* was intended to mean a fruit, because *Endrina* clearly means "sloeberry." But Corominas sees a type of ambiguity here: *Melón* means both "melon" and "badger." In the Archpriest's time, the badger was considered a shrewd and predatory animal that ate berries and preyed on orchards, and was the nightmare of farmers and mountaineers. Corominas buttresses his observations with detailed etymological analyses. Because Corominas' arguments are persuasive, we have adopted his interpretation.

58. Álvaro Gómez de Castro, sixteenth-century

humanist from Toledo, recorded in his notes (MS) thirty lines from the *Libro,* four of which appear to be part of the stanzas missing here: "Non avedes, amiga, de carne el coraçon, / sino de uesso duro mas fuerte que leon, / por mucho que vos digo, siempre dezides non: / ¡qual, ya mujer tan dura, fueras para varon!" ("My friend, you do not have a heart of flesh; it is made of hard bones, harder than a lion's. Although I say many things to you, you always answer 'no.' You should have been a man; you are too tough to be a woman.")

The passage appears to be spoken by Trota-conventos in response to Sloeberry's harsh words. Then, apparently, the lady recounts a fable to exemplify her reluctance to leave what she has in order to marry again. In this fable, the wolf, who has abundant bacon to eat, is urged by some good omens to search for something better. He proceeds to do so, but he meets disaster.

59. The lacuna of thirty-two stanzas may be the result of mutilation (see also n. 61 below) or the folios here may simply have fallen out of the manuscript. At this point the old woman tells the lover that the lady's parents have decided to marry her off to someone else.

60. *la Rama:* a pun on the name of Lady Sloeberry's mother.

61. As after stanza 781, thirty-two stanzas are missing at this dramatic point in the tale; the folios involved here were probably destroyed by a mutilator with moral scruples. The corresponding scene in *Pamphilus* goes as follows: the old woman, making an excuse that a neighbor is calling, leaves the young man and the lady alone. The impetuous lover makes his advances; the lady makes a show of resistance. By turns she is fearful of discovery, pleased, angry, and disconsolate. She begins to weep. The lover tries to console her and takes all the blame for what has happened. As the *Libro* resumes, Sir Badger has gone, and Trotaconventos is defending herself.

62. The text has *non porque a mi vino*, which can also be translated as "not because it happened to me," meaning, i.e., "it didn't happen to me."

63. The mention of Ferrand García here is quite some distance from his earlier appearance in the poem (stanzas 110–23). Corominas argues that the earlier Ferrand García episode was added in the "version" of 1343, because the Portuguese MS that represents the 1330 version has a lacuna between 110 and 123. See the Introduction, above, pp. 25–26.

64. The name *Urraca* means "magpie"; there is a pun on this in 920.

65. Corominas suggests that many of the names of the go-between can be organized into categories—

e.g., instruments with which to drag or convey (viz., the lady), to soothe or calm, to cover, to summon, or to catch game or fish.

66. The mountain-girl episodes (stanzas 950–1042) take place in the Guadarrama range, north of Madrid. For useful and interesting descriptions of the range and the dress and customs of the mountain girls, see C. Bernaldo de Quirós, "La ruta del Arcipreste de Hita por la sierra de Guadarrama," *La Lectura* 15 (1915): 145–60, and E. Pérez de King, "El realismo en las cantigas de serrana de Juan Ruiz," *Hispania* 21 (1938): 85–104. Ruiz may be synthesizing various journeys he made in these mountains; it seems clear that he is describing them from experience. The following places mentioned in the text are all in the Guadarrama range: Loçoya, Malangosto, Sotosalvos, Somosierra, Fuentfría, Ferreros, Ríofrio, Cornejo, and Tablada.

67. St. Paul, I Thess. 5:21: "Omnia autem probate, quod bonum est tenete."

68. Cejador says that the date is March 8, but the feast of St. Emeterius falls on March 3.

69. Moya today is a city in the province of Cuenca, but other villages of the same name might have existed in the Archpriest's day.

70. The meaning of *dalgueva* is obscure. In a long and sometimes delightful display of erudition, Chiarini argues forcefully that the term can be made to

mean "gold-digger" ("donna interessata e venale, che nulla concede gratis o sulla parola ma esige immediate concrete controprestazioni in cambio persino di una frugalissima refezione"). Some scholars take it to be the name of the mountain girl, fundamentally a variation of the name Eve. Corominas suggests the emendation *de la cueva* ("from the hut"), which we have adopted. There is also the possibility that *algueva* is a place name, though no trace of it survives in that region today.

71. The meaning seems to be: by running downhill, the Archpriest can at least warm himself, even if in the process he loses his way.

72. James 1:17.

73. See John 12:4–8, where Judas considered himself cheated of the money for which the ointment could have been sold.

74. This episode is interpreted by A. Serrano y Jover, "Un enxiemplo de Juan Ruiz," *La Ilustración Española y Americana* 77 (1904): 238–39, as a protest by Ruiz against excessive Lenten mortifications. For all the geographical references, see Aguado, *Glosario*.

75. *Castro Urdiales* is a small town near Santander on the Cantabrian coast. It was chosen as Lady Lent's headquarters because of the abundance of fish there.

76. *Alí*, probably after the fourteenth-century

Sultan Ali, is a generic name for the Moslems, the traditional enemy of the Spaniards. The Sultan sent his son into Spain to fight the Christians, but he was disastrously beaten by Alfonso XI in October, 1340.

77. *Alarcos* was the site of the Arab victory over the Christians in 1195, in the province of Ciudad Real.

78. *Speculum:* the *Speculum iudiciale* by Guillaume Durand (1230–96), professor of law at Bologna. *Repertory:* the *Breviarium seu Repertorium aureum juris,* also by Durand. *The man of Ostia:* Henry of Susa, Bishop of Ostia, professor at Bologna and Paris, author of the *Summa super titulis Decretalium. Innocent IV:* Pope and author of the *Apparatus seu quinque libros Decretalium. Guido:* Guido of Baisio, thirteenth-century author of the *Rosarium Decreti,* a compendium of the *glossa ordinaria* on the *Decreta.* See also Lecoy, *Recherches,* p. 197.

79. The "tough oak" is the hardened sinner; the "sweet wood" is the *dulce lignum* or wood of the Cross.

80. *Medellín* is a city in Extremadura. Sir Carnival's route follows the cattle trail from Calatrava to Segovia.

81. For a detailed study of the musical instruments, see R. Menéndez Pidal, *Poesía juglaresca y juglares* (Madrid, 1924), pp. 65–72. The Orabin is

a Moslem singer. The qanum and the half-qanum are Moslem instruments.

82. *La Mota* is a large castle in Medina del Campo.

83. *Bordones* is probably S. Pedro de Bordones in Galicia.

84. At the end of each of these six stanzas, Ruiz uses tags from the liturgy for Easter, somewhat as he did in the parody of the canonical hours (374–87). *Venite, exultemus* comes from the *invitatorium* for matins in the daily office: "Venite, exultemus Domino, jubilemus Deo, salutari nostro: praeoccupemus faciem ejus in confessione, et in psalmis jubilemus ei."

85. *Te, Amorem, laudamus:* a parody of *Te Deum laudamus,* the great hymn of thanksgiving. In the liturgy, the *Te Deum* is recited (or sung) at the end of matins. The "Preachers of St. Paul" are the Dominicans; see Cejador, II: 145–149.

86. *Exultemus et laetemur* comes from the liturgy for Easter; it is the antiphon used in lauds and the other hours of Easter, and the gradual for Easter Sunday and for Saturday of Easter week: "Haec dies, quam fecit Dominus: exultemus et laetemur in ea."

87. *Benedictus qui venit* is certainly from the offertory for Saturday in Easter week: "Benedictus qui venit in nomine Domini: benediximus vobis de

domo Domini: Deus Dominus, et illuxit nobis, alleluia, alleluia." (Chiarini cites the Gospels, but the passages there refer to the entrance of Christ into Jerusalem on Palm Sunday.)

88. *Mane nobiscum, Domine* is the versicle for vespers of Saturday in Easter week and for Low Sunday.

89. In this allegory, the year begins with November, the first month in the liturgical year in the Mozarabic rite. Note that Ruiz' seasons begin one month earlier than ours (Spring in February, etc.)

90. For "the longest beam" the text has *la viga de Gaula,* which may be an allusion to the lance of Amadis; "milady's head" is *un cabello de Paula,* "a hair of Paula," but the name, probably used to suit the rhyme, means "any woman." Corominas, however, suggests that *paula* may be a Mozarabic form for *polilla* or "moth."

91. Probably in the region of Córdoba.

92. A saint of Gascon origin. There is a pun here on *quitar,* "to take away."

93. According to E. K. Kane, "The electuaries of the Archpriest of Hita," *Modern Philology* 30 (1933): 263–66, the "electuaries" were well-known aphrodisiacs and philters introduced into medieval Europe by the Arabs.

94. *abbatis* is obscure; presumably it is the geni-

tive of the Latin *abbas*, abbot, and is the name of a special preparation.

95. The nun's name means "bride" in Arabic, a fact that has encouraged allegorical interpretations of this episode.

96. The features that Ruiz attributes to himself are the traditional features of the virile man (pointed ears, large mouth, etc.) according to medieval conventions. See E. K. Kane, "The personal appearance of Juan Ruiz," *Modern Language Notes* 45 (1930): 103–8.

97. There is a possible allusion in the Spanish *la su vida muy linpia en Dios se deleitava*, to Prov. 8:30–31: ". . . et delectabar per singulos dies ludens coram eo omni tempore, ludens in orbe terrarum; et deliciae meae esse cum filiis hominum."

98. In this dialogue (1509–1512), there are four Arabic words: *lêš nedrí* ("I don't know"); *lâ wa llâh* ("No, by Allah"); *'uskut* ("Be quiet"); *'imší* ("Go away"). Lida de Malkiel, *Two Spanish Masterpieces*, p. 46.

99. *tomorrow*: the text has *cras cras*, which combines the Latin *cras*, "tomorrow," and the cry of the raven.

100. This is a feature of the conventional assault on death. The meaning is that death, by ravaging the senses, is preparing for itself a loathsome abode.

101. The armor of the Christian may be schematized thus:

| Sins | Works of Mercy | Gifts of Holy Spirit | Virtues | Sacraments |
|---|---|---|---|---|
| Covetousness | clothing the naked | Wisdom | Justice | Baptism |
| Pride | sheltering the poor | Fear of the Lord | Temperance | Confirmation |
| Avarice | * | Piety | Faith | Holy Orders |
| Lust | refreshing the thirsty | Might | Fortitude | Matrimony |
| Anger | visiting the sick | Understanding | Hope | Penance |
| Gluttony | feeding the hungry | Knowledge | Prudence ** | Eucharist |
| Envy | burying the dead | Counsel | Charity | Extreme Unction |

* The work for Avarice should be to visit the imprisoned, but the text has giving alms to the poor.
** Prudence is not perfectly clear as the virtue

against Gluttony. Corominas believes that the letters on the shield of Good Counsel are *S.C.*, i.e., the initials of *spiritus consilii* and the first letters of *scutum*.

102. *Era de mill e trezientos e ochenta e un anos* (1381) = 1343. The Spanish *era* was reckoned according to the Caesarian, which preceded the Christian by thirty-eight years. (See also n. 31.)

103. In his edition, Ducamin placed the two "Songs of the Blind Men" after the "Song of the Talavera Clergy" and numbered the stanzas 1710–1728. Following more recent editors (Corominas, Chiarini, Mrs. Malkiel), we have placed them between the second "Students' Song" and the "Ave Maria," though retaining Ducamin's numbering.

104. At this point, the Gayoso MS ends with this postscript in the hand of the copyist: "Fenito libro, graçias a Domino nostro Jesuxristo. Este libro fue acabado jueves XXIII dias de jullio del ano del nascimiento del nuestro Salvador Jesuxristo de mill e tresientos e ochenta e nueve anos." ("The book is finished, thanks to our Lord Jesus Christ. This book was completed on Thursday, July 23, of the year of the birth of our Savior Jesus Christ 1389.")

105. This is a possible allusion to Ruiz' imprisonment in the city of Toledo.

106. The meaning of the Latin line seems to be: "We are to send [her] away, because it is sweet."

360 / NOTES TO TRANSLATION

Pidal, *Poesía juglaresca y juglares*, pp. 206–7, cites the *Consultatio Sacerdotum* of Walter Map as the major source in this episode. The ultimate source is Psalm 134:3: "Psallite nomini ejus, quoniam suave." The *double entendre* is clear from Map's line, "quisque presbyter cum sua suavi," and from common literary practice, cited by Chiarini, pp. 337–38. "With tears in my eyes and great grief" also echoes Map's "O quam dolor anxius, quam tormentum grave."

107. Of the several ecclesiastics who, besides the canons, form a chapter, only three have spoken; since stanza 1708 does not follow directly on 1707, there is apparently a lacuna here.

108. The text at the end appears in the Salamanca MS in the hand of the copyist Alphonse of Paradinas: "Este es el libro del arçipreste de hita el qual conpuso seyendo preso por mandado del cardenal don gil arçobispo de toledo. Laus tibi Xriste quoniam liber explicit iste. Alffon Patinen."

# SELECTED ANNOTATED BIBLIOGRAPHY

The reader interested in further pursuing large and small problems may find the following bibliography useful, apart from specific works cited in the notes. For a full bibliography, see R. Mignani, "Bibliografia compendiaria sul 'Libro de buen amor,'" *Cultura Neolatina* 25 (1965): 62–90.

## Editions and Translations

Ruiz, Juan, Arcipreste de Hita. *Libro de Buen Amor.* Edición y notas de Julio Cejador y Frauca. Madrid: La Lectura, 1913. 2 vols. Copiously annotated.

————. *Libro de Buen Amor.* Edizione critica a cura di Giorgio Chiarini. Milano-Napoli: Riccardo Ricciardi, 1964. The first critical edition, with many useful notes in Italian.

————. *Libro de Buen Amor.* Edición crítica de Juan Corominas. Madrid: Gredos, 1967. The most reliable critical edition, with excellent notes.

————. *Libro de Buen Amor.* Edición crítica por Manuel Criado de Val y Eric W. Naylor. Madrid: Consejo Superior de Investigaciones Científicas, 1965. Contains the text of all three MSS and of the fragments; corrects some of Ducamin's readings.

———. *Libro de Buen Amor*. Texte du XIV˙ siécle, publié pour la premierè fois avec les leçons des trois manuscrits connus par Jean Ducamin. Toulouse: Privat, 1901.

———. *The 'Book of Good Love' of the Archpriest of Hita, Juan Ruiz*. Translated into English verse by Elisha Kent Kane. New York: Rudge, 1933. The first complete English translation, in the meters of the original. Free, lively, interpretive, at times inaccurate. Illustrated with line drawings. Reprinted, without illustrations, with an introduction by John Esten Keller. Chapel Hill: The University of North Carolina Press, 1968.

———. *Libro de buen amor*. Texto íntegro en versión de María Brey Mariño. Valencia: Editorial Castalia, 1954. Excellent translation into modern Spanish.

*Scholarship and Criticism*

Aguado, Jose María. *Glosario sobre Juan Ruiz, poeta castellano del siglo XIV*. Madrid: Espasa-Calpe, 1929. Fundamental work.

Castro, Américo. *The Structure of Spanish History*. Princeton: Princeton University Press, 1954. A revision of Castro's *España en su historia* (Buenos Aires, 1948), in which he proposes his views on the non-Western influences on Ruiz.

Green, Otis H. *Spain and the Western Tradition.* Madison: University of Wisconsin Press, 1963. Volume I, pp. 27–71, interprets the poem generally (though not in all its parts) as "an index and a supreme manifestation of medieval laughter."

*"Libro de buen amor" Studies.* G. B. Gybbon-Monypenny, ed. London: Tamesis Books, Ltd., 1970. A collection of recent studies by several authors on different aspects of the *Libro.*

Hart, Thomas R. *La alegoria en el Libro de Buen Amor.* Madrid: Revista de Occidente, 1959. Allegorical interpretations of some sections of the *Libro.*

Lecoy, Félix. *Recherches sur le "Libro de Buen Amor" de Juan Ruiz, Archipretre de Hita.* Paris: Droz, 1938. Includes practically everything known on Ruiz and his work up to 1937—metrics, textual criticism, and sources especially.

Lida de Malkiel, Maria Rosa. *Two Spanish Masterpieces: The "Book of Good Love" and the "Celestina."* Urbana: The University of Illinois Press, 1961. In the first three chapters (pp. 1–50), Mrs. Malkiel presents the major arguments for the non-Western interpretation of the *Libro.*

Menéndez Pelayo, Marcelino. *Orígenes de la novela.*

Madrid: N. B. A. E., 1905–1915. 4 vols. For his seminal views, see Vol. 3, lviii–lxvi.

Puyol y Alonso, Julio. *El Arcipreste de Hita. Estudio crítico.* Madrid: Sucesora de M. Minuesa de los Rios, 1906. This was the first general critical study of the *Libro.*

Richardson, Henry B. *An etymological vocabulary to the "Libro de Buen Amor" of Juan Ruiz.* New Haven: Yale University Press, 1930. Fundamental work.

Sánchez-Albornoz, Claudio. *España, un enigma historico.* Buenos Aires, 1957. On pp. 451–533, the author disputes the theses of Castro and argues for the traditional interpretation.

Spitzer, Leo. "Zur Auffassung der Kunst des Arcipreste de Hita," *Zeitschrift für romanische Philologie* 54 (1934): 237–70. Searchingly presents the case for the allegorical interpretation of the *Libro.*

Weisser, F., "Sprachliches Kunstmittel des Erzpriesters von Hita," *Volkstum und Kultur der Romanen* 7 (1934): 164–243 and 281–348. A stylistic analysis of the *Libro.*

Zahareas, Anthony N. *The Art of Juan Ruiz Archpriest of Hita.* Madrid: Estudios de Literatura Española, 1965. A study of the style and of the literary values of the *Libro.*